Venceslas Kruta # celts

photographs Dario Bertuzzi / Werner Forman /
Erich Lessing

contents

Introduction 4 /

PART ONE: HISTORY 11

The rediscovery of the ancient Celts 12

Celts, Gauls, Galatians, Celtiberians and Bretons 15 / Druids and megaliths 16 /

Vercingetorix, the iconic national hero 20 / The Gauls of Marzabotto and the origins of Celtic archaeology 22 /

The gates to another world 23 / La Tène, the region that gave its name to La Tène culture 25 /

The question of origins 26

The Celts according to Herodotus, c. 500 BCE 28 / The earliest written evidence of a Celtic language 30 /

The emergence of the historical Celts and La Tène civilization (6th–5th century BCE) 35

Závist, a power-centre in the heart of Bohemia 43 / The origins of a Gaulish people – the Remi 'ancestors' 51 /

Palmette, lotus and mistletoe 57 / The Hallstatt Scabbard: another view of the Celts of the 5th century BCE 60 /

Pitchers for princely banquets 63 /

The Transalpine invasion of Italy (4th century BCE) 64

Coral and hidden faces 72 / 'Red-figure' vases 75 /

The Great Expedition (3rd century BCE) 76

The sacred treasure of Delphi 78 / Celtic mercenaries 85 / The birth of a Gaulish people: the Parisii 88 /

The Galatians of Asia Minor 86 /

The development, expansion and decline of the Celtic urban centres (2nd–1st century BCE) 94

The Iberian Celts 97 / Celtic coinage 100 / The oppidum, cornerstone of the city-states 102 /

The Boii: the turbulent history of a great tribe at the heart of Europe 105 / The cavalry, crack troops of the cities 110 /

The Celts in pre-Christian Britain and Ireland (1st century BCE to 5th century CE) 118

PART TWO: CIVILIZATION 135

A world-view centred on a distant past 136

The Celtic calendar according to the Coligny inscription 141 / The triskele, a Celtic emblem then and now 144 /

Peasants and artisans 152

Magicians of the forge and the furnace 161 / Enamel: colours borne of fire 163 /

A society in transition 168

Women's jewellery, an expression of rank and ethnic identity 175 / The great feast at Tara 182 /

Gaulish society in the middle of the 1st century BCE, as described by Julius Caesar 185 /

The heroic ideal of the warrior 190

Warriors and dragons 201 / Sacrificial arms and battle trophies 202 /

Images of the gods 208

A masterpiece of Celtic art: the Brno-Maloměřice flagon 213 /

The Gundestrup Cauldron: dumb images of a Celtic pantheon 224 /

Epilogue 232 / Chronology 236 / Index 238 / Bibliography 240 / Picture credits 240 /

Poured-bronze head at the end of a flat iron bar.
Possibly a chariot trapping, from the Křivoklát castle area, probable site of the oppidum *of Stradonice (Bohemia) or its environs. The picture emphasizes the remarkable power of the essential image of a deity that might have come from any age and any religion.*
2nd–1st century BCE. Height: 23 mm. Prague, Národní Muzeum.

Introduction

The Celts are very much in fashion. Over the past fifteen years, they have been the subject of exhibitions, scientific congresses, books and films. Celtic music is popular at music festivals, and there is an array of costumed re-enactments and events to celebrate the great feasts of the Celtic calendar; some even go beyond neo-druidism and use supposedly Celtic rituals to make political points.

There are many different reasons for this passion for all things Celtic. They range from the quest for roots – which involves not only the twenty-two European countries with a Celtic past, brief or sustained, but the millions of New World inhabitants of Irish, Breton, Galician or Scottish descent – to the need to escape from the constraints of a bland modern world, to nostalgia for the sense of community that is rightly or wrongly attributed to our distant ancestors.

The imprint of a Celtic past

Such a variety of motivations inevitably leads to very different images of the Celts; as does the paucity of the historical record. Whereas ancient Greece and Rome left us abundant and varied contemporary literature that gave us vivid insights into their cultures, Celtic myths and legends were transmitted orally. They were only transcribed long after Christianity had been adopted, when the religious ban on written records was lifted. By then, only the insular Celts who had remained independent had an intellectual elite versed in this lore. Several centuries of Roman domination had led to the abandonment or marginalization of traditional learning among the Continental Celts as it had long been useless to those who wanted to belong to the social elite or to follow a career in the administration. For such aspirants, a knowledge of Latin, or possibly Greek, the languages of culture and intellectual exchange, was indispensable. The only texts that exist, therefore, are late accounts reworked by Irish or Gallic monks to their own agenda, downgrading Celtic lore in favour of Christianity and embroidering it with elements from classical antiquity. The principal versions that have come down to us were written between the 11th and 15th centuries.

Similarly, Greece and Rome have left us stone and concrete architectural relics that survive to this day. Celtic monuments, on the other hand, were made almost exclusively from wood, which has long since rotted away to nothing. Only slopes of crumbling ramparts, constructed of wood and banked dry-stone, nowadays reveal to the informed observer the site of an abandoned fortification. Others have been well buried under towns that have grown over generations, notably in Gaul, where many capitals were built on the site of a Celtic settlement and may even bear a name of Celtic origin, generally that of a tribe. Thus Paris perpetuates the name of the Parisii, Vannes that of the Veneti, Bohemia the Boii, Arras the Atrebates, and Reims the Remi. Milan is built on the site of Celtic Mediolanum, Geneva on the port of Genava, Berne on Brenodurum. Prague originated from the nearby fortress of Závist, and Bratislava from a Boii settlement. Budapest and Belgrade also have Celtic origins.

Opposite
View of the 'Kleinaspergle' burial-mount in Asperg (near Ludwigsburg, Baden-Württemberg).
This 60-metre (197-ft) tumulus contained graves of members of the princely dynasty that lived in the neighbouring fortress of Hohenasperg in the 6th century BCE. The central tomb of the monument was robbed in ancient times but a lateral chamber, explored in 1879, contained an inhumation together with a splendid drinking service that included a beaked pitcher of Celtic workmanship, the sheet-gold decorations of a pair of drinking horns and two Attic goblets also decorated with sheet-gold appliqués. They are displayed in Stuttgart at the Württembergisches Landesmuseum, and may date from the second half of the 5th century BCE.

So, while it remains for most of us invisible and inaudible, the distant Celtic past has nevertheless profoundly influenced our contemporary landscape. It is also present in our customs, such as the use of mistletoe at Christmas, in our way of measuring time – the fortnight derives from the subdivision of the Celtic month – and in the majority of our great festivals each year, which are Christianized versions of those celebrated by the Celts.

Increasing awareness of the importance of this Celtic inheritance, coupled with the limited nature of the evidence we do have, has doubtless contributed to the current vogue for the ancient Celts. Imagination can run riot when reliable landmarks are sparse and when the accounts of ancient writers about their Celtic contemporaries are suspected, often rightly, of presenting a distorted image. Incomprehension, and sometimes even a desire to promote certain aspects at the expense of others, often simply reflects the fraught relationship that has always existed between the Celts and the Mediterranean world. In the 19th century the image of the Celt as an unpredictable savage threatening civilized order was tempered only by the assumption that he was at least capable of learning, of being transformed into a good Roman citizen. In this way he was used as a contrast with the German, the destructive barbarian responsible for the fall of Rome

The Gaul of children's stories

One might hope that this image of the Celt – or the Gaul, the two names being synonymous for their contemporaries – has now been totally revised. And indeed, although the quaint 19th-century vision of Gaul persists in the adventures of Asterix and his merry crew, those willing to delve a little deeper can find a wealth of recent research that sheds unprecedented light on these people.

One of my favourite childhood books was the story of Vercingetorix, the first in a series of lavishly illustrated volumes on the great figures of French history. The images from that book have always remained vivid in my memory: Gauls like those who appear on Gauloises cigarette packs, decked out in winged helmets (actually an Italian Bronze Age model), cuirasses and swords that also went back to the

beginning of the first millennium BCE. They were untidy, disorderly figures of fun, accompanied by women and children on wagons, and invariably a white-robed druid playing the harp. Together they formed a lively, multicoloured rabble processing towards their prey, possibly Rome. In the distance there would be the implacable precision of the Roman army marching with measured tread, led by a centurion with attendant standards and trumpets, and boasting fiendish ballistae. Ultimately, inevitably, it would prove to be no contest. However, in reality, just as in the Asterix comics, the Gauls were not always a pushover for Imperial Rome. At Allia, for instance, an army of young, inexperienced Roman recruits broke rank and fled in terror when confronted by yelling hordes of Gauls banging their swords on their shields.

The rehabilitation of the noble savage

While the pictures from this book have always stayed with me, I had forgotten Héron de Villefosse's elegantly written text until I rediscovered it recently. His prose reflects ideas current at the time (the book was published in 1937), which now seem as quaint as any Asterix cartoon. For instance, the book begins: 'Three thousand years ago, nature alone ruled over our country, France. Egypt already had the pyramids and Babylon its temples but our country had no towns, roads or bridges, nor even beautiful fields cultivated in regular furrows. Between the valleys lay huge rivers, immense forests populated by wolves, aurochs, lynx and boar, mountains inhabited by bears. A few sparse villages that struggled to find a place in the clearings sheltered several tribes that had migrated from central Asia.' So much for the landscape. Here is what Villefosse says about the inhabitants: 'We need not conceal the fact that our ancestors were true barbarians, very brave but very belligerent, who enjoyed lengthy feasts and recitals of heroic exploits … Other civilized countries thought them prone to childish rages and mocked their singular custom of shooting arrows skywards when it thundered, of marching sword in hand ahead of tempests and floods … In fact, they were much feared by their neighbours.' In other words, the Gauls were volatile but likeable children in a man's world.

Opposite
**Detail of a stone head from
Mšecké Žehrovice (Bohemia).**
*One of the best-known works of
Celtic sculpture (see p. 95).*
2nd–1st century BCE.
Prague, Národní Muzeum.

Nowadays, we can offer the same patronizing smile to Villefosse as he offered to the Gauls. His concept of the noble savage was, of course, essentially drawn from Greek and Latin accounts, and as such it gives a wholly inaccurate picture. Nevertheless, while we now understand a great deal more than this amateur historian from the 1930s, our knowledge of Celtic civilization still falls far short of what we know of the great Mediterranean civilizations of antiquity. And some of the gaps will never be filled because of the absence of consistent texts. However, new discoveries and the constant progress of research mean that we are learning more all the time. While there are no Celtic texts to give us an insight into their spiritual universe, we do have a number of important artworks of remarkable quality that offer a key to this domain. However, to appreciate their value, we must first reject the common preconception that these artworks are merely attempted copies or adaptations of Greek, Etruscan or Roman models. Second, we must make a great effort really to *see* the objects. The particular characteristics of Celtic art mean that these works, which are often small and difficult to view, do not always reveal themselves at first glance. We must learn how to look at them, allowing the play of light, the sense of the moment, the inspiration to reveal their multiple facets. To be understood, this inspiring, interactive art demands a patient, lengthy apprenticeship, a total intellectual openness and enormous sensitivity. If this course is followed, it provides the best and most stimulating way to establish a direct dialogue with these distant ancestors.

Speaking images

It is therefore impossible to discuss Celtic civilization without access to many detailed photographs, of the type that appear in this book. These pictures should lead to a better understanding that the Celts did much more than mould the landscape in which they lived: they had such a profound impact on civilization that we are still feeling the effects today in virtually everything we do.

Following page
**Detail of the upper part of the incised decoration
on the plaque of an iron scabbard from
Cernon-sur-Coole (Marne).**
*The first impression is of a totally freestyle creation
directly inspired by the artist's imagination. In fact, this is
a highly original interpretation of the warrior emblem of
a pair of serpentine monsters framing a palmette: only
the right half is shown on this side. This remarkable
work, typical of Celtic art at its height, also testifies to
the skill and the experience of the craftsman who drew it
freehand, with no halt or hesitation to be seen, even
when viewed under a microscope.*
First half of the 3rd century BCE.
Length: 50 mm. Châlons-en-Champagne (Marne, France), Musée Municipal.

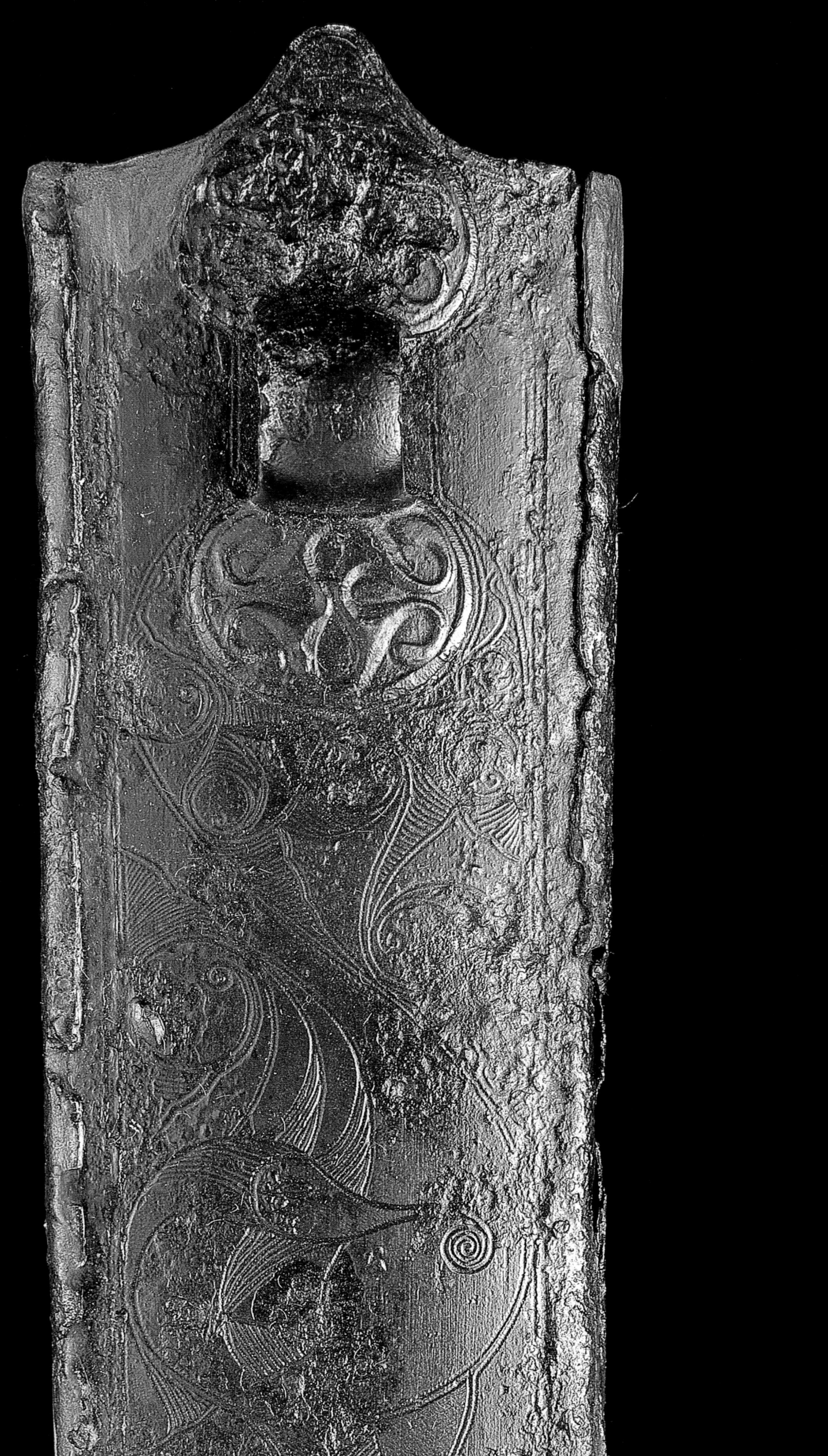

HISTORY

From the centre of Europe to the Mediterranean,

from the Atlantic to the Carpathians,

origins,

expansion,

decline,

heritage

Left
The Dying Gaul.
Generally thought to be a Roman copy of a monument erected in 227 BCE by the ruler of Pergamon, Attalos I, in the Temple of Athena to commemorate his victory over the Galatians. The statue was originally part of a group that also included The suicide of a Gaul and his wife. *It expresses well the respect and admiration of the sculptor for the pride and indomitable courage of these redoubtable enemies who braved death in heroic nudity (see p. 204).*
Roman. Life-size.
Rome, Musei Capitolini.

The rediscovery of the ancient Celts

Greek and Latin classical writings constitute the oldest and richest source of information on the customs and history of the Celts. But any passages dealing with them obviously reflect the vicissitudes of Mediterranean history, notably the incursions of Celtic armies against the cities of Greece and Italy. The first of these was the invasion of Italy by the Transalpine Celts at the beginning of the 4th century BCE. From then on, historians paid close attention to the Celts who settled in the Italian Peninsula and to their struggles against Rome that persisted until the beginning of the 2nd century BCE. In this period, specifically around 280, Celtic armies campaigned as far as Delphi, Thrace and Asia Minor in the so-called 'Great Expedition'; thereafter, Celtic mercenaries in the service of Hellenic and Galatian rulers became a force to be reckoned with. Then came the struggles of Iberian Celts against Carthage and Rome; links established during Hannibal's expedition across southern Gaul and the Alps and into Italy; and the later conquest of Gaul by Julius Caesar, who left the most detailed textual commentary on any ancient Celtic territory. There is also a little documentation relating to the Celts of Central Europe in the 1st century, and somewhat more on the struggles of the British Celts against the Romans.

Any information we have is therefore unequally distributed over time and place, and often chronicles events some time after they had occurred. As a result, this is a distorted history, with some events exaggerated for effect, others gleaned from myth or legend. Moreover, all of these accounts were written from a perspective that tended to emphasize, more or less consciously, the beneficial and irreversible character of a model urbanized society, such as was found in the Greek and Roman worlds. The resounding success of this model would eventually have permanent repercussions for the Celtic way of life. Much later, especially during the Middle Ages, subtle retouches to the legendary epics and genealogies of insular literature attempted to anchor the Celts into the traditional progression of history from the Trojan Wars onwards.

Nevertheless, despite such reservations, these historical, ethnological and geographical testaments are invaluable. They furnish us with precious information on the time frame of events, especially in relation to the conflicts between the Celts and the Mediterranean peoples. They give us a window into Celtic social structure, economy, religion and customs, and into the various tribes and their geographical situations. Finally, they describe the characters who for several centuries stood shoulder to shoulder with the giants of mythology, the Amazons and the Persians as the personification of the wild and disorderly barbarian world. Recently we have been able to look afresh at these resources, thanks to developments in Celtic archaeology, which have both illustrated and complemented the documentary record.

Scholars were first drawn to the ancient Celts as a result of the latter's occasional appearances in histories of Rome. Events such as the Gauls' sack of Rome and Julius Caesar's conquest of Gaul caught the attention of researchers who took special interest in passages describing the ancient histories of their countries. However, a scientific approach to the Celtic past developed only gradually, chiefly in the insular regions where the Celtic languages were still spoken.

Opposite
View of the great central way of the principal *oppidum* **of Bibracte, city of the Aedui.**
It is situated in France on Mont Beuvray (southern Morvan region), an isolated 820-metre (2,690 ft) hill at the conjunction of the valleys of the Yonne, Loire, Seine and Saône rivers. Occupied and probably also fortified from 5,000 years BCE, the site reached its apogee in the 1st century BCE, when a double rampart enclosed an urban centre of around 200 hectares (500 acres). It was gradually abandoned towards the end of that century in favour of the new town of Augustodunum (Autun). This picture shows it as it was before the excavations that have been carried out at the site since 1984. See p.18.

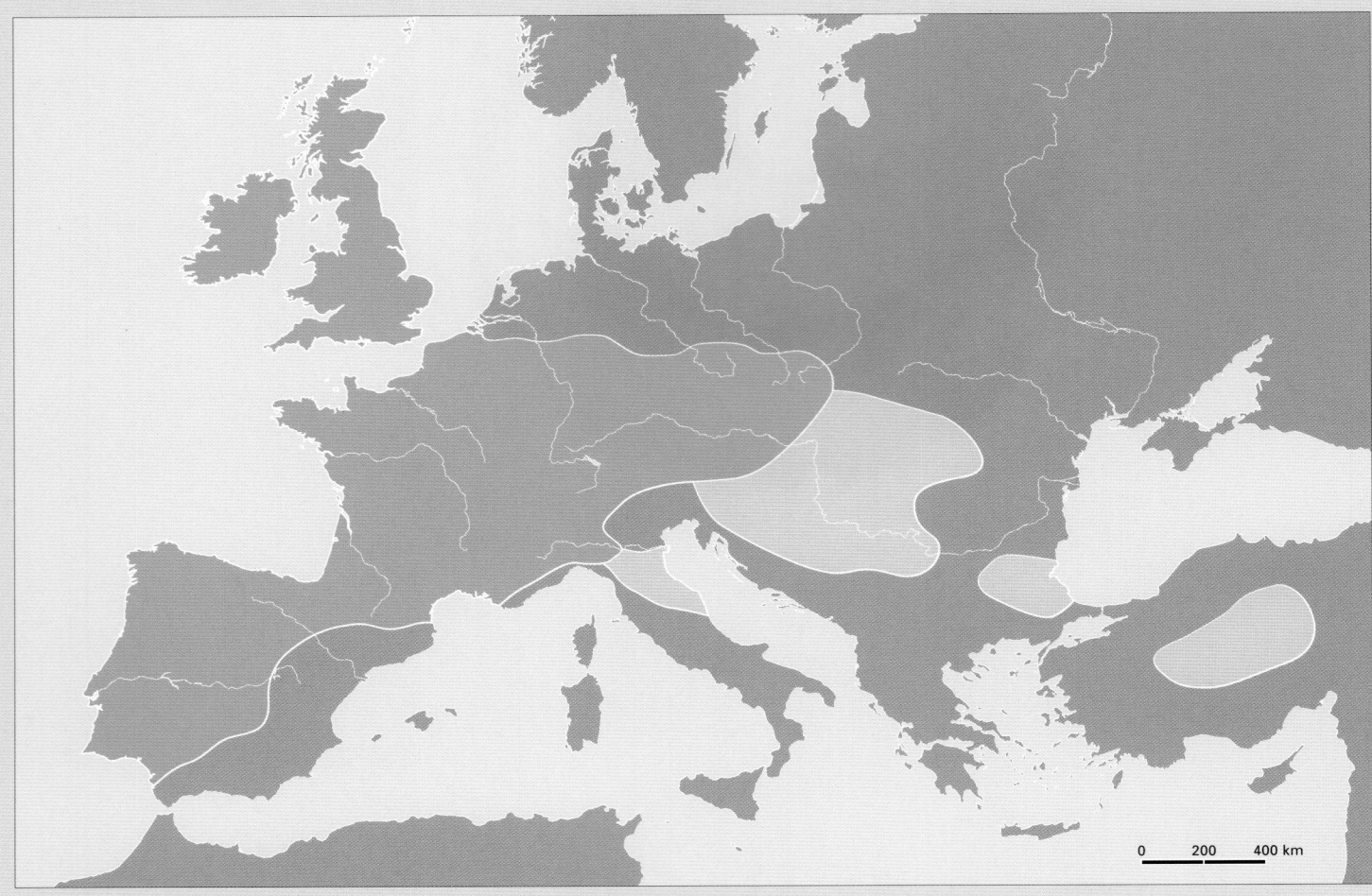

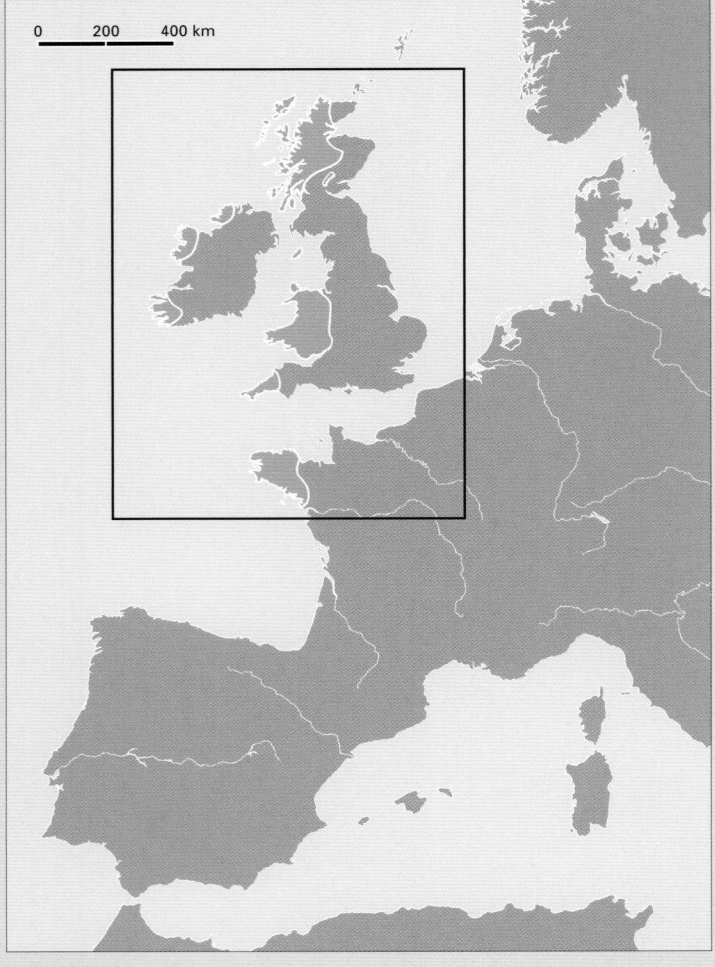

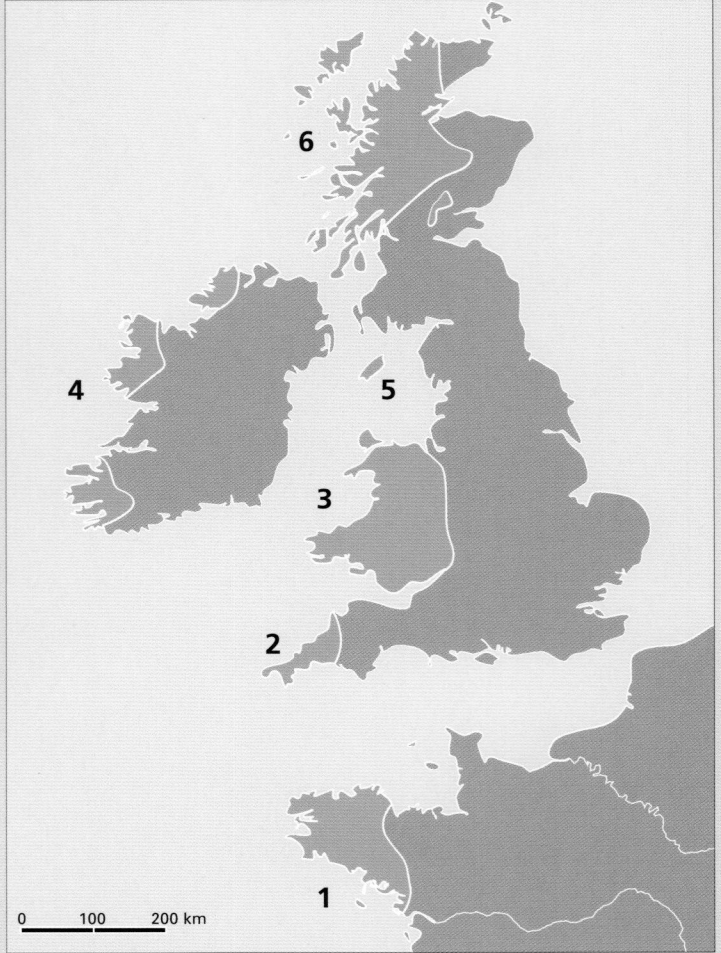

The ancient Celts (top).

Map showing the maximum expansion of Celtic tribes in the 3rd century BCE. The deepest colour indicates territories long settled almost exclusively by Celts; not shown are enclaves inhabited by non-Celtic tribes, especially in parts of the Pyrenees and the Alps. The lighter areas indicate zones of historical expansion with strong indigenous substrata of non-Celtic origin: Italy south of the Po River (early 4th century BCE), Danube regions, modern Bulgaria and Galatia in Asia Minor (early 3rd century BCE).

The Celts today (bottom).

Map showing the extent of Celtic languages that are currently spoken or that became extinct after the 18th century: Breton [1] includes four Brythonic dialects, introduced from the 5th century via Britain, corresponding to four regions (Léon, Cornouaille, Trégor, Vannes); Cornish [2] became extinct towards the end of the 18th century; Welsh [3], an insular Brythonic language formerly spoken in regions up to Scotland; Irish [4], the Gaelic of Ireland; Manx [5], the Gaelic of the Isle of Man, extinct from the middle of the 20th century; Scottish [6], which includes the Gaelic dialects of the Highlands and the Hebridean islands.

Celts, Gauls, Galatians, Celtiberians and Bretons

Classical writers indiscriminately used various terms corresponding to today's *Celts, Gauls* and *Galatians* to designate the groups of people who occupied vast territories from the Atlantic coast to the Danube Valley. The first term they employed, *Keltoi* or *Keltai* (Latin *Celtae*), approximates to our word *Celts* and was probably in use by Greek writers from the 6th century BCE onwards. Its first certain appearance is in the *Histories* of Herodotus, written around the middle of the 5th century, but based on information probably gathered during the preceding century. Although its meaning is uncertain, it is undoubtedly of Celtic origin, and was still used several centuries later in the Iberian Peninsula. Nowadays it is considered to be the most general term, the one that encompasses all of the ancient and modern peoples belonging to the Celtic linguistic family. In antiquity, similarly, it embraced a mosaic of great and small tribes who described themselves in emblematic terms: thus, the Boii were 'the Terrible Ones', the Remi 'the First', the Senones 'the Veterans', and the Aedui 'the Raging Ones'. Their southern, Mediterranean neighbours considered them related by their languages, their religion and their customs.

The Latin term *Galli* (*Gauls*) was used by the Romans from the beginning of the 4th century. Its Greek form, *Galatai* or *Galatae*, did not appear until the beginning of the following century. It is probably not a totally different term designating a group of Celts but rather a different form of the same name that may originally have meant 'the Brave', an appellation appropriate to the reputation of these tribes.

Nowadays, however, the word *Gaul* tends to mean specifically the inhabitants of Cisalpine and Transalpine Gaul, while *Galatae* is applied to those who settled in Asia Minor around 278. One of St Paul's letters was addressed to these 'Galatians'.

The equivalent term *Celtiberians* was introduced in classical times to designate the Celtic populations of the Iberian Peninsula, who were strongly influenced by the Iberian culture of its Mediterranean seaboard. Today, the peninsular peoples of Celtic origin – which includes many tribes from the Atlantic side – are collectively described as *Hispano-Celts*.

The insular Celts were known as *Pritani* (*Bretons* or *Britons*), a term used in the Greek adjectival form by the navigator Pytheas of Massilia (Marseille) to designate the British Isles from the time of Alexander the Great. The creation of the Roman province of Britannia consolidated the geographical use of the name, which by the 5th century also signified Armorica (modern Brittany), populated at that time by insular migrants. Bretons are the modern inhabitants of this Continental 'Britain', while the Welsh descendants of the insular Britons style themselves *Cymru* ('Companions'). The Gaelic-speaking Irish and Scots belong to another linguistic branch of the Celtic family.

Left
Engraving by Matthäu Merian the Elder showing the capture of Rome by the Gauls led by Brennos, from the *Historical Chronicle* of Johann Ludwig Gottfried published in Frankfurt, Germany in 1630.
Illustrators of the period gave the Celts arms and equipment identical to those of the Romans or to those they depicted in Old Testament scenes. As for the portrayal of Rome, it features monuments at least 500 years later than the events shown, such as Castel Sant Angelo, the mausoleum of the emperor Hadrian converted to a fortress by the Popes.

Left

The fortress of Tre'r Ceiri (Caernavonshire, Wales).
Situated on an exposed height, it dominates the northern coast of Wales some 20 km (14 miles) south of the island of Anglesey.

Opposite

Coloured print showing the Gaulish emissaries taking the oath to the military standards, from *The Illustrated History of the World for Everyone* **by J.G. Vogt published in Leipzig in 1893.**
The picture perpetuates the romantic idea of the Celts that developed around the end of the 18th century.

> The whole race which is now called both 'Gallic' and 'Galatic' is war-mad, and both high-spirited and quick for battle, although otherwise simple and not ill-mannered.
>
> STRABO, *Geography*, IV, 4.

Languages and literature

Following the success of William Camden's *Britannia*, first published in 1586 and going into several later editions, the Welsh scholar Edward Lhuyd's *Archaeologia Britannica* (1707) gave the first account of the Celtic languages still spoken in his time, with a basic grammar and lexicon. This was the forerunner of Celtic philology, which developed rapidly from the second quarter of the 19th century. It is no longer based solely on comparative study of the medieval and modern Celtic dialects, as it now has at its disposal several hundred inscriptions made by the ancient Celts themselves using different alphabets derived successively from Etruscan, Greek, Iberian and Latin. The distinctive characteristics of several ancient Celtic dialects have also recently been isolated. We can now differentiate between the languages of the Celts of Lombardy/Piedmont (traditionally but incorrectly classified as 'Lepontic'), the Celtiberians and the Gauls. This has led to the abandonment of the traditional model, developed in the 19th century, of two great founding branches of the Celtic family of languages – the Goidelic and the Brythonic – successively associated with the great migrations of Celtic peoples and their presumed ancestors.

Interest in ancient Celtic literature developed in the 1760s with the immense success of the Ossianic pastiches of the Scot James Macpherson. These were quickly translated into most European languages and enthusiastically hailed as the expression of a literary sensibility in tune with the pre-Romantic age. Translations of Welsh and Irish writings poured forth in the wake of Macpherson's work. Complementing the literature was an upsurge in interest in traditional Celtic music.

The Celtic 'founders of the nation'

Nowadays accepted as founding elements in modern European culture, in some countries the Celts have become symbolic representatives of the nation's purest and deepest roots. In France the Gauls had opposed the Franks, who were considered to be the ancestors of the privileged nobility and monarchy of the *ancien régime*. The Gauls therefore came to be seen as the forerunners of liberal, radical democracy, the true 'founders of the nation'. Obviously the assumptions behind this Celtic entry on to the French political scene do not bear close scrutiny. The chief influence came from Amédée Thierry's *Histoire des Gaulois* (1828), which propounded the idea of a Gallic race whose direct heirs were the French. Thierry's work consisted of a series of clichés that thereafter coloured the work of many historians of Gaul. Sometimes these 'histories' verged on caricature, especially after French defeat in the Franco-Prussian War of 1870/1, when anti-German chauvinism was at its height.

Druids and megaliths

The Celtic intellectual elite – the druids – first aroused the interest of historians in Britain and France at the beginning of the 16th century. From this point onwards they were invariably associated with the megalithic monuments of the Atlantic regions. Druids were considered philosophical originators of the doctrine of the immortality of the soul; and by the 18th century they were also seen as experts on the harmony between man and nature that contemporary science was just beginning to rediscover. The neo-druidic associations that sprang up at the time constituted something of a Celtic variant of Freemasonry, reinventing traditions and ceremonies that centred on the great solar festivals of the year. In Britain their locus was naturally the great megalithic monuments – especially Stonehenge and Avebury – that since the 17th century had been thought to be druidic sanctuaries. This idea was developed in the mid-18th century notably by William Stukeley, and it was warmly received in France, where the writings of La Tour d'Auvergne (*Origines gauloises [Welsh Origins]*, 1796), Jacques de Cambry (*Monuments celtiques [Celtic Monuments]*, 1805) and others suggested that the Breton megaliths were druidic astronomical sanctuaries. The anachronistic association thus established between monuments constructed in the 5th–3rd millennia BCE by pre-Indo-European (and therefore pre-Celtic) peoples and the Celts of the Iron Age was wildly popular in the mid-19th century. It survives in France in the popular 'Gallic' folklore brilliantly illustrated in the Asterix comics.

Vercingetorix, the iconic national hero

The unhappy torch-bearer of Gaulish resistance against Caesar in 52 BCE, the young Arvernian leader Vercingetorix was cast by Thierry as the first French national hero. This role was confirmed in the *Histoire de France* (1837) of Henri Martin, who in 1865 even devoted a 'heroic drama' in verse to Vercingetorix. Soon his proud surrender before Alesia became one of the first illustrations in the history-books of generations of young French scholars, in the chapter dedicated to 'our ancestors the Gauls' that invariably followed that on the *Pax Romana*. Statues were raised to him anywhere that could be linked to his exploits. He was often paired with Joan of Arc as a hero of the Republic. The zenith of this glorious ascent into legend is the magisterial *Vercingetorix* (1901) by Camille Jullian, the great historian of Gaul.

But thereafter voices began to be raised against this iconic figure, and they continued throughout the 20th century. He was accused by some historians of blundering, incompetence and even of collaboration with the Roman enemy. Finally, now that the passion has died down, Vercingétorix has become a subject of *modern* history, offering a valuable insight into the mores of 19th-century France rather than ancient history or the writings of Julius Caesar. The latter are explored in depth in Jullian's book, which remains essential reading on that topic. However, since Jullian wrote his seminal work, archaeology has been able to provide a picture of Gaul in the middle of the 1st century BCE that is incomparably richer and more nuanced than it was at the beginning of the 20th century CE.

Historians and archeologists

The study of artefacts from the prehistoric past happily allowed the development of a new approach to the ancient Celts. Hitherto, the identification of possibly Celtic archaeological remains was rather slow, and the Celts were frequently associated with anything strange or picturesque that pre-dated the Roman era. Stone Age axes, jewellery and weapons from the Bronze Age and the Merovingian period were all hailed as 'Celtic' at one time or another. Rarely, objects that genuinely did come from the Iron Age of the historical Celts were identified in the same way. In 1862, Bronze Age weapons discovered at Alise-Sainte-Reine – presumed to be the site of Alesia (the scene of Vercingetorix's surrender to the Romans) – during a dig ordered by Napoleon III were immediately hailed as 'fallen from the failing hands of the defenders', thus helping to feed the 'Gallic' iconography that has survived to our own time.

The 'Alesia' dig fostered interest in everything pre-Roman, and several burial-sites, especially in Champagne, subsequently yielded numerous artefacts. These eventually enriched the collections of the new National Museum of Antiquities. Study of these artefacts led in 1871 to the attribution of characteristic Iron Age tools to the historical Celts – the Transalpine invaders of Italy – and, the next year, to the subdivision of this epoch into two cultural periods: the first called the 'Hallstatt' (first Iron Age) culture, after a burial-ground in Austria; the second known as 'La Tène' (second Iron Age) culture, after a Swiss lakeside site near Neuchâtel.

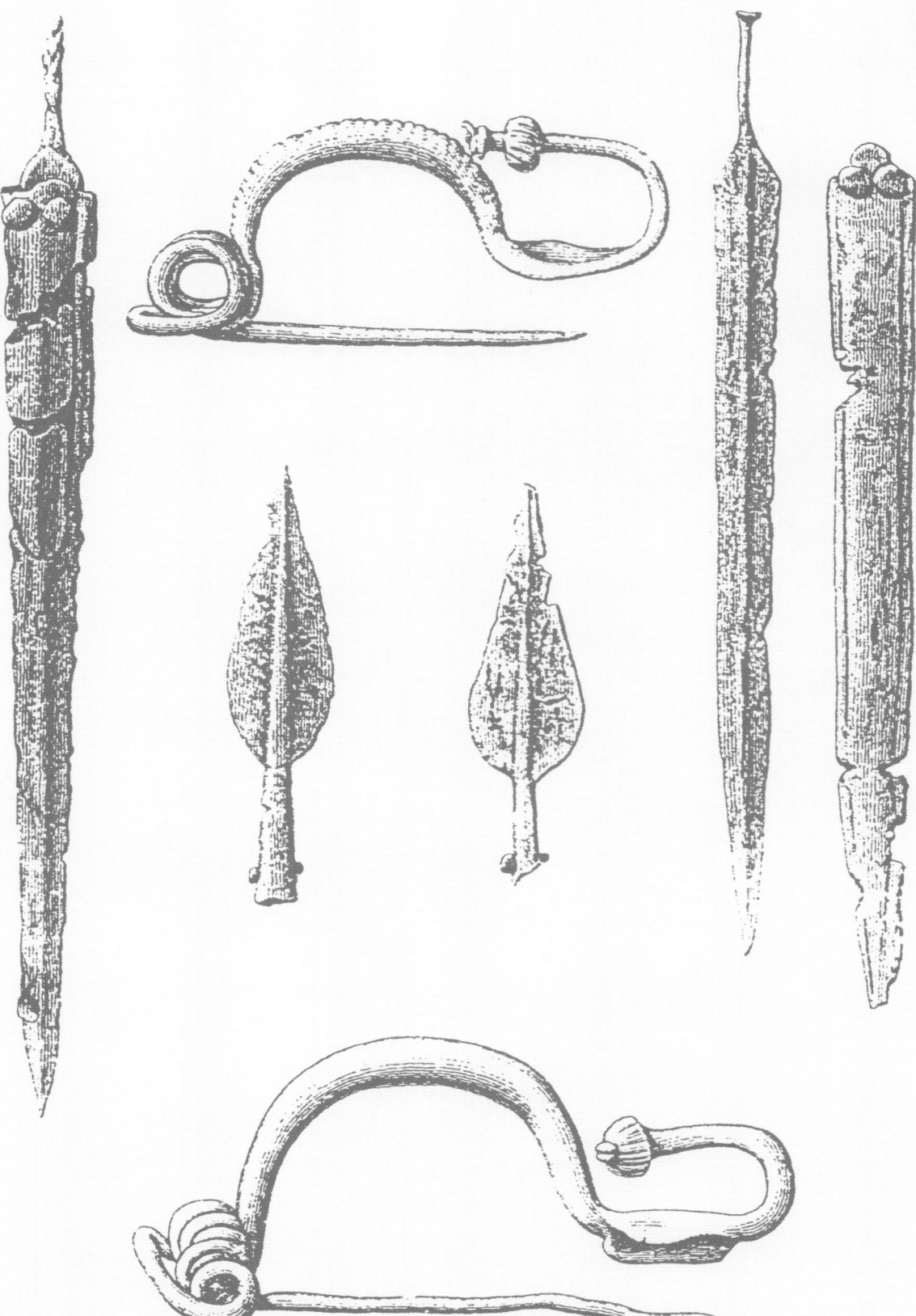

Left

Gaulish artefacts from Marzabotto; plate illustrating the article by Gabriel de Mortillet published in 1871 in *La Revue Archéologique.* *Here the author compares weapons and ornaments (1, 3, 5) found on this site of an Etruscan town near Bologna with similar objects (2, 4, 6) found in the Champagne region of France, in the Musée des Antiquités Nationales de Saint-Germain-en-Laye, created several years earlier. The appearance of this article can be considered, together with the International Congress on prehistoric anthropology and archaeology that took place in Bologna the same year, 1871, as the decisive moment in the birth of Celtic archaeology.*

The Gauls of Marzabotto and the origins of Celtic archaeology

In Bologna in 1871, an International Congress of Prehistoric Anthropology and Archaeology (two rapidly expanding new disciplines) gave scholars from all over Europe an opportunity to visit several archaeological sites in northern Italy. The excavations at Marzabotto, some 20 km (12 miles) from Bologna, on the site of an Etruscan town, had been explored for a decade by a distinguished Bolognese amateur, Count Gozzadini. A small burial-ground had just been discovered, containing male and female interments, accompanied by unusual objects for the region: long iron

swords, curious brooches and other jewellery. Two visiting scholars, Frenchman Gabriel de Mortillet and the Swiss Emile Desor, immediately recognized archaeological evidence for the presence of Gaulish invaders from the beginning of the 4th century. The objects in question were familiar to both archaeologists as similar ones had already been gathered in their hundreds from the Champagne burial-sites and La Tène. Celtic archaeology was born!

The presence of this burial-ground in the ruins of an Etruscan town was long

considered proof of the destructive character of the Celtic invasion. But we now know that the artefacts identified in 1871 came partly from an Etruscan tomb dating from the end of the 5th century (the silver brooch), and partly from Celtic tombs that can be dated approximately to the end of the 4th century or the beginning of the 3rd, thus excluding all direct connection with the invasion. It is currently thought that the town was abandoned because of the collapse of trade routes rather than as a result of the violence of the Celts.

Historical Celts and others

Once the La Tène artefacts were attributed to the Celts, evidence of their presence was recognized even in regions where classical writings made no mention of them. Thus, from the end of the 19th century, it became possible to take the first tentative steps towards painting a picture of the ancient Celts based on a combination of textual and archaeological data.

The evolution of Celtic archaeology took a huge leap forward when excavations began on a larger scale: where colonies had sprung up around cemeteries or isolated tombs, be they simple villages or *oppida* (large, fortified, urbanized areas). The particular attention paid to certain categories of artefact – such as works of art – and increased sophistication in dating and analysis also shed new light on the existing documentary evidence.

The identification of ancient Celtic-language peoples belonging to neither Hallstatt nor La Tène culture – or at least not originally, as in the case of the Golasecca Celts in modern-day Lombardy and Piedmont – prompted a re-examination of

One thousand lbs. of gold was fixed as the ransom of a people destined ere long to rule the world. This humiliation was great enough as it was, but it was aggravated by the despicable meanness of the Gauls, who produced unjust weights, and when the tribune protested, the insolent Gaul threw his sword into the scale, with an exclamation intolerable to Roman ears, 'Woe to the vanquished!'

Titus Livius, *The History of Rome*, V, 48.

the overly exclusive link between La Tène culture and the Celts. This led to the introduction of the concept of the La Tène (or historical) Celts: those who were the protagonists of great events described in classical literature – the invasion of Italy and the Danubian expansion.

The gates to another world

Modern 'Celtomania' is often found in unexpected places. *Here, a German beer from the end of the 1980s: the modern aluminium bottle proclaims it 'the beer of druids' and 'splendid Teutonic elixir'! A bearded druid crowned with oak leaves and perched on an oak tree is cutting mistletoe.*

According to Irish tradition, the ancient Celts who inhabited the island integrated the impressive monuments that already dominated the landscape when they arrived into their mythological topography. They were venerated as the constructions of a mythical race and the dwelling-places of gods, as well as doorways to the other world, entries that opened temporarily at the feast of Samain. The great royal sites (Tara, Emain Macha, Cruachan) and their surroundings, and the megalithic monument of Lough Crew, have yielded a cache of inscribed bone plaques, probably dating from the 1st century CE, that may have been intended for ritual or magic use. Nevertheless, it is impossible either to prove that these places were used in ceremonies linked to astronomical events, or to reconstruct what actually happened there.

La Tène, the region that gave its name to La Tène culture

Lake Neuchâtel used to rise and fall alarmingly. In 1857 it sank to a very low level, which led to the discovery of the sunken site of La Tène at La Thielle, on the northernmost tip of the lake. With the first systematic lowering of the Jura lakes from 1868 to1883, the site became completely dry, enabling a local teacher, Paul Vouga, to conduct archaeological excavations. Vouga uncovered the remains of two bridges that crossed La Thielle, and the site rapidly became world famous because of the number of artefacts found there. In 1872 La Tène gave its name to the second Celtic Iron Age. The artefacts recovered during the excavations (which continued until 1917) included wooden items that have been submitted to dendrochronological analysis (based on the decomposition rates of annual rings in the wood). This gave the following dates: 251 BCE for the 'Vouga Bridge' (upstream); 229 BCE for a wooden shield; 38 BCE for a walkway laid out in the temporarily dry bed of the La Thielle River under the 'Desor Bridge' (downstream). The site's function and the significance of the hundreds of metal objects – arms, tools, ornaments – discovered there remain debatable. There are two principal theories. First, it has been suggested that it was a place of transit linked to a settlement that was destroyed by catastrophic floods. The important conjunction of a water-crossing (the former bed of the River Aar) with land routes may explain the concentration of craft activities. Alternatively, some have said that it was the site of a cult, with the bridges being used primarily as platforms for the sacrifice of objects, animals and humans. One must have reservations about both of these theories. There is, though, an undisputed connection between the construction of the bridges – in the first half of the 3rd century BCE, as is confirmed by a neighbouring Celtic bridge discovered at Cornaux in 1965 – and the development of a network of long-distance trade routes in which Switzerland played a pivotal role. Exclusively ritual use therefore seems unlikely.

Left
View over the site of La Tène (Marin-Épagnier, Switzerland).
Taken from the west bank of Lake Neuchâtel. On the horizon, the Jura mountains.

Left
***In situ* reconstruction of a
5th century BCE tumulus at
Tübingen-Kilchberg
(Baden-Württemberg).**
*The burial mound is surrounded
at the base by a circle of large
stones and topped with an
anthropomorphic stele.*
Diameter of the mound: approx. 13 m (43 ft).

The question of origins

Once La Tène Celts had been identified through archaeology at the end of the 19th century, their distribution was studied using a combination of texts and remains. The plan was to make accurate estimates of when the Celts first appeared in various regions. This method was employed for the 4th and 3rd centuries BCE and it worked very well: the appearance of characteristic La Tène weapons and ornaments in areas where they represented a new, non-indigenous, element corresponded with classical writings on the irruption of the Transalpine Celts into the Po Valley and with all available information on Danubian expansion and the 'Great Expedition' of 280 BCE. But it was much more difficult to explain the Celticization of other parts of Europe in this way, and the origins of La Tène culture itself remained unclear. Long after the Second World War, it was still thought that the development of La Tène culture must have been the result of a new wave of immigration, even in those regions where Celts had been long established, such as Champagne.

The issue of the La Tène cultural substratum was eventually settled by casually assigning features of the Hallstatt culture to the Celts of those regions that stretched between the Alps and the great plains of the north, from the west of France to Bohemia. But this still left areas where there was strong evidence of a Celtic presence that could not possibly be associated with the (supposedly Celtic) Hallstatt culture, and where any La Tène elements seemed rather too late and inconsequentially few in number. This is notably the case with the Iberian Peninsula and the British Isles, which remained in classical times the last bastions of independent Celts.

Because of these inconsistencies, a theory of *earlier* Celtic migration, especially towards the end of the Bronze Age (the end of the second millennium BCE), was devised. This was a time when vast territories of Central and Western Europe displayed considerable cultural uniformity, including the widespread practice of cremation and burial of the remains in urns. Some of the features of this 'Urnfield' culture can be attributed to people of Celtic origin.

Moreover, the obvious cultural frontier that separated Central Europe from the 'Lusatian Urnfield' culture of Northern Europe can be seen as the boundary between two great ethnic groupings: Celtic in the south, Germanic in the north. In Bohemia this boundary approximates the course of the River Elbe; along its banks villages of each culture are separated by only a few kilometres. They share the same agricultural activities but the shapes and decoration of their fine ceramics are markedly different.

But again this scenario does not fit all situations. The similarity of ceramic forms, often inspired by widely available metal vessels, and the cremation rite point to more general tendencies that are not exclusively linked to ethnic variations. For instance, they might be customs linked to new beliefs. It has been noted that some Urnfield groups occupied territories that were later settled by obviously non-Celtic people, for example in north-western Spain, which was inhabited in the 6th and 5th centuries BCE by people of Iberian descent. In short, models of Indo-European and Celtic expansion that were developed in the 1930s – and associated with a contemporary theory of the evolution of these languages that has recently been challenged – are now thought to be unnecessarily complicated and based on inaccurate assumptions.

Classical writings do not give much help towards resolving the question of origins. Herodotus was the first to provide reliable documentation, but he states, on the one hand, that the Celts lived near the source of the Danube (a region with features of the central-western Hallstatt culture, thought in the 1930s to be Celtic), and, on the other, that they lived on the south-western tip of the Iberian Peninsula.

Opposite
**Statue of a man, found broken in three pieces at the
foot of the Ditzingen-Hirschlanden tumulus
(Baden-Württemberg).**
*Wearing a conical hat and a large closed torc, the figure is
otherwise naked except for a belt with a round-hilted dagger.
This remarkable sculpture is generally related to Greek models.*
6th century BCE. Height: 1,500 mm (4 ft 11 in).
Stuttgart, Württembergisches Landesmuseum.

The Celts according to Herodotus, *c.* 500 BCE

Herodotus wrote his *Histories* around the middle of the 5th century BCE. Born in Asia Minor, the 'Father of History' travelled extensively throughout the Greek colonies of southern Italy, and it was probably there that he gathered the information on Western Europe that he included in his writings. He mentions the Celts in two passages. The first (Book Two, 33) describes the Danube (Istros), 'which has its source amongst the Celts near Pyrene and flows right through the middle of Europe (the Celts live beyond the Pillars of Hercules, next to the Cynesians who are the most westerly people of Europe), to reach the Black Sea at the Milesian colony of Istria'. The second passage (Book Four, 49) simply summarizes and confirms the first: 'All these rivers discharge into the Danube, that mighty stream which, rising amongst the Celts, the most westerly, after the Cynetes, of all

European nations, traverses the whole length of the continent before it enters Scythia.' Herodotus seems to have used two sources, reflecting the probable situation at the middle or end of the 6th century BCE. The first probably comes from Greek trading posts in the Iberian Peninsula. The second must have originated in Marseille and seems to be based on the stories of merchants or travellers who sailed up the Rhône Corridor to reach the upper Danube. Archaeological discoveries confirm this hypothesis: the Hallstatt fortress of Heuneburg, situated on the upper course of the Danube, has yielded much pottery imported from the Mediterranean, fragments of black-figured Attic vases and shards of Marseille wine amphorae; its fortifications have also been reconstructed following a plan based on rectangular bastions, derived from a style

known in greater Greece, and therefore probably built by an architect from that region. Herodotus' Celts who lived in the south of modern Portugal were probably those who settled in the region of Cape St Vincent. They were still called *Celtici* or *Keltikoi* several centuries later. According to the geographer Strabo, groups of these tribes gradually migrated northwards, establishing themselves near Cape Nerion, known in classical times as Celticum promontorium (now Cap Touriñan).

These distant Atlantic coasts were therefore inhabited from that era by tribes said to be Celtic, although no Hallstatt- or La Tène-type artefacts have been found in the region. So Herodotus' consistent testimony shows that recognizably Celtic-type settlements were established in Western Europe from very early times.

Above
The Hallstat fortress of Heuneburg near Sigmaringen (Baden-Württemberg).
An isolated hill crowned with a triangular plateau that dominates the left side of the Danube valley, 30 km (18¹/₂ miles) north of Lake Constance, it is now the best-known 'residence and princely burial ground' complex, frequently cited and used as a reference. Strong Mediterranean influences have been noted: not simply imports but also the intervention of a military architect probably trained by Western Greeks.

New data on Celtic origins

Clearly, Herodotus' writings directly contradict the theory of the distribution of Celtic populations that postulated a relatively late expansion from a Central European nucleus. However, many popular books still stand by this late-expansion hypothesis. Their maps illustrate a bean-shaped original settlement somewhere north of the Alps – in the area where La Tène culture developed in the 5th century – with arrows radiating out from it in all directions. Some of these arrows bear dates that are wholly fantastical, but others – those pointing towards Cispadane Gaul, the Danubian territories and Asia Minor – do at least correspond with genuine Celtic expansion.

The late-expansion model took another knock with the discovery of inscriptions in modern-day Piedmont and Lombardy. These inscriptions, although written in characters taken from the Etruscan alphabet, are of the Celtic language-group, yet certainly pre-date the invasion of the beginning of the 4th century BCE. The tribes who made the inscriptions were culturally related to the complex of north Italian cultures. They constituted a western branch named 'Golasecca culture', after an important site in the upper Po Valley between the Rivers Ticino and Adda, recognized since the 19th century. Once again, their Celtic credentials were unconvincingly attributed to minor infiltrations by Transalpine Hallstatt or La Tène groups in the 5th century BCE, but this theory falls down because the earliest inscriptions (of which there are many) date from the end of the 7th century BCE, and this particular form of inscription persisted up to the 1st century BCE. One can therefore confidently say that it was a well-established local practice, as with the neighbouring Veneti, who also adopted the Etruscan alphabet. The idea that such inscription was employed by non-indigenous Transalpine tribes who integrated with the local population as a kind of advance guard for the 4th-century invasion seems utterly unlikely in comparison.

This therefore raised the possibility that tribes speaking Celtic languages could belong to distinct cultural locations that were neither Hallstatt nor La Tène. This observation was as interesting as the evolution of the Golasecca culture, and it implied continuous Celtic habitation from as far back as the end of the second millennium BCE or even earlier.

The ancient Celts and their roots

So the available information seems to indicate that Celts started to migrate from well before the 6th century BCE. Thereafter, they formed several culturally differentiated groups that occupied most of Central and Western Europe. In the centre groups settled between the massif of the Alps and the southern edge of the great northern plains of Europe. This was to become the birthplace of La Tène culture, which flourished from the middle of the 5th century to the second half of the 1st century BCE, when Roman and Germanic domination of formerly Celtic territories became complete.

The earliest written evidence of a Celtic language

Inscriptions written in a Celtic–Etruscan alphabet – also traditionally, but incorrectly, called 'Lepontic', after the Lepontines, a small tribe known to have lived in the Ticino Valley north of Lake Maggiore – can be divided into two major series. The earliest inscriptions cover a period ranging from the end of the 7th century (inscription from Sesto Calende, in the neighbourhood of Golasecca on the left bank of the Ticino as it flows out of Lake Maggiore) and the beginning of the 6th century (on a vase found in a grave at

Castelleto Ticino, opposite Sesto Calende-Golasecca, on the Piedmontese side of the river) to the end of the 5th century BCE. They consist principally of graffiti on pottery, generally simply the name of the owner. But inscriptions carved on stone have also been found; outstanding among these is the one found at the urban centre of Como-Prestino that can be dated to the end of the 6th century or the beginning of the fifth. It is a dedication carefully carved on a long stone lintel, between two lines, following a layout used in other lapidary

inscriptions in the region. This characteristic is typical of the Etruscan seaboard, indicating that the borrowed script did not come from northern Etruria (Po Valley) but via the routes that linked the great lakes with the Gulf of Genoa.

The second, more recent, series dates chiefly from the 2nd century BCE and the beginning of the following century. It includes not only inscriptions on pottery and stone – some of them in both Celtic and Latin, such as a funerary inscription from Todi (central Italy: a long way from the normal locale of

Above and left

**Detail and diagram
of the Como-Prestino
inscription.**

*Leftwards reading, it was
very carefully incised
between two lines, in letters
borrowed from the Etruscan
alphabet, on a very long
stone lintel or step. It
consists of a dedication in
the language of ancient
populations of Celtic origin
in what is now Lombardy
and Piedmont.*

End 6th–early 5th century BCE.

Length of the monolithic block:

3,750 mm, including 1,900 mm for

the inscription in the centre.

Como (Italy), Museo Civico

Archeologico P. Giovio.

these inscriptions, whose epicentre seems
to be the territory of the powerful Insubres
tribe of Lombardy) – but several monetary
inscriptions on drachmas inspired by issues
from Marseille, of which the oldest may
date back to the 4th century BCE.

The continuity of usage of this writing over
several centuries in the same geographical
location, as well as no evidence of writing
among the 4th-century Celtic immigrants –
notably the Cenomani, who installed
themselves north of the Po between two
indigenous populations, the Insubres (direct
descendants of the Golasecca Celts) and the
Veneti – prompts caution over suggested
distinctions between the languages of both
series: 'Lepontic', defined as Celtic (it refers
to a language related to Gaulish, but with
several distinctive features), for the earlier
series; Gaulish for the later series. This
differentiation is supposed to have been
made by Transalpines of this period, but
knowledge of the ancient Celtic languages
and their geographical and historical
variants is still too fragmentary to permit
such assumptions.

Left
The *oppidum* of Ulaca.
View of the altar, carved into the rock, of the oppidum *of Ulaca (Solosancho, Spain), situated on a high plateau dominating the plain of Avila, 20 km (12¹/₂ miles) south-west of the town. On the horizon, towards the south, lie the peaks of the Sierra de Gredos. This was one of the centres of the powerful Celto-Lusitanian tribe of the Vettones.*

Since the 1870s, La Tène culture has been recognized as that of the 'historical' Celts – those described in the writings of Greek and Latin commentators – who invaded Italy at the beginning of the 4th century BCE and, in the following century, penetrated as far as the Balkans, threatened the sacred site of Delphi and even settled in Asia Minor, in the plains around Ankara, which for that reason was called 'Galatia' (now modern Turkey).

However, analysis of the northern Italian inscriptions indicates that Celts were established long before the 4th-century invasion in what are now Lombardy and Piedmont, where they founded settlements that were the forerunners of several great modern cities. The Celtic name of the most important one, Mediolanon (now Milan), means 'the centre of the territory'. This was the capital of the Insubres, a powerful tribal confederation documented since the 4th century BCE. These early Italian Celts do not seem to have adopted any elements of La Tène culture – except possibly weapons – until the 3rd century BCE.

The only other Celtic tribes of this period for whom we have documentary evidence are those described by Herodotus on the Atlantic seaboard of modern-day Portugal. Similarly, no Celtic inscriptions have been found anywhere between the Atlantic coast and the mountains of Central Europe. However, it seems probable that the Celts constituted – with several exceptions, such as the ancestors of the Basques of northern Spain and southern France, and the Rhètes of the Alps – the major people of the region. It is clear that this situation was the result of a long, complex process of integration with different and considerably earlier aboriginal populations.

There is no indisputable theory for how Celtic peoples evolved, but it seems likely that their ancestors were among the earliest Indo-European groups to reach the Atlantic coast, where they gradually achieved domination over the descendants of the tribes who had constructed the megaliths. This would have taken place towards the middle of the third millennium BCE and would have been perpetrated by groups descended from the 'Battle-Axe' or 'Corded Ware' folk – Indo-Europeans who occupied Northern Europe around the beginning of the millennium, penetrating as far as Switzerland and the Rhine Valley. These energetic people settled in the British Isles, the Iberian Peninsula and even North Africa. They were traditionally associated with the spread of metalworking and were known as the 'Beaker' folk, after a drinking vessel typically found in their graves, sometimes accompanied by a bow and arrows. Were they Celts? On the one hand, they do not appear to have been entirely homogeneous, so they could not be labelled as such. However, their language probably formed the template for all of the Celtic languages (as well as some related but distinct languages, such as the Lusitanian dialect of the Douro Valley).

Recently, a spectacular burial-site of one of the Beaker folk has been excavated near Stonehenge. As well as yielding exceptionally rich artefacts, the discovery of this grave allowed DNA analysis to be made of a member of the Beaker elite. It seems that he was Alpine in origin.

Opposite
The Dürrnberg mountain, near Hallein (Austria).
It dominates the course of the Salzach 20 km (12¹/₂ miles) upstream from Salzburg. The site owed its importance in the protohistoric era to mining and trading in salt. Very rich burial-grounds (5th–3rd century BCE) have been discovered and explored on its summit and slopes (see p. 62).

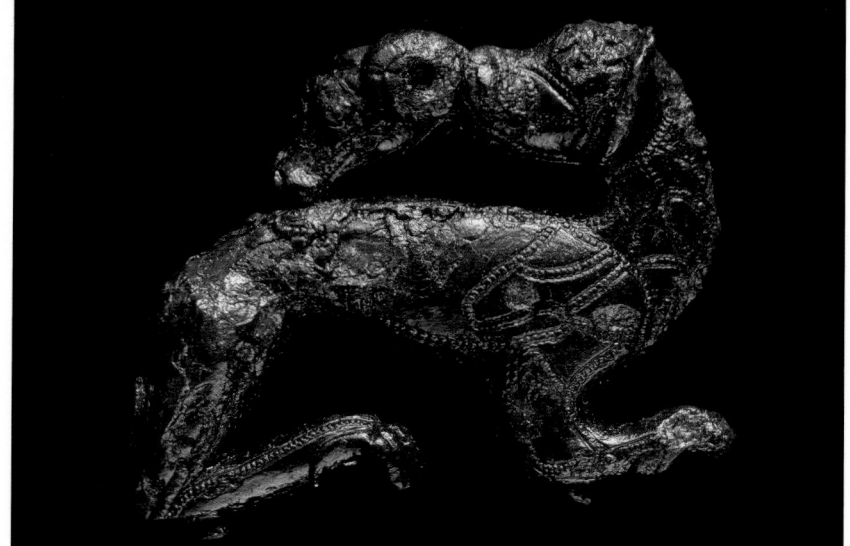

Left
Bronze statuette showing a lion with a ram's head in front of his muzzle.
Found in the excavated section of a large structure built against the exterior of a rectangular enclosure at Droužkovice (Bohemia) in the foothills of Monts Metalliferes, a site that has also yielded fragments of Attic black-figure ceramics, the statue would have originally been fixed to the rim of a ceremonial pitcher. The work is typical of the Celtic transformation of borrowings from the Mediterranean repertoire – probably Etruscan in this case.
Second half of the 5th century BCE. Height: 40 mm.
Chomutov, Oblastní Muzeum.

The emergence of the historical Celts and La Tène civilization (6th–5th century BCE)

The 6th century BCE saw an unprecedented development of interaction between the Mediterranean cities, Central Europe and the Atlantic seaboard. The foundation of the Phoenician colony of Massilia (Marseille) around 600 BCE provided an outlet for goods and merchants coming from as far afield as the Paris Basin and the valleys of the Rhine and the Danube. Further west, beyond Gibraltar and Ceuta, the Phoenicians, who had already been established for several centuries at Gadeira (Cadiz), sailed along the Atlantic coast to the mouth of the Sado River. They even reached north of the Tagus Estuary (modern Lisbon), as recently discovered trading-posts in the region prove. In a four-month voyage the Carthaginian explorer Himilco explored the islands off the southern coast of Armorica (modern Brittany). The inhabitants of these islands had existing trade links with two far larger islands: Ierné (Ireland) and Albion (Great Britain). It should be added here that Keltos, the mythical ancestor of the Celts, was said to be the son of Heracles. He in turn, according to legend, had been the first Greek to venture to the Atlantic. It is in this general context that Herodotus collected his information about the Celts.

The chief reason for this interest in the extreme west among the great powers of the time was undoubtedly its rich metal deposits. These were common knowledge because of the stories of expeditions such as that of the Phoenicians to the opulent kingdom of Tartessos (in the Huelva region). Tartessos was ruled by Arganthonios, a sovereign whose name is derived from the Celtic word *arganto* (silver). However, it was not silver, nor even gold, that most interested the Phoenicians. Rather, they sought tin, which was essential in the manufacture of bronze. Although iron was by now being widely used (and would give its name to this epoch), bronze remained the pre-eminent material for metalworkers. The tin used in its manufacture came from deposits along the Atlantic coast. These were mined and transported across Gaul along well-established riverine or land trade routes, or by more recently charted seaways.

It is likely that there were also tin mines in Central Europe, in Monts Metalliferes, Bohemia. The metal from there would move south along already ancient paths that had been used for many centuries by merchants transporting amber from the Baltic. However, while neither the west–east nor the north–south trade routes were new, increased demand and a proliferation of outlets considerably increased the traffic in the middle of the 1st millennium BCE. The nature of certain merchandise that sustained the northern trade – metal or pottery Greek and Etruscan vases – enables us to appreciate its ebb and flow, and its impact, especially in the Transalpine regions. The effects of this commercial expansion are most evident today in the part of Europe that was the cradle of the historical Celts.

The principal beneficiaries were the leaders of the warrior caste, the heirs to a function that dates back at least to the Bronze Age and equates to that of the tribal king described in Irish writings. These Celtic 'princes' apparently played a central role in the spiritual and social lives of their communities. They can be identified by the elaborate funerary rituals that developed especially from the 7th century BCE. These are probably, to some degree at least, echoes of similar Italian funerary customs from the preceding century, in the 'orientalized' form used by the Etruscan-Italian elite. However, as is generally the case with Celtic borrowing from Mediterranean cultures, the funerary rituals were not blind imitation but rather the integration of elements of a new model into an existing ideological system that can be traced back at least to the preceding millennium.

Opposite
Detail of the mask decorating the hook of the bronze belt-hook from Želkovice (Bohemia).
See p. 39.
Second half of the 5th century BCE. Full height of the mask: 33 mm.
Prague, Národní Muzeum.

Armorican vase with incised and stamped decoration, from Kélouer-Plouhinec (Finistère), used as a funerary urn.
This is an excellent example of the ceramic production of the region, inspired by the ornamentation of metallic vases. The chief decoration is formed of a chain of overlapping S's, filled in with stippling. Around the beginning of the 5th century BCE, Armorica was one of the sites from which styles of decoration on metal and pottery spread throughout the British Isles, typifying La Tène culture.
5th–4th century BCE. Saint-Germain-en-Laye (Yvelines), Musée des Antiquités Nationales.

Flat-bottomed terracotta flagon from Hlubyně (Bohemia) with finely engraved and stamped decoration.
This pottery shape, typical of the initial phase of La Tène culture in Bohemia and the region bordering the Danube valley is to be found as far west as the Dürrnberg site, south of Salzburg. It was specially designed and used for the service and consumption of drinks such as hydromel, beer or wine.
Second half of the 5th century BCE. Height: 330 mm. Prague, Národní Muzeum.

The tombs of princes

Apart from the monument – a mound of earth and rocks, sometimes surmounted by a stele, later even a statute, over a large wooden funerary chamber – the most spectacular element of a princely burial is the presence of a ceremonial four-wheeled chariot, possibly symbolizing the solar chariot, on which the body is laid. The vehicle was probably used to transport the deceased to his last resting-place, as in Herodotus' account of a Scythian royal burial.

Another indicator of princely status is the presence of a set of drinking vessels, generally made of bronze. These point to the ancient tradition of ceremonial consumption of an alcoholic drink: beer, mead or, with the development of trade, mulled wine from the south. The drinking vessels were apparently not used privately but during banquets when the whole community gathered together on the great feasts of the Celtic year. At these feasts the princes would indulge in ritual intoxication in order to ascend closer to the gods.

The utensils used at these banquets and buried with the princes provide eloquent evidence that merchandise of Mediterranean origin reached the Celts. As well as drinking vessels, fragments of amphorae usually originating from Marseille, pitchers, cauldrons and other bronze vessels of Greek or Etruscan workmanship, sieves used to filter impurities from wine, and ceramic Attic goblets have all been unearthed. It seems likely that merchants' goods would also have included other products to enhance the prestige of the Celtic elite. However, many of these would have been perishable and therefore have not survived. We do, though, have fragments of silk-embroidered cloth that must have come from a distant land, and ivory appliqués that were originally attached to wooden furniture imported from Greece or Italy. A sumptuous bronze couch or bed discovered in a princely tomb at Hochdorf near Stuttgart illustrates another element in the commercial exchanges of the Transalpine world: it was probably made by Celts of the Golasecca culture of northern Italy. The little figurines mounted on wheels that support the bed display another novelty: inlays of coral, which was thought to have magical powers and was highly valued by the Celts.

Phalera (harness ornament) from the Hořovičky (Bohemia) chariot burial. Iron, covered with embossed sheet bronze.
Second half of the 5th century BCE. Diameter: 150 mm. Prague, Národní Muzeum.

Flat terracotta bowl from grave No. 66 of the Manětín-Hrádek (Bohemia) burial ground, richly decorated with stamped motifs arranged in concentric circles around the central *omphalos*.
This type of ceramic decoration developed in Central Europe, being jointly influenced by the decoration of metal or Attic black-figure vases and of the stamped pottery of the Golasecca culture in North Italy (see p. 40).
Second half of the 5th century BCE. Diameter: 173 mm. Prague, Národní Muzeum.

Towards the end of the 6th century BCE and continuing in the following century female burials of the 'princely' type became much more common. One of the most famous of these was that of the 'princess' of Vix. Such rituals clearly indicate that power in Celtic society could be held by women as well as men, and this continued for many centuries, as is shown by the later appearance of Queens Boudicca and Cartimandua in Britain.

These splendid male and female princely tombs (which have usually been found near fortified areas) have fascinated ancient historians for decades. Indeed, such has been the focus on them that equally significant evidence from rural sites in regions on the periphery of the princely world has often been neglected. In Bohemia, where the roots of Celtic settlement can be traced in an unbroken line back to the second half of the 3rd millennium BCE, fragments of Attic ceramics and even a local imitation of a black-figured drinking cup have been found in several small excavated settlements. This shows the extent of long-distance trade and a 'capillary' penetration of imported goods equal to that in the rural centre

of Italy, south of the Po, at the same time. Bohemia was clearly a special case where trade was concerned, though, probably on account of its abundant local metal deposits. In general, it stands out from more westerly regions because it can boast so many princely burials, particularly from the 6th century BCE onwards. Tombs with ceremonial chariots, mostly found on the fertile plains in the middle of the country, belong almost exclusively to the 7th century BCE.

The following century saw the rise of large fortified centres that indicate a major concentration of power. By the middle of the 6th century BCE Závist, the best known, had surpassed other Transalpine fortified sites as much by its exceptional size as by the importance of the constructions there. However, oddly, no princely burial from the period of its expansion, or even later, has yet been identified there. It is difficult to attribute this to their subsequent destruction or lack of visibility; more likely is that the region had by then left behind the tributary-chieftain phase and had evolved a system of centralized power that was collegial rather than individual.

Opposite

Detail of a phalera from Hořovičky (Bohemia).

This phalera (boss), an iron harness ornament covered with repoussé sheet bronze, from the chariot tomb of Hořovičky (Bohemia), was discovered in 1863. Also found were another similar piece, ten other smaller pieces decorated with a single row of heads that have since disappeared, and other metal items from the harness of the two yoked horses, as well as the remains of the chariot, a broadsword, an iron firedog and other items. The head shown is linked with the mistletoe-leaf motif that surrounds the face and that also appears above the headdress. This type of image of the chief masculine deity is one of the principal themes of the initial period of Celtic art. See p. 37.

Second half of the 5th century BCE. Diameter: 150 mm. Prague, Národní Muzeum.

Above

Bronze belt-hook, found in the 19th century in a tumulus burial, Želkovice (Bohemia).

The artist very skilfully emphasized the contrast between the vigorous, expressive relief of the fastening (see p. 34) and the finely engraved 'rocked-chisel' decoration of the plaque that covers the fixing for the leather part.

Second half of the 5th century BCE. Height: 62 mm. Prague, Národní Muzeum.

Following page

Detail of the Manětín-Hrádek (Bohemia) bowl. *See p. 37.*

Page 41
Detached terminal of a bronze fibula from Kšice (Bohemia), discovered in a tumulus inhumation burial.
This minuscule work represents the head of a bearded and moustached man, whose face remains very expressive, despite enlargement. It illustrates the remarkable quality of the modelling and cire perdue casting of Central European Celtic artists from the beginning of the La Tène age.
Second half of the 5th century BCE. Height: 16 mm.
Prague, Národní Muzeum.

Opposite
Mounting from a princely burial found in a tumulus, Chlum (Bohemia).
This was found with a beaker and two bronze bowls of Etruscan or North Italian origin, a long La Tène sword, an iron axe, a finely engraved cylindrical bronze case and two pots. Now incomplete, it is made up of a bronze plaque, decorated with compass-work on the silvered (tinned?) reverse, covered with sheet-gold openwork and embossed. Originally the iron points would have held pearls and round cabochons, probably in coral. This sort of object, designed to enhance the prestige of high-ranking persons, is fairly common in the Rhineland where it has been found in several richly furnished burials.
Second half of the 5th century BCE. Length: 52 mm.
Prague, Národní Muzeum.

Závist, a power-centre in the heart of Bohemia

The fortress of Závist dominates one bank of the Vltava River about 12 km (7 miles) upstream from Prague. It occupies a strategic location facing the former confluence with the Berounka River, where the stream leaves the woods for the more open countryside of central Bohemia. Settled since Neolithic times, although with several interruptions, the site became a fortified settlement of about 50 hectares (125 acres) around the end of the Bronze Age, in the 10th or 9th century BCE. However, its most significant expansion took place over nearly two centuries of continuous occupation beginning in the first half of the 6th century BCE. During this period an imposing system of ramparts made of wood, earth and dry-stone was gradually built around the hilltop plateau. By the end of the 6th century, an area of around 100 hectares (250 acres) was thus enclosed. This was an exceptionally large site in the Transalpine world of that time.

Major excavations carried out on the site over twenty years from 1963 revealed not only the long and complex history of the defence system but the principal stages of occupation of the interior space. The most remarkable discovery was on the plateau of the 'acropolis', where there was evidence of successive transformations of an area that may have been a cult centre. This was the central sanctuary of a vast territory, initially a rectangular enclosure formed by a palisade, in front of which were aligned, on each side of the path leading to the entrance, large buildings of equal size and shape. Around the middle of the 5th century BCE the complex was enclosed by a massive rectangular rampart behind a large trench carved out of the rock. Inside were high dry-stone platforms – still nearly 5 metres (16 feet) high – five rectangular and one triangular, which seems to have been a kind of astronomical observatory. The largest (27 m x 11 m/88 x 36 feet) is thought to have been an altar, or the base of a wooden temple inspired by the Etruscan model of a temple standing on a podium. Before the end of the 5th century, the space between these foundations was deliberately filled in to form a single platform.

This is the most important stone-built monumental ensemble of the period in the northern Mediterranean region yet discovered. Subsequently the site was almost completely abandoned for more than two centuries. It was reoccupied towards the end of the first quarter of the 2nd century BCE and then became the starting-point for the building of a network of Bohemian *oppida*.

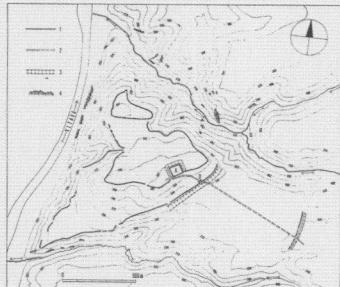

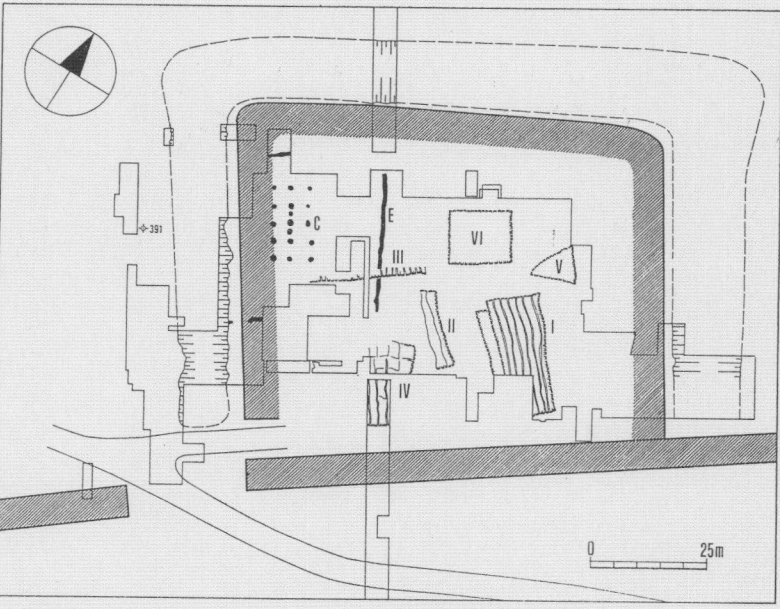

Left
Plans of the fortress of Závist.
On the left, a plan of the fortress complex in the 5th century BCE. On the right, detail of a plan showing the penultimate state of the rectangular enclosure of the acropolis, with a rampart protected by a large ditch and, inside, the monumental drystone foundations.

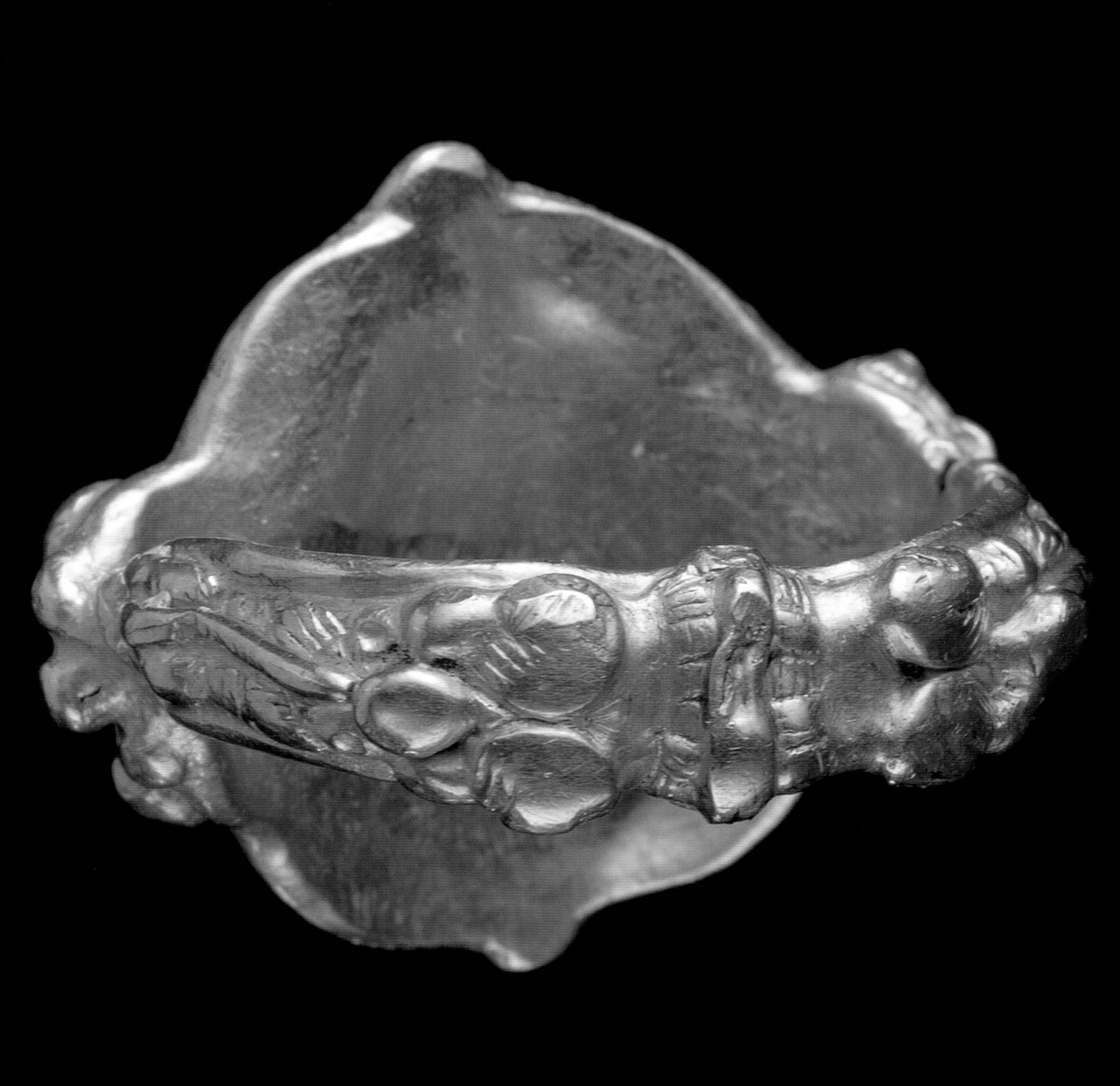

Preceding pages
Gold ring from the Hořovice region (Bohemia).
Probably inspired by an Etruscan model, this jewel for a person of high rank illustrates the quality of the Central European jewellers' workmanship, as well as the refined taste of their patrons.
Second half of the 5th century BCE. Height of the bezel: 25 mm. Prague, Národní Muzeum.

> ... they amass a great amount of gold, which is used for ornament not only by the women but also by the men. For around their wrists and arms they wear bracelets, around their necks heavy necklaces of solid gold, and huge rings they wear as well ...
>
> DIODORUS SICULUS, *Historical Library*, V, 27.

The emergence of Celtic peoples

Due to the impressive richness of its burials, the princely system is often considered the sole model of Celtic society of the 6th–5th century BCE. However, it was the dominant form of society in only some of the Celtic regions. Elsewhere, other types of community may have lacked the spectacular burial chambers of a social elite, but they seem to have been even more dynamic. Such was the case, for instance, in Champagne, on the periphery of 'princely burials' territory. Here a non-indigenous population, probably originating in the south-east,

established itself around the middle of the 6th century BCE, to become the nucleus of a 'Jogassian' settlement (named after Les Jogasses in Chouilly, where an important burial-ground was discovered). This settlement grew tremendously over the next a hundred years, and by the end of the 5th century Champagne had become densely populated with historical Celtic communities. Just as at Závist, no ostentatious princely burials occurred here: a burial might include a single four-wheeled chariot, but it was invariably poorly equipped, as no doubt was the tomb in which it was buried. However, grave goods found in the area are generally as fine as those excavated in the princely region.

In Switzerland, the essential gateway for traffic to and from Italy, graves with princely type furnishings are few in number and generally fairly old. Nevertheless, from the second half of the 5th century BCE this region would flourish impressively as a La Tène settlement. Its burial-grounds indicate local conformity in dress and funerary customs, but in contrast to Champagne the torc worn by women is generally accompanied by ankle-rings. These distinctions in feminine dress indicate the rank of the individual, and also her membership of a large community, a tribe.

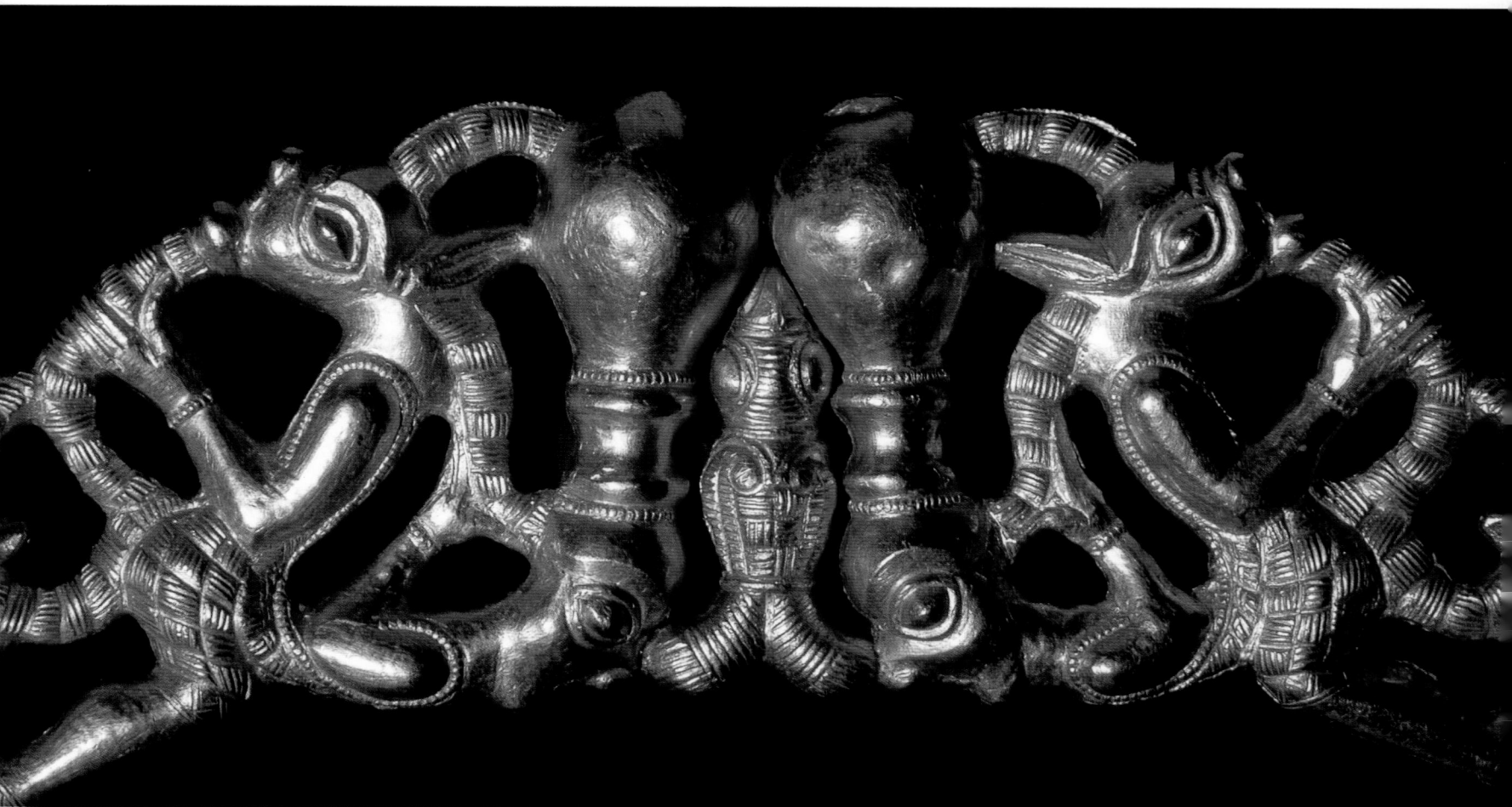

Above and opposite
Detail of two gold torcs from Erstfeld (Switzerland).
Four fine gold torcs and three gold bracelets were discovered under a rock in Erstfeld (Uri). Generally held to be the hoard of a jeweller or a merchant, the find may actually be a votive offering designed to attract the gods' favour before crossing the the Alps. The central part of the torc above displays an astonishing melange of monstrous vegetal, animal and human elements, arranged around a bird flanked by two bulbous shapes, possibly fruits.

In different style, the torc on the right has a central part formed of false terminals, flanked on each side by monstrous siren-type creatures, whose wings and tail are palmettes, and the head that of a quadruped with human eyes. The ensemble forms two interlaced S-scrolls with opposing movements.
End 5th–early 4th century BCE. Actual length of the detail: 80 mm.
Zurich, Swiss National Museum.

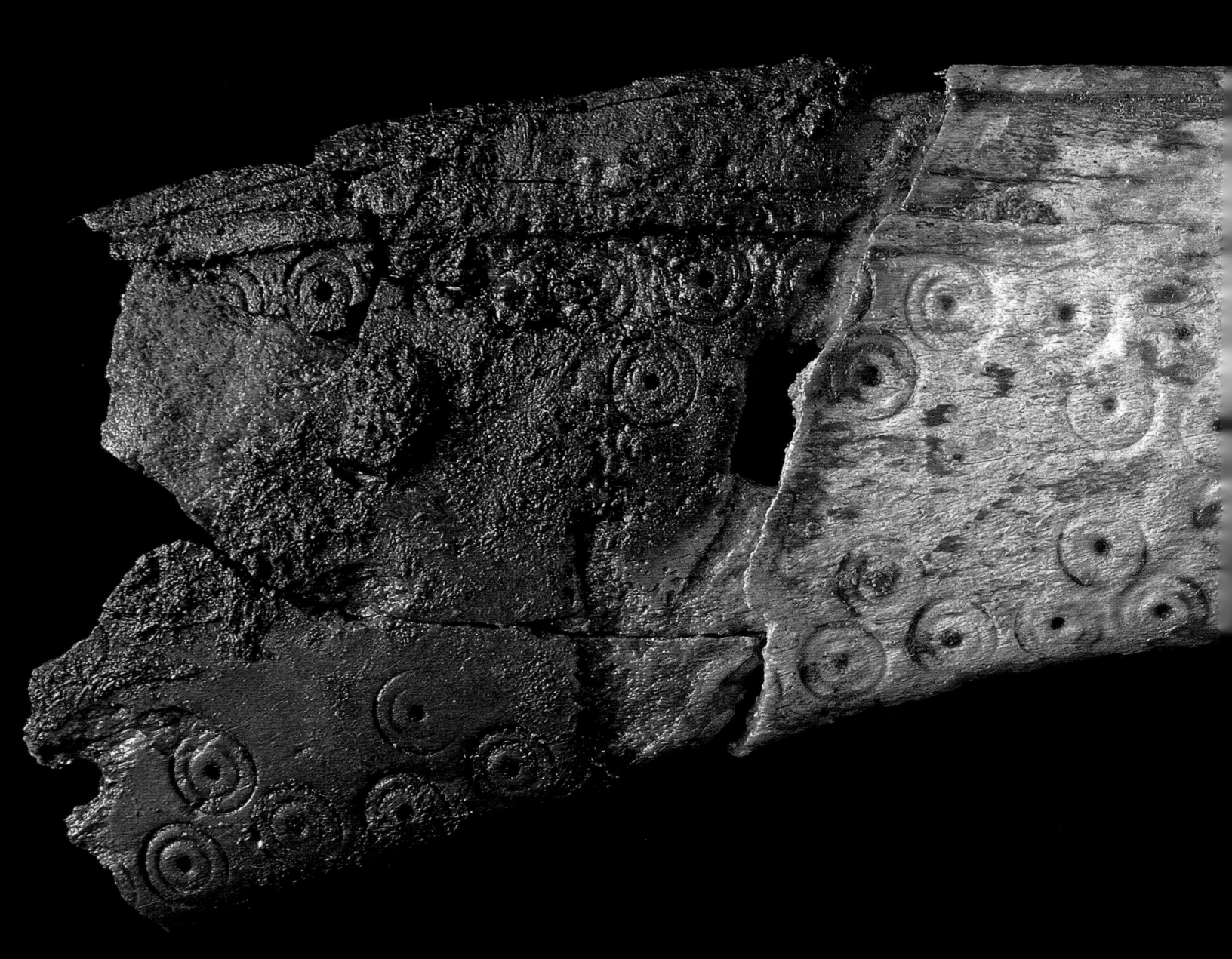

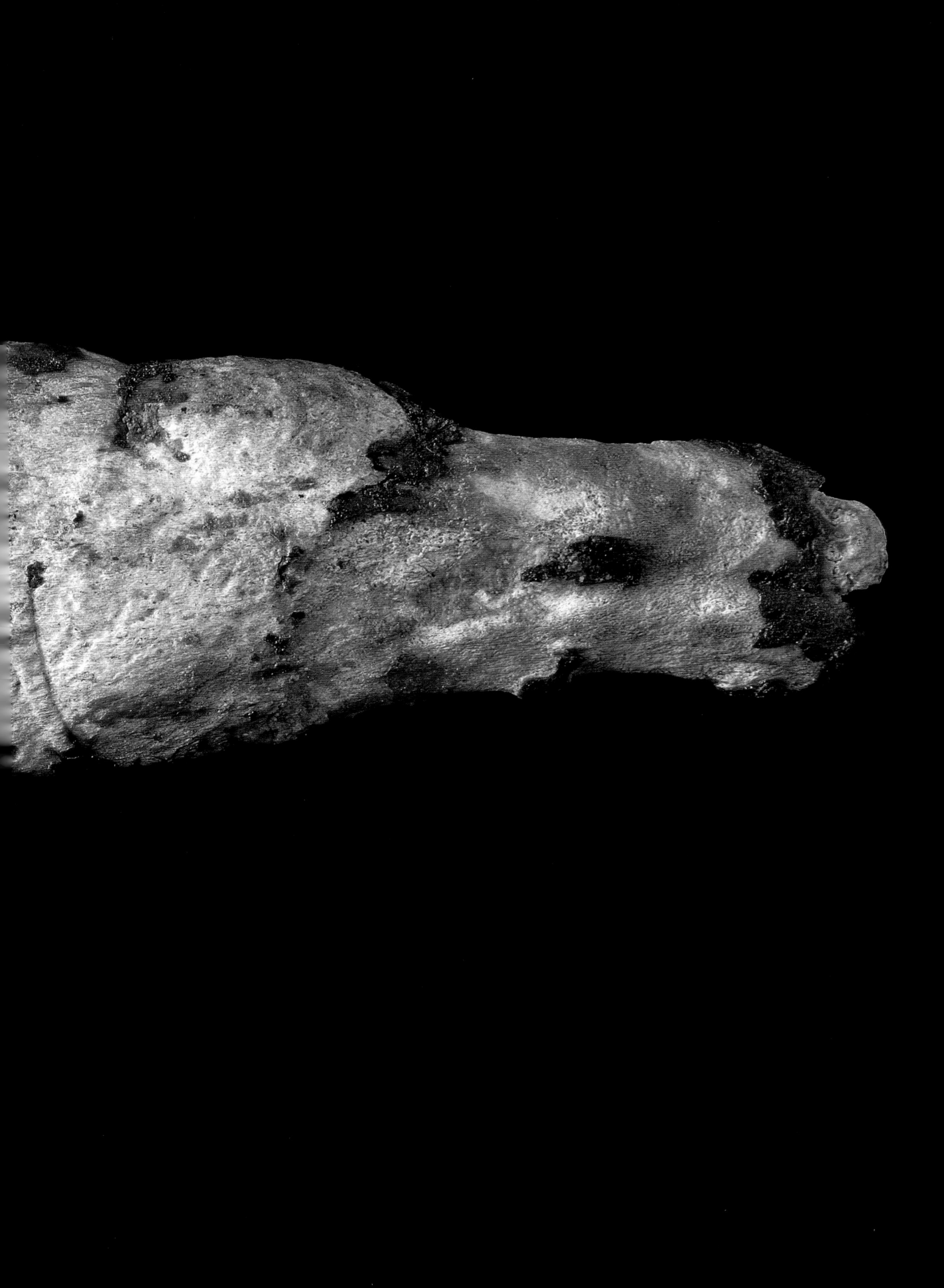

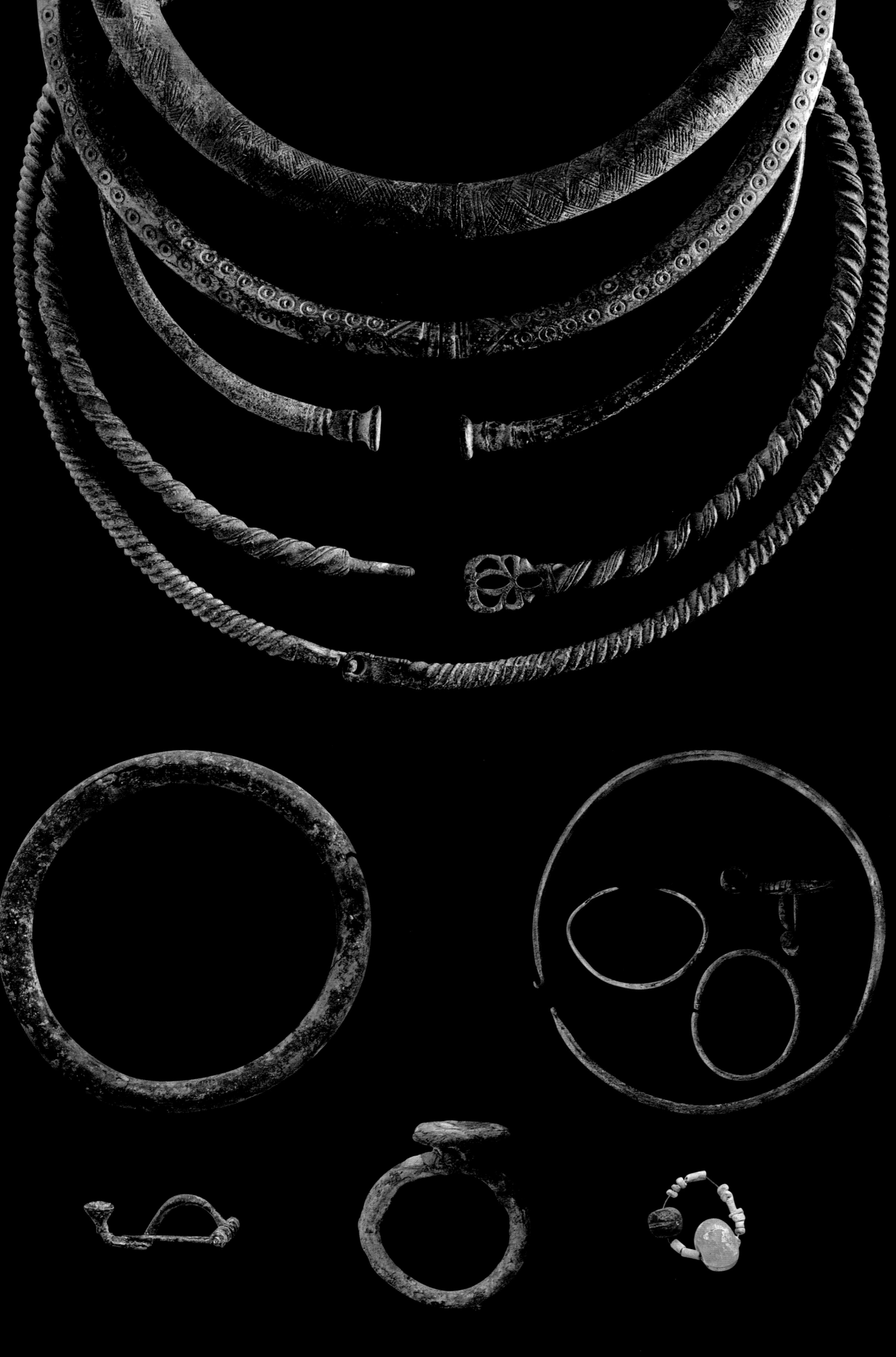

The origins of a Gaulish people – the Remi 'ancestors'

Thanks to chalky subsoil, which allows for the easy detection of ditches, the plains of Champagne have been extensively explored by archaeologists. Thousands of Iron Age burial-sites have been excavated since the early 19th century. The first useful publication dates from 1829 and tells of a necropolis discovered at Bergères-les-Vertus, and identified since then as a Gaulish burial-ground. This area experienced a remarkable continuity of settlement from the 6th century BCE right up to the Gallo-Roman era. Among its foremost inhabitants were the Remi, a powerful tribe whose name lives on in the place name Reims. The tribe's appellation seems to have come about by dropping the initial 'P' from Premi ('the First' or 'the Ancestors').

The initial nucleus of the Champagne Celts comprised of a 'Jogassian' Tardo–Hallstatt strain whose origins remain obscure. However, they do not appear to be linked with any local substratum and therefore were probably non-indigenous immigrants. This group, at first localized, enjoyed a spectacular demographic explosion in the 5th century BCE to become one of the cradles of La Tène culture. It is possible to trace the progressive transformation of ornaments (torcs, bracelets, brooches) and the chief weapon (a short dagger and its scabbard) into typical La Tène forms around the middle of this century. Traditionally known as 'Marnian', as it was centred on the Marne region, these early La Tène features coincided with expansion and an unusual density of population. The cemeteries of the relevant half-century period form a tight network over the considerably expanded territory, each only a few kilometres apart, or even less.

The remarkable homogeneity of 'Marnian' culture is attested by the uniformity of ceramic shapes and decoration, burial customs and clothing. High-ranking women wore torcs, generally in the shape of a curved rod with free terminals, and a pair of bracelets worn symmetrically. Weapons also displayed similar features, including the first La Tène long-swords with their characteristic scabbards. These innovations developed gradually and coexisted for a period with Tardo–Hallstatt designs.

The situation changed abruptly around the end of the 5th century BCE, when there was a dramatic slump in population. The majority of the burial-grounds were no longer used and only the region around Reims remained continuously occupied during the following century; it alone does not seem to have suffered a noticeable reduction in population. While it is impossible to pinpoint any obvious modification in funerary customs or dress in this latter period, new styles from the Celtic-Italian region do seem to feature strongly. There was, for instance, in the second half of the 4th century, a short-lived fad for Graeco-Etruscan 'red-figured' vases. The continuing occupation of the region, to this day still linked to the name Remi (which is appropriate if one takes into account the region's age with regard to the neighbouring areas), can be traced to the Gallo-Romano period.

A slender iron dirk in a bronze scabbard, from grave No. 22 of the burial ground at Jogasses à Chouilly (Marne).
This type of scabbard later evolved to originate the typical La Tène form of this object.
End 6th–early 5th century BCE. Length: 398 mm. Épernay (Marne), Musée Municipal d'Archéologie et du Vin de Champagne.

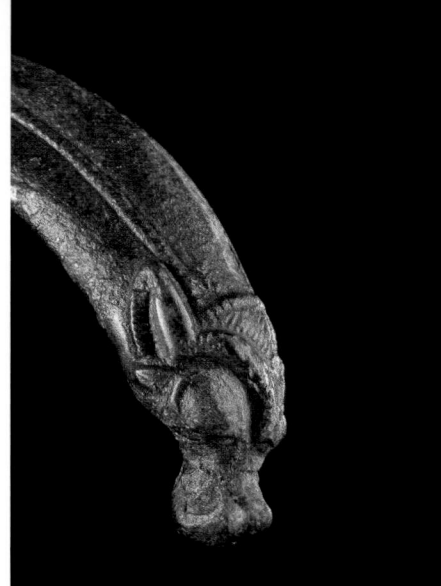

Left

Detail of a bronze fibula, its bow encrusted with coral, from Libčice-Chýnov (Bohemia).
The end that topped the long spring, now missing, had the head of an animal with pointed ears and round eyes. See p. 53 onwards.
Second half of the 5th century BCE. Actual height of the detail: approx. 18 mm. Prague, Národní Muzeum.

From the second half of the 6th century BCE Armorica (Brittany) developed in an unusual fashion, apparently being strongly influenced by northern Italy, possibly due to the insular tin trade. As in other regions, continuity of occupation can be traced up to the time of the Roman conquest, and evidence shows that Armorican tribes were formed during this period. These included the Veneti of Morbihan and those whom the navigator Pytheas called Ostimioi, of the Oestrymnides, or the islands and peninsula of Brittany. These people became the Osismii of Finistère of Julius Caesar's time; their name means 'the last, the most remote', which of course accurately describes their geographical location.

Archaeological evidence therefore identifies the period from the 6th century to the beginning of the 5th century BCE as an epoch when at least part of the territories long inhabited by the Celts underwent significant mutations that were accentuated and highlighted by contacts with Mediterraneans. Sadly, we have no textual information from this period, but there are hints of early Celtic forays into Italy at this time. For instance, Livy relates the story of Ambicatus, king of the Bituriges in the centre of Gaul, and his nephews Bellovesus ('he who can kill') and Segovesus ('he who can conquer'), who left in search of new territories, taking with them part of the population. Such tales no doubt accurately reflect the existence of internal tensions leading to migratory movements and conflicts.

We are no better informed as to why, at the end of the 6th century and the beginning of the 5th century BCE, the supply of imports to Central Europe via Marseille trading-posts apparently came to an abrupt halt. It was probably due to a shift in the complex balance of power between Greeks, Etruscans and Carthaginians in the Western Mediterranean at that time. The result of this was a significant increase in the export of Etruscan objects north of the Alps during the 5th century. This trade was probably conducted largely by Golaseccan Celts acting as middlemen, and the development of the Como-Prestino urban centre testifies to their economic expansion. This trade was clearly much more energetic than it had been in the 6th century, as the 5th-century imported goods have been found over a much wider area than their earlier equivalents.

The consequences of Transalpine contacts

Objects of characteristic northern Italian or Transalpine origin – such as brooches featuring the heads of aquatic birds, generally inlaid with coral – have also been found in large quantities both north and south of the Alps. They testify to the extent, depth and multiplicity of Transalpine contacts from the beginning of the 5th century; such contacts would certainly have led to the migration of individuals or small groups. Pliny the Elder tells of the Helvetii smith Helicon, who plied his trade in Italy before returning to his own country laden with dried figs, grapes, oil and wine to incite his compatriots to conquer this land of plenty.

This explains why most early examples of La Tène culture found antecedents or sources of inspiration in the Italian Peninsula. One such was the two-wheeled war-chariot, which replaced the four-wheeled ceremonial chariot of the Hallstatt culture in funerary rites. Similarly, pottery became rounded, and ceramic decoration became characteristically Italian. Furthermore, bronze vessels, such as pitchers and sieves, started to be used, and new jewellery designs – ship-shaped earrings, new forms for sets of rings, disc-shaped brooches inspired by Etruscan models, others derived from an Etruscan–Po Valley type called 'La Certosa' and anthropomorphic or zoomorphic 'mask' brooches – were adopted. As has been mentioned, the final reconstruction of the sanctuary at Závist, with its dry-stone undercrofts, was also inspired by an Etruscan model.

The repertory of the new La Tène art, generally considered to be the high point of Celtic art, is particularly indicative in this respect. Almost everything that distinguishes it from the geometric art of the Hallstatt culture is the Etruscan–Italian in origin. This is true not only in the vaguely 'oriental' motifs and themes involving monsters, divinities and flora, but in the sophisticated designs engraved with the aid of compasses.

Opposite, left
View of the upper part of the bronze fibula from Nová Huť (Bohemia)
See p. 55.
Second half of the 5th century BCE. Length: 55 mm.
Plzeň (Czech Republic), Západočeské Muzeum.

Opposite, right
Bronze fibula from Libčice-Chýnov (Bohemia).
See p. 52 and 54.
Second half of the 5th century BCE. Length: 68 mm. Prague, Národní Muzeum.

Upper part of a bronze fibula from Kyšice (Bohemia).
This object was found many years ago with others, during excavations on six tumuli. The terminal represents a bearded human head with prominent eyes. On the bow, two superimposed and overlapping 'masks' look in the same direction; the one on top has the pointed ears of an animal, the eyebrows of the other end in scrolls. They are, therefore, faces with the same attributes as those of the Nová Huť fibula (see p. 53), but assembled differently.

Second half of the 5th century BCE. Length: 61 mm.

Plzeň (Czech Republic), Západočeské Muzeum.

Bronze fibula from Libčice-Chýnov (Bohemia), detail of terminal.
This jewel was discovered in 1901 in a burial ground that originally contained around 60 tumuli. The terminal is a head with pointed animal ears, a tight beard running down the neck and bulbous eyes topped with arched eyebrows that start from the base of the nose. The other end bears the head of an animal. See p. 52 and 53.

Second half of the 5th century BCE. Height of the head: approx. 15 mm.

Prague, Národní Muzeum.

Bronze fibula from Kyšice (Bohemia), detail of terminal.
See p. 54.

Second half of the 5th century BCE. Height of the head: approx. 20 mm.

Plzeň (Czech Republic), Západočeské Muzeum.

Bronze fibula from Nová Huť (Bohemia), side view.
This jewel was recovered from one of the 60-odd tumuli explored on the site between 1907 and 1911. The terminal is composed of a griffon's head with a long, lightly curved beak. The bow bears two almost identical opposing heads, joined by their headdresses: only the pointed animal ears differentiate the head turned towards the griffon from the other one, which instead has eyebrows running from the bulbous eye to terminate in scrolls. See p. 53 and 55.

Second half of the 5th century BCE. Length: 55 mm.

Plzeň (Czech Republic), Západočeské Muzeum.

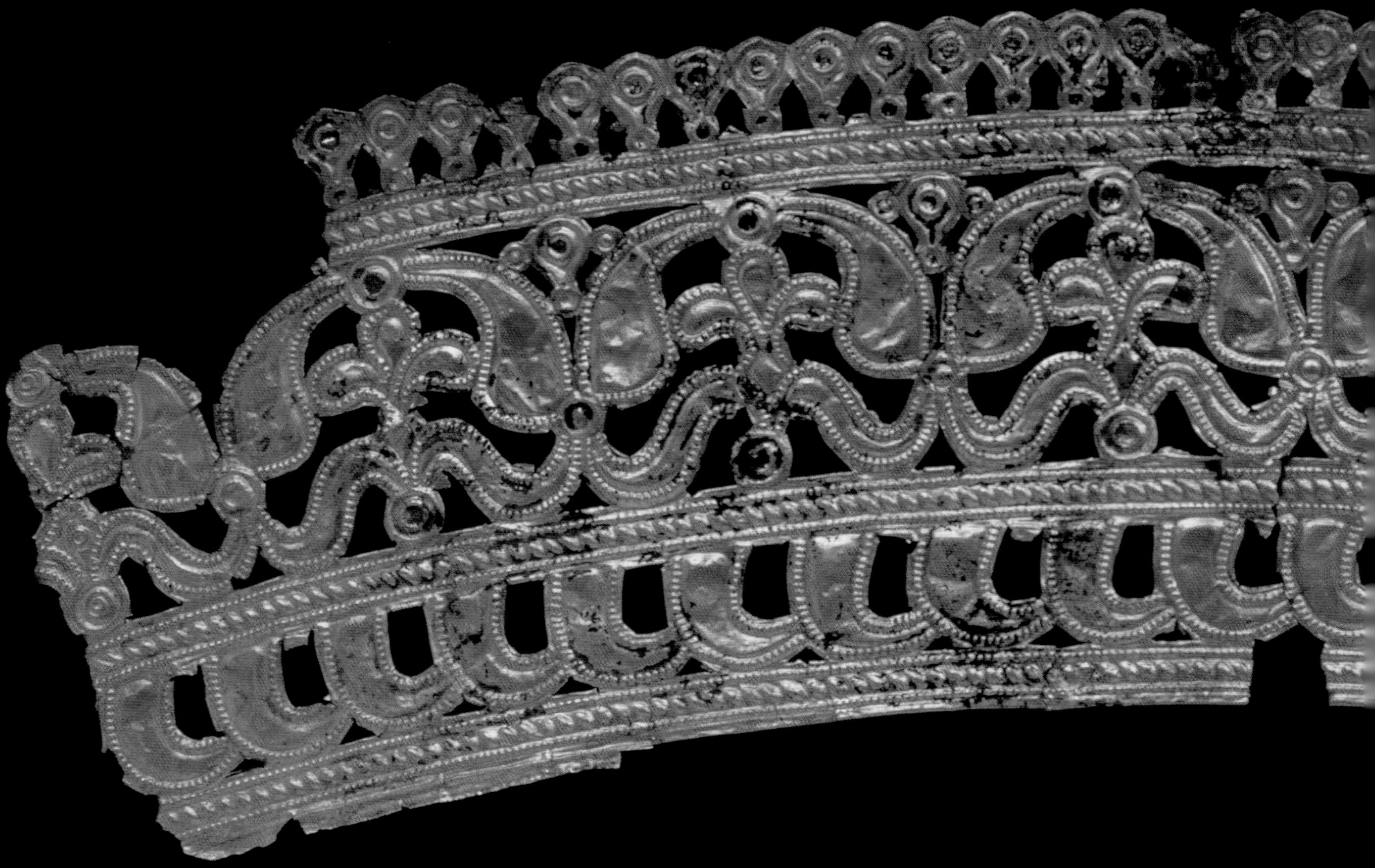

Right

Two possible readings of the vegetal frieze from the mounting for a drinking horn, Eigenbilzen (Belgium).

The Greco-Etruscan original is subtly transformed by the way the lotus petal tips are joined by a circular motif. Alternatively, this part of the composition may be read as a double mistletoe-leaf.

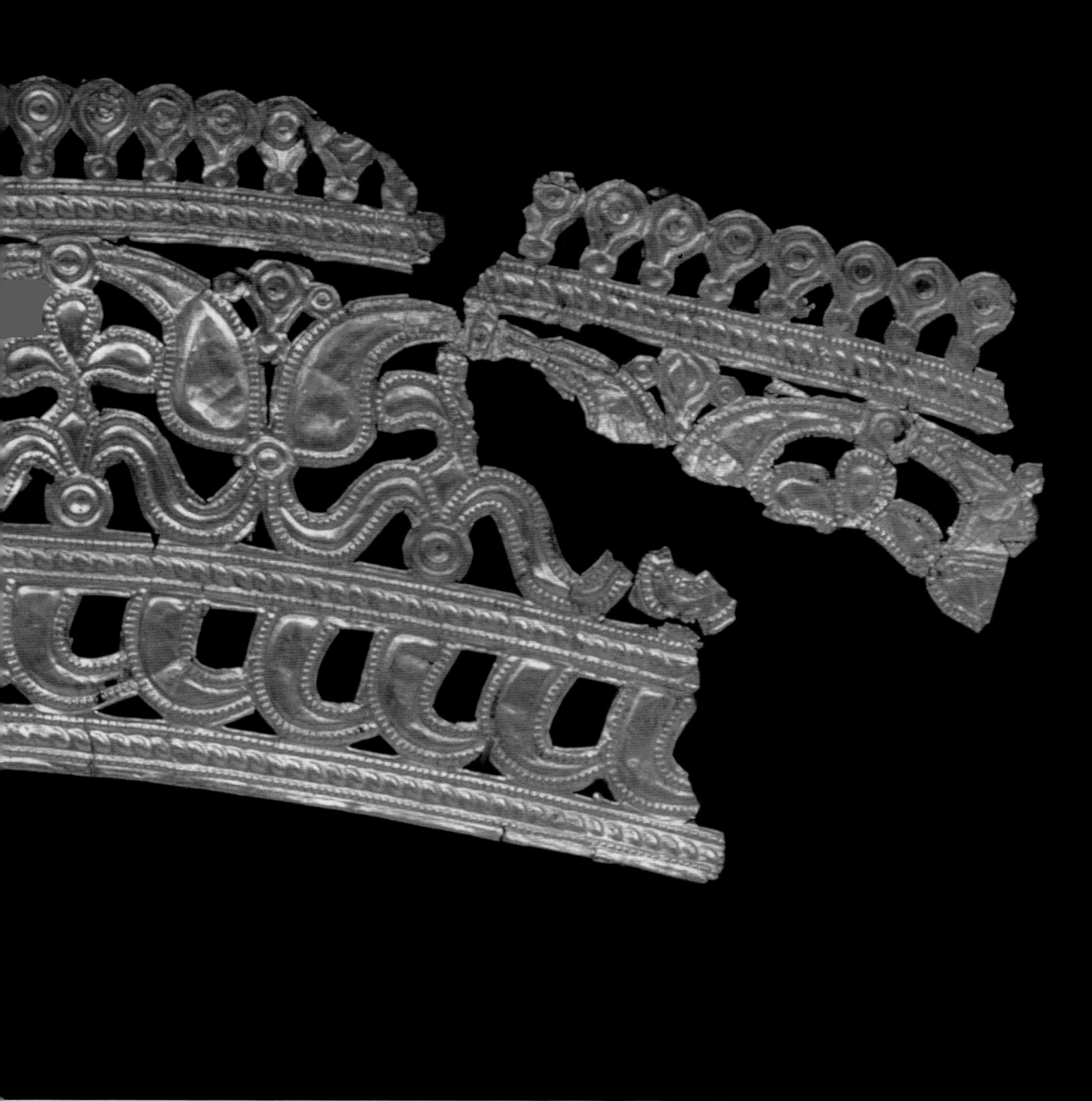

Left
**Decorative panel from
a drinking horn**
*Openwork sheet gold
finely worked in repoussé,
discovered in 1871 at
Eigenbilzen (Belgium),
in a princely tomb that
also contained a Etruscan
wine pitcher and a
'corded' situla (a sort
of sheet bronze bucket)
that contained the ashes
of the deceased. Directly
inspired by an Etruscan
frieze of alternating
palmettes and lotus
flowers, this ornament
is one of the most
striking examples of the
Celts' transformation of
vegetal motifs in the
5th century BCE.*
Mid-5th century BCE.
Height: 65 mm.
Brussels, Musées Royaux d'Art
et d'Histoire.

Palmette, lotus and mistletoe

With their first borrowings from the repertory of
Mediterranean art, Celtic artists demonstrated a
remarkable capacity for diverting, by subtle retouches,
the original meaning of a variety of images towards their
own ends. Over several centuries, through systematic
and deliberate adaptation, they integrated the imported
models into traditional Celtic imagery.

The openwork gold-leaf decoration of a drinking horn
found in a princely tomb at Eigenbilzen (Belgium), dated
to the second half of the 5th century BCE, perfectly
illustrates the Celtic transformation of a Graeco-Etruscan
motif: the frieze of alternating palmettes and lotus
flowers. Apart from the reduction of the palm-leaf
segments to three – no doubt due to the significance that
the Celts attached to this number – the difference from
the original may seem slight at first glance: little circles
join the tips of the lotus-flower petals.

However, this detail probably represents the leaf of the
mistletoe, the plant that, according to Pliny the Elder
(*Natural History*, XVI, 249), was most venerated by the
Celts. This motif, associated with an important male
deity, was extremely popular in both the earliest phase
of Celtic art and later, when it was often accompanied
by the palmette, a symbolic representation of the tree
of life.

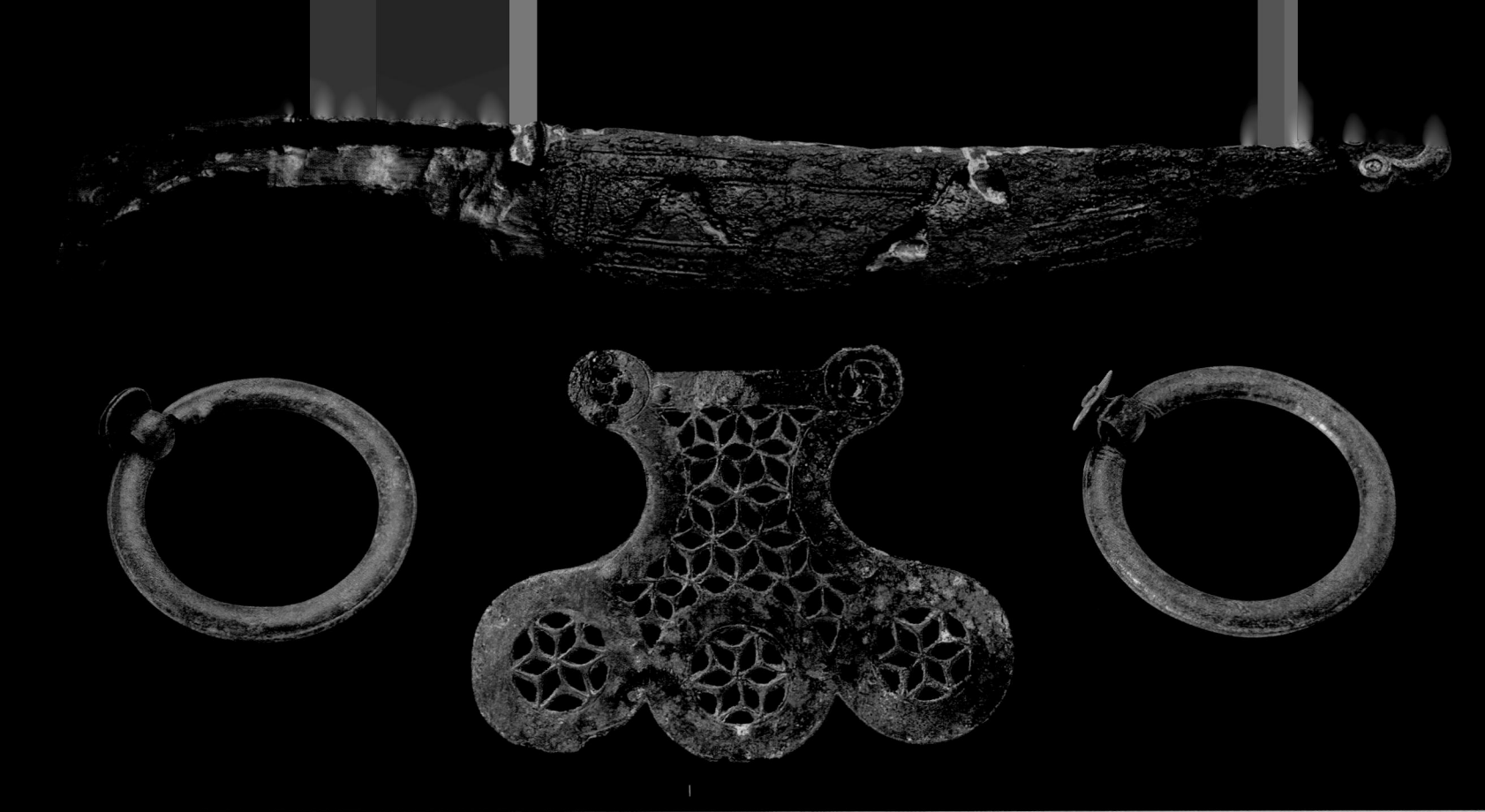

Above, top

Broadsword found in grave No. 2 of funerary mound No. 1 in Léglise (Belgium).

This slashing hand-weapon was very common among the Celts of the second half of the 5th century BCE. The Léglise example has retained its leather scabbard, now mineralized, with finely embossed decoration terminating in a bronze guard.

Second half of the 5th century BCE. Length: 280 mm.

Libramont (Belgium), Musée des Celtes.

Above, bottom centre

Harness-plaque in bronze openwork, from chariot burial No. 1 of funerary mound No. IV, Léglise (Belgium).

On the upper part can be discerned the triskele, frequently associated with the horse, an avatar of the Celtic sun god.

Second half of the 5th century BCE. Height: 60 mm.

Libramont (Belgium), Musée des Celtes.

Above, bottom right and left

Bronze suspension rings to attach a weapon – broadsword or épée – to a belt, from Este (Italy).

The presence of this typically Transalpine-type suspension dating from the second half of the 5th century BCE in a Venetian burial ground confirms the direct contacts that existed between the two regions at the time.

Second half of the 5th century BCE. Diameter: approx. 80 mm.

Este (Italy), Museo Nazionale Atestino.

A prosperous, powerful and ordered world

Other innovations were more practical. The weapon that was to become one of the mainstays of Celtic armies appeared and developed at this time: the versatile long-sword that was equally well suited to slash and cut, for cavalry and infantry. During the second half of the 5th century BCE, however, this sword was issued to only a limited number of warriors. It appears in about one in five of the Champagne burial-grounds, and still fewer to the east, where the curved broadsword was the standard hand-weapon. (At this time, the spear or javelin was the most widely used long-distance offensive weapon found in warrior graves.)

Initially La Tène culture apparently developed in a minority of the Celtic populations, and it was first apparent only in the social elite: the last representatives of the old Hallstatt dynasties and the new warrior chieftains, buried near two-wheeled chariots used for battle or hunting. But the second half of the 5th century BCE witnessed the increasing spread of the culture from the borders of Champagne to the western border of the Carpathian Basin.

This was the maturation period of a Celtic world that thereafter broke away from the rigid framework of the princely caste system to undergo profound transformations in its social structure. It was a stable environment, densely populated, prosperous and attached to its traditions; proud of its uniqueness, it nevertheless remained open to southern influences that were successfully integrated.

Opposite
The atmosphere of the temperate forest, filled with shadows and rays of light, changing with the seasons, certainly contributed to the development of the sensibility reflected in the art of the ancient Celts. Now overgrown by the forest, the enclosure of the camp of Artus near Huelgoat (Finistère, France), on the southern boundary of the Arrée hills, is impregnated with the Celtic past: in the 1st century BCE, it was the site of a large oppidum of the Armorican Osismes.

The Hallstatt Scabbard: another view of the Celts of the 5th century BCE

The 19th-century – and even much later – image of the army of Transalpine Celts that invaded Italy at the beginning of the 4th century BCE is of a wild and disorderly horde whose chief strengths were its numbers and a mindless, death-defying impetuosity. The finely engraved military parade on the right-hand brass panel of a La Tène scabbard found at Hallstatt (Austria) presents a quite different picture. It is probably a mythological episode, possibly the same as that featured on one of the panels of the Gundestrup Cauldron (Denmark) about three centuries later (see p. 112). It shows infantrymen armed with lances and shields, helmeted cavalrymen equipped with long spears and breastplates, probably made of leather, extended by a kilt. The third man in the rank carries a short sword whose hilt can be clearly seen. Apart from the ornamental band with varied, probably

multicoloured, motifs, there is little difference between these images and those of Etruscan military equipment of the 6th–5th century BCE.

This is not an exception, restricted to an Alpine site that had grown rich through salt-mining and trading. The recently discovered stone statue and fragments of three others from Glauberg (near Frankfurt) clearly show that similar equipment was adopted by the military elite of the Transalpine Celts. It is also illustrated in statuary found in the French Midi – particularly the seated figures from Roquepertuse, recently dated to the same period. Metal items found in tombs have been identified as horse tack or appliqués on leather breastplates or helmets. This, therefore, is how we should visualize the Transalpine army that descended on Italy and crushed the Roman legions on the banks of the River Allia in 390 BCE.

Male dress in the second half of the 5th century BCE – a tunic, a kind of overcoat, fitted hose or breeches (*bracae*), shoes with turned-up points – is equally well depicted on several brooches of this date found in Central Europe. Again, this is far removed from the 'barbarian' fantasies imagined by 19th-century artists.

The incised decoration on the right-hand bronze panel from the scabbard found in grave No. 994, Hallstatt (Austria).

The central part shows a parade of three infantrymen armed with spears and oval shields with different emblems, followed by four helmeted cavalrymen armed with spears and, in one instance, a La Tène-type sword with the typical guard; the horse-trappings include round phalerae like those from graves of the same period. The two pairs of facing figures holding a wheel that frame the middle part illustrate well the daily costume of the Central European Celtic elite: banded woven stockings, probably multi-coloured, a sort of surcoat. The triangular battle-scene at the tip terminates with a half-palmette, topped with a trilobed palmette surrounded by a pair of serpentine monsters on the guard. Many elements with a clear religious symbolism can be identified, indicating the mythological nature of the scenes represented.

Second half of the 5th century BCE.

Total length: 680 mm. Maximum height: 60 mm.

Vienna (Austria), Naturhistorisches Museum.

Detail of a bronze fibula inlaid with amber from grave No. 4, Manětín-Hrádek (Bohemia).

The figure wears, in La Tène local style of the 5th century BCE, a long tunic reaching to mid-thigh, stockings, and shoes with turned-up points.

Second half of the 5th century BCE.

Total length: 80 mm.

Length of detail: 48 mm.

Prague, Národní Muzeum.

Above

Bronze appliqués from Dürrnberg bei Hallein (Austria).

Originally mounted on a wooden pitcher, they were found in the rich chariot tomb No. 44/2.

Second half of the 5th century BCE. Height of the central piece (head): 80 mm.

Hallein (Austria), Keltenmuseum.

Pitchers for princely banquets

The drinking service used during banquets organized by tribal kings for their entourage or the community was usually buried with them. In the 6th and 5th centuries BCE it constituted one of the most obvious indicators of their status, and the design is clearly inspired by Graeco-Etruscan models. Coinciding with the adoption of wine from the Mediterranean, the first receptacles and utensils designed for its consumption – cauldrons, *stamnoi* and other large vessels, sieves, pitchers – appeared in the burial-sites of Transalpine princes. These later inspired Celtic artisans towards the middle of the 5th century BCE to create their own versions. The most important item of the service appears to have been the pitcher. It is not only the utensil most often found, but the one in which all of the elements of the new La Tène repertory come into play. The vessel lends itself well to such style, both in its dimensions and because of its function as the ceremonial dispenser of an intoxicating liquid considered a gift from the gods. It was used for imported wine, of course, but also for drinks that had been consumed by the Celts for centuries: possibly *cerevisia*, a beer made from fermented barley, and certainly mead. Recent meticulous analysis of the contents of two pitchers from the second half of the 5th century BCE found in the princely tombs of Glauberg revealed that one had contained 4 litres (7 pints) of mead made from 2 kilos (4½ pounds) of honey, while the other had contained the same volume of a liquid, possibly imported wine, to which had been added around 200 grams (7 oz) of honey. La Tène flagons were made of bronze, terracotta or wood with metal inlays. There are two principal shapes: either with an open, beaked spout, inspired by a widespread Etruscan model, or with a tubular spout, probably also derived from Etruscan–Italian prototypes. Around a dozen bronze flagons have been found, including the sumptuous examples from Reinheim, Kleinaspergle, Borsch, Basse-Yutz, Dürrnberg (near Hallein, Austria), Waldalgesheim and two recently discovered at Glauberg. We also have evidence of half a dozen wooden vessels, identifiable thanks to their metallic attachments; these are all of the tube-spouted variety and have been dated to between the second half of the 5th century to the first half of the 3rd century BCE. This was when the wooden bucket seems to have replaced the pitcher as the receptacle used for ceremonial consumption of the intoxicating brew, as shown most notably by the outstanding example from Brno-Maloměřice.

The flagon found in Grave 44/2 at Dürrnberg is one of the oldest examples, coming from a burial of the second half of the 5th century BCE. It was accompanied by a two-wheeled chariot, and outstanding weapons and armour: a metal helmet, a sword with openwork double-hooked fastening, arrow or javelin tips, and two large spearheads. A broadsword deposited near a haunch of pork and other objects, such as a large bronze platter with beaten gold-leaf appliqués and amber beads, testify to the importance of the individual buried there. The drinking service comprised the flagon, a black-varnished Attic cup and a large *situla* – a bucket covered in sheet bronze – with a capacity of almost 90 litres (20 gallons). There was also a straight-sided round flagon, also in sheet bronze, with a cylindrical neck, mounted on four little representations of human legs. It has a capacity of around 18 litres (4 gallons), and traces of mulled wine were found in it.

The appliqués on the flagon feature themes found on other Celtic vessels of this kind: the head of a male divinity with the mistletoe leaf and the palmette. Here, uniquely, there is also a pair of counter-rotating triskeles, a motif that often accompanies the image of the sun god and his avatar, a man-headed horse, especially on coins.

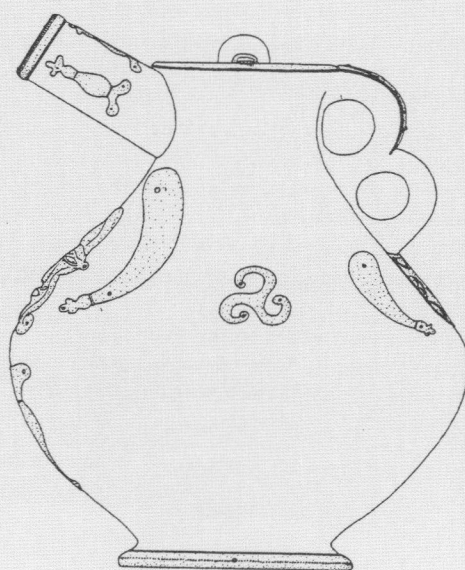

Left
Hypothetical reconstruction of the wooden jug with metal fittings from grave No. 44/2, Dürrnberg bei Hallein (Austria).
Height: approx. 240 mm.

The Transalpine invasion of Italy
(4th century BCE)

The arrival in force of Transalpine Gauls in Italy is the first certain event in Celtic history. They established themselves south of the Po and penetrated as far as Rome, inflicting a bloody defeat on the Roman legions at the Allia River and temporarily occupying the city. News of this unexpected triumph spread far and wide. Plutarch recorded that the philosopher and astrologer Heraclides Ponticus, a follower of Plato, had noted that 'an army, proceeding from the Hyperboreans, had taken a Greek city called Rome, seated somewhere upon the great sea'. Other Greek writers of the 4th century BCE were equally well informed.

The defeat had a profound effect on the collective Roman psyche. Although Rome would much later become the most powerful force in the Mediterranean, this unhappy episode in its history was repeatedly cited as evidence of an enduring 'Celtic threat'. This is turn was used to justify a policy of conquest of the Celtic territories, and was always included in the story of Rome's long march towards world dominion. However, the original story underwent many revisions designed both to save Rome's face and to emphasize the danger represented by the unpredictable nature of the Celtic 'barbarians'.

The various versions therefore differ in details, but all writers agree on most of the seminal points: large groups of Gauls crossed the Alps, passed the Po and occupied Etruria south of that river. Then an army led by a chieftain named Brennos (supported, according to some writers, by the Senones, who had recently settled beyond Ancona on the Adriatic coast) laid siege to the Etruscan town of Clusium (Chiusi) and claimed part of its territory. Roman ambassadors were sent to negotiate on behalf of the city, but in breach of custom they took the side of Clusium, where upon the Gauls organized a punitive expedition against Rome. The 70,000-strong Celtic army met the legions about 15 kilometres (9 miles) north of Rome, near the confluence of the Allia and the Tiber. The crushing defeat of the Roman troops, whose survivors took shelter in the neighbouring town of Veii, left Rome defenceless, except for the Capitol, where the few men still capable of bearing arms entrenched themselves with rations and enough supplies to maintain the principal urban services.

This Battle of Allia took place on 18 July 387 BCE, and thereafter the date was considered ill-fated in Rome. The Gauls entered the city three days later, and occupied it for seven months. However, they never managed to seize the Capitol; one nocturnal attempt failed because the sacred geese in the Temple of Juno raised the alarm. Brennos' armies were finally persuaded to leave in exchange for a ransom of a 320 kilos (1,000 [Roman] pounds) of gold. According to writers in the age of Augustus, this ransom was never paid, or was recovered shortly afterwards by the intervention of Camillus and his troops, who were said by some sources to have driven the Gauls out of the city and slain Brennos. These later versions are contradicted by the earliest account we have, though. The Greek historian Polybius, writing in the middle of the 2nd century BCE, describes the orderly retreat of the Gauls. His account is based primarily on the work of the Roman annalist Fabius Pictor, who was related to the Roman ambassadors sent to Clusium and was therefore undoubtedly well informed. According to Polybius, the Veneti invaded the territory of the Gauls, who 'then concluded a treaty with the Romans, giving them back their town and returning to their country'. Nevertheless, they organized a new expedition thirty years later (around 357/6 BCE), and, despite their restored forces, the Romans 'did not dare, this time, to set their troops against them because the suddenness of the invasion had taken them by surprise and they had not had time to rally the forces of their allies'. The story of the immediate revenge of Camillus' army on the Celtic invaders therefore seems to be a late invention designed to safeguard Roman honour.

Design developments in two gold torcs.
Top, gold torc from the Waldalgesheim grave (Rheinland-Pfalz).
Bottom, torc of unknown provenance, British Museum, London.
Mid-4th century BCE.

Detail of the buffer terminal of a gold torc from Oploty (Bohemia).
Its decoration makes this ornament outstanding among works from the Celto-Italian region; the subtle allusion of this vegetal composition to a human face is brilliantly realised by the artists who worked it.
Mid-4th century BCE. Height of the detail: approx. 30 mm.
Vienna (Austria), Naturhistorisches Museum

Detail of one of a pair of identical golden bracelets from the Waldalgesheim (Rheinland-Pfalz) grave.
A richly jewelled woman – torc, a pair of gold bracelets and an armband, bronze ankle-rings – was buried with a two-wheeled chariot (see p. 169) and a drinking service: a situla (bucket) of Greek origin and a spouted flagon of Celtic workmanship.
Mid-4th century BCE. Height of detail: approx. 15 mm.
Bonn (Germany), Rheinisches Landesmuseum.

Polybius goes on to say that around 345 BCE the Romans gained their first success against a Celtic army. Fourteen or so years later a peace treaty was agreed between Rome and the Gauls that was rigorously respected for thirty years. However, hostilities between the Cisalpine Gauls and the Romans then recommenced and led to the defeat of the Senones in 283 BCE, followed by occupation of their territory. Neither the use of Transalpine mercenaries – who were wiped out at Cape Telamon with the Cisalpine army in 225 – nor an alliance with Hannibal's expedition into Italy succeeded in halting the inexorable rise of Rome that culminated in 191 with definitive victories over the Boii and the Insubres.

Documentary sources give scant information on the relations between newly arrived Celts and the other powers in the Italian Peninsula. Nevertheless, a passage from Trogus Pompeius (writing in the 1st century CE) cites a military alliance offered by the Gauls after the fall of Rome to Denys I of Syracuse, a tyrant with well-known expansionist ambitions. This alliance was presumably successfully concluded, and the Syracusan trading-post of Ancona, in direct contact with the Senones, became the principal recruiting-point for mercenary Celtic troops engaged in Denys' service. These warriors are known to have been present in the south of the peninsula, as well as in Greece, where Xenophon mentions them as forming part of the Syracusan expeditionary force mustered against the Thebans in 367 BCE. Contrary to the impression given by Roman historians, who dealt only with Romano-Celtic relations, these scraps of information clearly indicate that, thanks to their military skill, the newcomers soon became embroiled in the complex game of peninsular politics. In fact, they were (somewhat unwittingly) involved in Italian political machinations even before the invasion. It seems likely that their arrival was carefully planned with the help of local accomplices, a situation referred to discreetly by Livy in an anecdote about Arruns of Clusium. Seeking revenge on his wife's seducer – who may have been a local king – Arruns baited the Gauls by introducing them to the delights of wine, then led them into Italy.

Archaeology fully confirms the date and method of the invasion indicated by classical writings. There seems to have been a sudden influx of La Tène artefacts in the north of Italy from the Alps to the Apennines, with the exception of the territory of the native Celts of the Golasecca culture, who were apparently bypassed by the invaders. The impact of the invasion is particularly evident in the distribution of La Tène swords. Only a few examples from the 5th century BCE have been found in the foothills of the Alps, but the characteristic shapes of the 4th and 3rd centuries BCE have turned up everywhere that classical writers said was visited by the Celts. They have also been found in neighbouring territories – the Veneto, Liguria, Umbria, Picenium – in the Etruscan region, and in the south of Italy, where their presence must be due to raids or mercenary activity. The fact that local people adopted these La Tène weapons is the best indication of the military prestige enjoyed by the Celts in the peninsula at this time.

Detail of the relief decoration of a torc from the Waldalgesheim (Rheinland-Pfalz) grave.
This composition results from the transformation of a Greek original, probably created in the Celto-Italian region.
Mid-4th century BCE. Height of detail: approx. 20 mm.
Bonn (Germany), Rheinisches Landesmuseum.

Disc-shaped appliqué (perhaps a phalera, a boss or decoration for a helmet, shield or sword), from Auvers-sur-Oise (Val-d'Oise, France), in bronze covered with worked gold sheet with coral-inlaid openwork.
The central cylinder and the two lateral studs held red enamel; the alternating lotus flowers and palmettes are modified and assembled to suggest human faces, a process characteristic of the Celto-Italian milieu.
First half of the 4th century BCE. Diameter: 100 mm.
Paris, Bibliothèque Nationale, Cabinet des Médailles.

Transalpines from Gaul and Central Europe

As for the invasion itself, it remains difficult to attribute to it particular objects of Transalpine origin, since they cannot be sufficiently precisely dated to distinguish them from any that may have been acquired through earlier trade. Only a brooch discovered in the votive repository of the sanctuary of Nemi in the Alban Hills may provide evidence of the first serious Celtic incursions into Italy. This massive brooch representing an aquatic bird is unquestionably related, in both shape and method of production, to Central European examples that have been dated to the end of the 5th century or the beginning of the 4th century BCE.

However, we are able to make an educated guess as to the origin of the invaders thanks to their names. The tribes who settled in Italy, and the territories attributed to them, are well documented and point to certain Transalpine regions. The two best-known peninsular Celtic populations – the Cispadane Gauls (those living south of the Po River) belonging to the Senones and Boii tribes – both had Transalpine namesakes. The former lived in the south of the Champagne region of France, where they eventually gave their name to the town of Sens; the latter were from Central Europe, where their name lives on to this day in Bohemia, the Boiohaemum of classical writers. There is evidence that around the end of the 5th century BCE both of these Transalpine regions suffered a significant decrease in population. One explanation for this is the emigration of large numbers of people. As has been mentioned, in Champagne many burial-grounds were abandoned seemingly overnight.

In Bohemia the dense network of necropolises and settlements of the central plains indicate a cultural shift. The bi-ritual, often tumular, cemeteries where incineration and regular deposition of pottery predominated gave way to flat necropolises devoted exclusively to burial, strictly *without* pottery. In these latter necropolises aspects of funerary ritual and types of female ornament are strongly reminiscent of those of people from the Swiss plateau. The shift is equally obvious in ceramic shapes, where, uniquely in this epoch, certain shapes specific to the initial La Tène phase no longer feature – for example, the lenticular flagon, which continued to be made in neighbouring regions right up to the 3rd century BCE. Most of the Hallstatt–LaTène settlements seem to have been abandoned, including the most important of them, Závist. However, unlike in the central and western plains, small groups in the south of the country maintained traditional practices: they cremated their dead and continued to deposit pottery in their graves.

Openwork bronze mounts, originally fixed to a perishable base (perhaps drinking horns), Čížkovice (Bohemia).
Two versions based on the same design from a Greek prototype. The one on the left is a continuous chain of vegetal elements:
foliage scrolls and palmettes form S's and triskeles, terminating in two small heads, one seen frontally, the other in profile (see p. 69).
That on the right juxtaposes leaves, S-scrolls and palmette, arranged around a face seen full on.
Mid-4th century BCE. Height: 62 mm.
Litoměřice (Czech Republic), Okresni Muzeum.

Left and opposite

Bronze beaked flagons from Basse-Yutz (Moselle, France).

The richness of the coral inlays and the champlevé red enamel, as well as the finely incised decoration link these two exceptional works to the turning point between the initial period of Celtic art and the innovations that followed the Transalpine settlement in Italy. The handle of one of the flagons ends in a head composed of S-scrolls, with a palmette headdress, partly transformed into a sketch of a face (detail p. 71).

Early 4th century BCE. Height: 380 mm.

Height of the handle: approx. 50 mm.

London, British Museum.

This shift in cultural practice was formerly explained as being due to conquest by armed bands of non-indigenous Celts, but it is difficult to accept that small groups of invaders could have ousted the densely populated, powerful, centralized societies suggested by the impressive fortifications at Závist. A much better explanation, for both Champagne and Bohemia, is that a significant portion of the population simply left of their own accord, and headed towards Italy, a land known and envied for its riches. To some extent, this is confirmed by similarities that may be discerned between the cultural practices of the Boii and the Senones and their Transalpine namesakes. Obviously these are just hints, but they are significant: the Boii practised bi-rituality, with a preponderance of cremations and a ritual bending of weapons that was characteristic of Bohemia in the second half of the 5th century BCE; the Senones of the Adriatic region invariably buried their dead, and women of rank wore torcs with terminals and a pair of matching bracelets. The fact that these practices also existed in indigenous Italian societies does not diminish the argument, because local tradition remained distinct; for instance, the use of flat stone chests for Ligurian-type cremations cannot be confused with the deposit of ashes straight into the ground, which was typical only of Bohemian tribes and the Boii.

In general, the communities of Cispadane Gaul that are considered to be Celtic are not homogeneous ethnic populations but a mixture of the original occupants – who themselves were already mixed – and immigrant 'Celtic' groups that were probably infused with many different ethnic groups during their migration to the region. Furthermore, contrary to a formerly widespread theory, the arrival of the Transalpines did not mean the disappearance of native populations or the dismantling of existing urban networks. The burial-grounds, notably those of urban centres, illustrate an ongoing cohabitation, especially between the Celtic and local elites. On the other hand, certain details of the funerary ritual suggest that indigenous men were buried with La Tène arms. This is further evidence that there was a degree of assimilation between Celtic immigrants and local populations with warrior traditions, notably the Umbrians and the Ligurians.

The repercussions of the invasion of Italy

For the immigrant Transalpines, the conquest of northern Italy allowed direct contact with the world of Greek and Etruscan cities and enabled them to establish strong trade links with their regions of origin. The 4th century BCE therefore saw an intensification of relations between the Cisalpine and Transalpine regions. People moved back and forth – warriors going to Italy in search of glory or wealth and then returning home to Champagne or Bohemia, maybe years later, with their booty – while stylish new products were carried north by merchants. It is hardly surprising that this increasingly busy traffic strongly influenced Switzerland (the inevitable intermediary in Transalpine trade) as well as Champagne and Bohemia.

Derived chiefly from direct borrowing from the Graeco-Etruscan 'vegetal' style – intricate compositions of palmettes linked by foliage and other devices – new forms of expression proved remarkably successful and were widely distributed, leading Celtic art to its most original creations. Thus, from the first half of the 4th century BCE Celtic-Italian society provided the earliest forms of those equivocal designs that can be interpreted in many ways: human or floral elements, symbols and sometimes even zoomorphic elements merge with one another to form ambiguous images. These were responses to the Celtic idea that the visible world conceals an obscure, but much more significant, aspect of existence.

Metal pieces richly decorated with coral, from a chariot burial in Condé-sur-Marne (France).
Left, decorative bronze ferrule ornamented with coral, 35 mm in diameter (perhaps a chariot piece).
Right, rectangular appliqué in iron, 80 mm high, probably from harness, openwork decorated
with coral discs or foliage in finely sculpted vegetal motifs (detail p. 73).
Mid-4th century BCE.
Châlons-en-Champagne Musée Municipal (Marne, France).

Coral and hidden faces

Coral was highly valued by the Celts from the 6th century BCE onwards because of the magical qualities they attributed to it. It was initially used in small quantities, mostly for inlay on objects made primarily from precious metals. However, when the Transalpines invaded Italy, they found great resources of coral in the fisheries of the Gulf of Naples, which they could access without recourse to too many intermediaries. It could be said that the 'amber route' – from the Baltic to the south – had its counterpart in the opposite direction with a 'coral route' that began in Campania, crossed the Alps, and then headed towards Bohemia or Champagne. The precious material was so popular that it prompted the design of a special brooch terminating in a boss to carry an inset piece of coral, called the 'Münsingen' brooch after the burial-ground in the Berne region of Switzerland where it is particularly well represented. If coral could not be obtained, coloured bone, a mosaic of red glass or even beaten bronze was used as a substitute.

The use of coral was not limited to a simple setting, an appliqué or an inlay. Some luxury objects were decorated with coral sculpted with such delicacy that the design cannot be fully appreciated without the aid of a strong magnifying glass. These include the ceremonial helmets of Agris, the cabochons of brooches and some items of warrior equipment. A chariot and accompanying harness discovered in a chieftain's grave in Condé-sur-Marne illustrate the high standards achieved in this work.

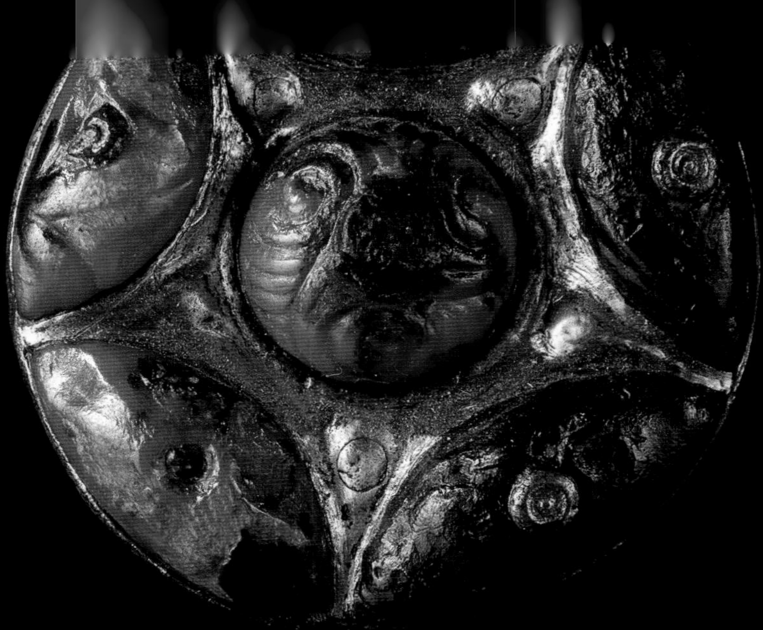

Discoidal ornament for a side ring from a horse-bit, Condé-sur-Marne chariot-burial.

The central coral cabochon is engraved with a triskele formed of three demi-palmettes; the five elements of the perimeter bear a four-leaved zigzag in the same lozenge shape. The presence of these almost invisible decorations must have served to indicate the prestige of the owner as well as to appeal to the magic protection of the divinity.

Mid-4th century BCE. Diameter: 21 mm.

Châlons-en-Champagne Musée Municipal (Marne, France).

Iron axle-pin, the head encrusted with coral, from a chariot-tomb in Condé-sur-Marne.

Mid-4th century BCE. Width: 50 mm.

Châlons-en-Champagne Musée Municipal (Marne).

Barely visible to the naked eye, the coral-work includes the triskele (one of the principal motifs of the Celtic symbolic repertory), S-shapes and peltas (motifs derived from the Celtic transformation of the palmette). The great openwork panel, sadly incomplete, illustrates another remarkable aspect of the art of the 4th-century Celtic–Italian artists: delicately sculpted coral appliqués are assembled to create a head with eyes made of inset cabochons and dressed with the double mistletoe leaf familiar from the iconography of the preceding century. One needs an informed eye to see this image, previously explicitly depicted in many different versions but here evoked only by allusion. It could almost be an optical game designed for initiates to test their powers of perception.

This type of image was very popular and is one of the most original aspects of Celtic art at its peak.

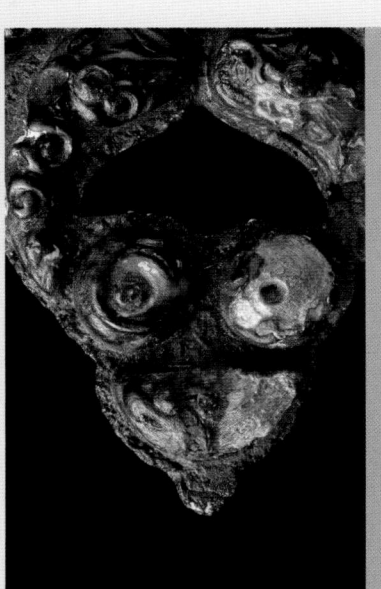

Detail of the rectangular appliqué from Condé-sur-Marne.

The shape and the arrangement of the coral pieces in the corners suggest the most characteristic motif of the first La Tène period: a head bearing the double mistletoe-leaf. It is no longer obvious but can be easily recognized by a trained eye.

Mid-4th century BCE.

Height: 35 mm. Châlons-en-Champagne Musée Municipal (Marne, France).

Pedestal vase from Beine-Prunay (Marne), decorated in the 'red-figure' technique.
The upper part of the body was painted with finely diluted clay, fired at high heat, in curvilinear motifs the same colour as the surface of the clay, then covered with a fine reddish glaze submitted to an oxidizing temperature.
Second half of the 4th century BCE.
Height: 350 mm.
Reims (Marne, France),
Musée Saint-Remi.

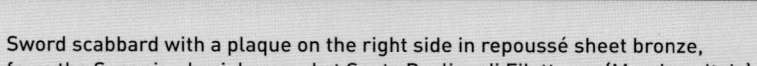

Sword scabbard with a plaque on the right side in repoussé sheet bronze,
from the Senonian burial ground at Santa Paolina di Filottrano (Marches, Italy).
The frieze of palmettes surrounded by foliage scrolls is transformed to form the outline of human faces, with triskeles and large S's at the junction; the rest of the lateral foliage scrolls also suggests a stag's antlers… Here we find in the same allusive image all the fundamental elements of the Celtic repertoire: human, animal, vegetal, as well as the two principal symbols.
Second quarter of the 4th century BCE. Length: 675 mm. Ancona (Italy), Museo Archeologico Nazionale delle Marche.

A Gallic citizen from Switzerland, named Helico, who had lived in Rome because of his skill as a craftsman, [and] brought with him when he came back some dried figs and grapes and some samples of oil and wine.

Pliny the Elder, *Natural History*, XII, 2, 5.

The influence of Celtic Italy

Evidence of contact between the Transalpine regions and Italy includes the sumptuous ceremonial helmets of Agris, richly decorated with coral, and those of Amfreville, in which red-glass mosaic was used to similar effect. But some instances are even more explicit. Thus, beaten sheet-bronze appliqués, probably made as a plate for a scabbard and then reused on an iron one discovered at Epiais-Rhus (near Paris), are exact matches of the scabbard decoration from Moscano di Fabriano, found in a rich Senonian grave of the middle of the 4th century BCE. Equally significant is the warrior burial-site recently discovered in Plessis-Gassot (north of Paris), which can be dated to the beginning of the 3rd century BCE. The dead man was accompanied by two Etruscan black-varnished cups, the only ones of that period found north of the Alps to date. They were buried along with the corpse, as was customary in Cispadane Gaul, thereby virtually proving that the warrior had spent time in the peninsula.

Italy was long considered to be a marginal region in the Celtic world, the theatre of a brief occupation whose chief interest came from the vicissitudes of the struggle against Rome. But it now seems that it was a key province, which, from the 4th century BCE, exercised a profound and durable influence, particularly in art, on the culture of all of the historical Celtic world.

The capacity for integration displayed by immigrant groups in Italy helps us to understand what happened in other territories during the historic migration. They rapidly built powerful ethnic groupings with those under their control, as did the Senones and the Boii. More surprising, on close examination, is the diversity of the Cisalpine Celts, in the variety of their origins and in the individual characteristics of each particular tribe. For example, throughout their autonomous existence of little more than a century, the Senones occupied a territory situated around ports they did not control, while for two centuries the Boii dominated a region with a long-standing, sophisticated urban network. This was later to be of fundamental importance in the development of the urban system of the Celts of Central Europe.

'Red-figure' vases

Design developments.
Top left, design on a ceremonial Celto-Italian helmet from Canosa (Pouilles, Italy), richly inlaid with coral. Bottom left, design on a vase from Beine-Prunay (Marne, France). The similarity of the two compositions is obvious.

The region between the valleys of the Vesle and Suippe rivers, east of Reims, did not suffer any perceptible fall in population towards the end of the 5th century BCE, when the majority of the burial grounds in the rest of the Champagne region were abandoned. Thereafter continuously occupied until the Roman conquest, it is the centre of Remi territory.

It was there, in the second half of the following century, an astonishing series of painted vases appeared, created in the workshop of a craftsman whose production was inspired by the Greek or Etruscan pottery technique known as 'red-figure', probably developed in Italy: diluted coloured clay that darkened with firing was used to sketch motifs that would then appear clearly on the terracotta.

The Great Expedition (3rd century BCE)

The success of the Celtic invasion of Italy, as well as the knowledge acquired through subsequent mercenary service both of the great riches and important weaknesses of the cities of the Mediterranean region, must have increased its attraction for adventurous elements in the Transalpine communities. However, the peace concluded with Rome during the last third of the 4th century BCE limited the scope of further military expeditions. Further east, Celtic penetration into the Carpathian Basin was slowed by belligerent local populations. Small groups of western Celts in search of new places to settle were by no means uniformly successful in their attempts to insinuate their way into these societies. Despite this, they gradually established themselves in that region from the end of the 5th century BCE onwards.

The push towards the Balkans and the eastern Mediterranean was, however, temporarily halted by a new Macedonian power. Ptolemy Lagos, one of Alexander the Great's generals, reported that Celtic emissaries were received by his sovereign in 335 BCE, during Alexander's campaign against the Triballes of Thrace (on today's Bulgarian–Romanian border). Coming from the Adriatic coast, these envoys must have been Senones, for the Celts never settled on the eastern seaboard of the Adriatic, which was difficult to access and inhabited by particularly bellicose tribes. The emissaries were probably sounding out Alexander about offering their services as mercenaries. However, any Celtic infiltration towards the south-east amounted to little until after the death of Alexander, when quarrels between his successors encouraged them to consider that the Macedonian kingdom's defences might be weak. This initially proved to be a misguided presumption, as a first expedition was wiped out in 298 on Haemus (modern Stara Planina, Bulgaria) by Cassander, the new king of Macedonia.

But in 281 the death of Lysimachus – ruler of Thrace, Macedonia and the western part of Asia Minor – followed by the collapse of his kingdom, created a favourable situation. The very next year three Celtic armies totalling 300,000 men began to march south. The first, commanded by Cerethrios, attacked Thrace. The second, led by another warrior called Brennos and Achichorius, invaded the Dardanelles and Thermopylae. The third, led by Bolgios, marched against Macedonia itself, where in 279 it crushed the feeble army of Ptolemy Ceraunos. The young king, wounded and captured, was beheaded by the victors, but Bolgios' army did not follow up its advantage and returned home.

There was similar indecision in the rest of the Celtic forces: a dispute led to the departure of 20,000 men commanded by Leonnarios and Lutarios. But Brennos and 68,000 soldiers continued on to Delphi, where they sacked the immensely wealthy sanctuary. However, thereafter Brennos' army withdrew. Tradition has it that the sanctuary was saved from total destruction by the intervention of the presiding deity, Apollo, and his acolytes. A festival, the Soteria ('Feast of Salvation'), was inaugurated to commemorate deliverance from the Celtic peril.

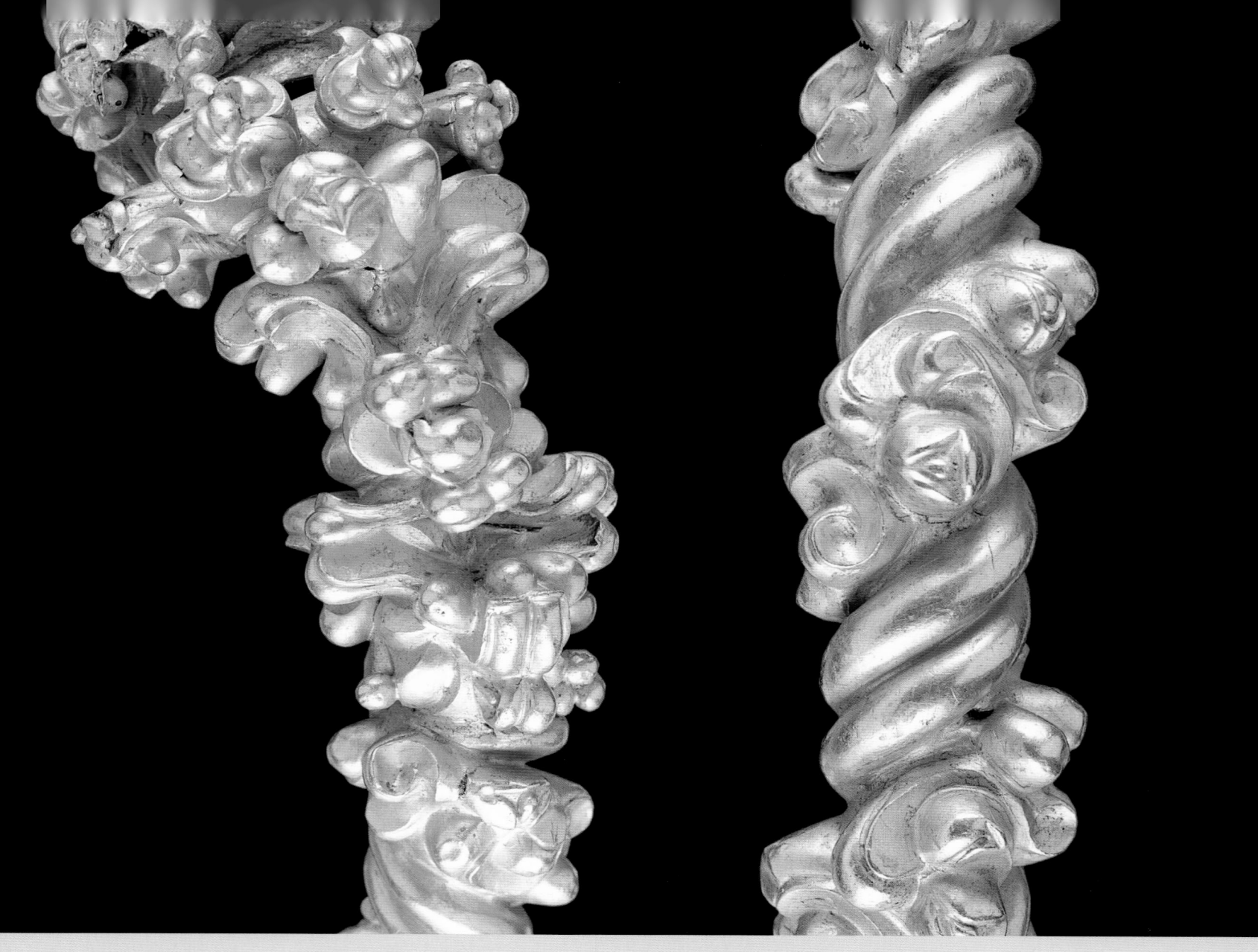

Details of a gold torc found in 1885, together with a gold armband, at Lasgraïsses (Tarn).
The decorative scheme takes its inspiration from Hellenistic floral crowns: clumps of floral motifs twine around the oblique spirals formed by the ribbon binding the stems of the flowers of the crown. Despite their high Baroque exuberance, these motifs follow a rigorous organizational structure where a sort of rosette suggests the mistletoe flower.
3rd century BCE. Toulouse (Haute-Garonne, France), Musée Saint-Raymond.

The sacred treasure of Delphi

The threat posed by Brennos' expedition against the sanctuary of Apollo in 279 BCE created shock waves in the Hellenic world. Several years later, the poet Callimachos penned these words for the god: 'From the extreme West the last of the Titans, raising against Hellas the sword of the barbarian, and the Celtic Ares rushed like snowflakes, numerous as the constellations that strew the celestial meadow, one day ... near my temple, were sighted enemy phalanxes already nearing my tripods, the swords and belts, the impudent armour and

the odious shields that for the Galatae, a frenzied race, marked the route of a cruel fate'.
Classical historians commented on the divine intervention that saved Delphi, and on the check to the Celtic enterprise; it was described by Polybius as a 'rout'. However, according to some, the sanctuary was pillaged by the Celts, and a wealth of booty was transported back to Toulouse by the Volcae Tectosages, who had taken part in the expedition. This 'gold of Toulouse', accursed for its sacrilegious provenance

and dedicated to the gods, was seized in 105 BCE by the Roman commander Q. Servilius Caepio, conqueror of the Volcae. He was subsequently exiled for sacrilege, while his two daughters, who were sent to brothels, died in disgrace. Strabo reported that the treasure amounted to 15,000 talents (equivalent to about 430 tonnes of silver) in gold and silver ingots that was pillaged from votive offerings that had been deposited by the Volcae in their sacred lakes and enclosures. (In this version, however, the treasure had actually been

Details of a golden armring from Lasgraïsses (Tarn).
This jewel, found with the torc opposite, is an elegant variation of the 'hollow egg' ring ornaments of the Danubian Celts.
3rd century BCE. Toulouse (Haute-Garonne, France), Musée Saint-Raymond.

mined in the region rather than looted from Apollo's shrine.)

Several remarkable gold objects typical of 3rd-century BCE La Tène culture have been discovered in the former territory of the Volcae. The first find, at Fenouillet in 1841, comprised seven torcs. One of these bore some resemblance to a jewel found in Gajic in Croatia, at the confluence of the Drava and the Danube, where the presence of Volcae was recorded by classical writers. The second find, at Lasgraïsses, consisted of a torc and armband of remarkable craftsmanship. The torc was inspired by a Hellenic motif of a floral crown tied with a twisted ribbon; the armband resembles the sets of rings with an oval decoration typical of Danubian Celtic sites. They are probably similar to ornaments worn by Gaulish chieftains described by classical writers that formed part of the victorious Romans' booty. Both sets of ornaments confirm the Volcae Tectosages' connection with the Great Expedition of 280 BCE.

Following pages
Detail of the fastening of one of the seven gold torcs discovered in 1841 at Fenouillet (Haute-Garonne).
The stem was formed by twisting a cross section of a rectangular bar, and the fastening was secured by a cuff decorated with vegetal incrustations, possibly inspired by the male catkins of the oak tree.
3rd century BCE.
Toulouse (Haute-Garonne, France), Musée Saint-Raymond.

Terracotta frieze from Civitalba (Marches, Italy).
The fleeing Gaulish raiders drop their booty, bowls with
omphalos and relief decoration in precious metal (right);
the Gaulish chieftain standing in his chariot is about to ride
over the body of one of his warriors lying on the ground (left).
See pp. 76–77.
First half of the 2nd century BCE. Height: 450 mm.

Ancona (Italy), Museo Archeologico Nazionale delle Marche.

Following the withdrawal from Delphi, part of the central army, consisting of Illyrians as well as Celts, settled in the Danube Valley at the confluence of the Sava and Morava rivers. Here they formed a new tribal confederation known as the Scordisci. The rest of the army turned towards Thrace, already occupied by the army of Cerethrios, where they were defeated by the king of Macedonia, Antigonus Gonatas, grandson of the brother of Alexander the Great. The small army commanded by Leonnarios and Lutarios crossed into Asia Minor, where several decades later they were allowed to settle, establishing themselves on the plains of Anatolia and becoming known as Galatians. Some of the remaining troops of the Great Expedition ended up in Thrace, where they established a powerful enclave that survived for several decades. Others entered the service of Antigonus Gonatas after their defeat at his hands.

So ended the last great documented military endeavour of the Celts. Despite the names of tribes involved – such as the Volcae Tectosages, which means 'Wolves Searching for Shelter' – this does not seem to have been a migration with the ultimate aim of settlement in new territory, as had been the case with the Transalpine foray into Italy in the previous century. Rather, it was a straightforward military campaign, a hit-and-run operation to secure booty. All available

archaeological evidence indicates that the forces of 280 BCE originated in the Danube Valley, which at the time was a densely populated region. Since no significant demographic reduction occurred at this time, it seems that it was a 'capillary' recruitment of very mobile contingents that could rapidly be mustered into an efficient fighting force. Nevertheless, leaders well versed in military techniques and endowed with indisputable authority would be needed to defeat the Macedonians. This role was probably played by elite warrior bands who came together from different tribes, temporarily or otherwise. These were professional soldiers who fought for adventure and riches. Such groups seem to have been gathered from a vast area, and this, coupled with the high mobility of their members, would have facilitated rapid transmission of information, enabling the recruitment of an army for mercenary service or other military adventures. The case of the Volcae Tectosages well illustrates the formation of new ethnic groups around the time of the Great Expedition and its aftermath. They probably settled in the Languedoc region of France around 275–260 BCE. Signs of their presence have also been found in Central Europe around the Danube, in Asia Minor (where the Tectosages were one of the three tribes that made up the Galatian community), and around the valley of the Ebro River. As is indicated by the

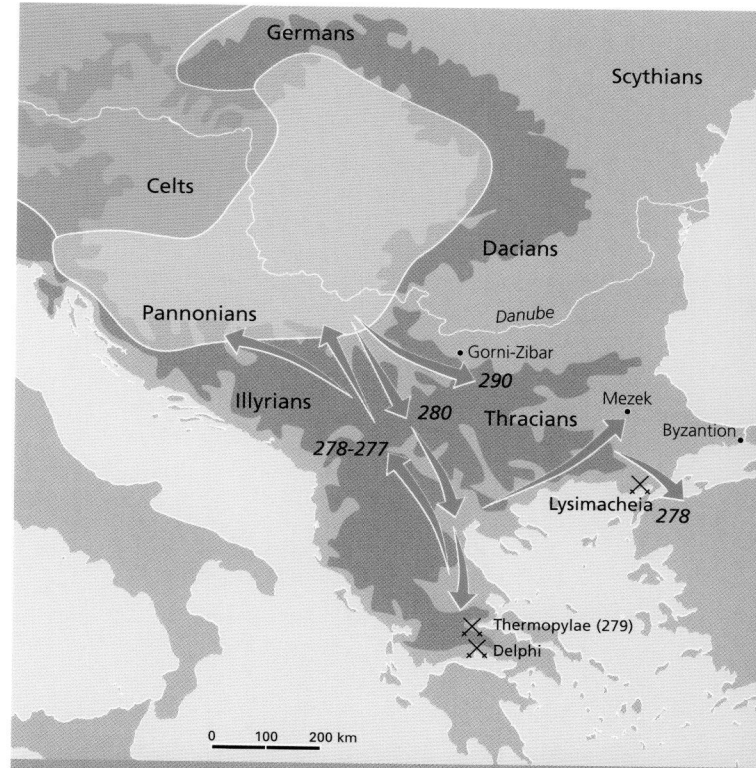

traditional association of the Volcae Tectosages with the pillage of Delphi, as well as by archaeological evidence of links with Danubian settlements, the tribe appears to have been established in Languedoc – and maybe on the other side of the Pyrenees, too – for so long that they might have been returning 'home' after the Great Expedition. But this should not been seen as displaying a desire to settle down. A Carthaginian recruiting-post was situated close by, which was probably a main attraction of the region for Celtic mercenaries eager for more campaigning.

At about this time, as is indicated by the presence of Danubian artefacts, there was a pronounced Celtic push further west. It is likely that the Rhône Valley was settled by a tribe whom Polybius called the 'Gaesatae', using 'a name that they [the Celts] give to mercenaries'. These were recruited around 232 BCE by the Insubres and the Boii of Cisalpine Gaul to fight alongside them. Polybius must have been referring to the Allobroges ('those who come from elsewhere'), a tribe that Hannibal found established between the Rhône and the Isere in 218 BCE.

The Great Expedition of 280 BCE and the successive incursions of the Celts into the Baltic Peninsula.
Territories occupied by the Celts before the end of the 4th century BCE are shown in a deeper colour; the lightest colour indicates the regions occupied in the first quarter of the following century, notably following the expedition of 280 BCE.

**Celtic imitation of a gold stater of Philip II
of Macedon, attributed to the Sequani.**
*The spread of this type of coinage among the Celts is probably
due to their mercenary activity; this Macedonian piece, struck
some time after the ruler's death, was one of the most
widespread in the 3rd and even the 2nd century BCE, being
generally used to pay the troops' wages.*
3rd–2nd century BCE. Diameter: 20 mm.

Paris, Bibliothèque Nationale, Cabinet des Médailles.

Celtic mercenaries

Mercenary service was a very attractive career for a
Celt, as it combined the warrior predilection of many of
them with a guaranteed wage and the possibility of
occasional loot. It is likely that this practice began
around the 6th century BCE, but it was first documented
about 480 BCE, when mercenary troops recruited from
around Narbonne (France) to fight for Carthage
participated in the Battle of Himera. Although it is not
certain that these were Celts, Ensérune, the principal site
excavated in the Narbonne region, is the only one from
the Midi to have yielded La Tène weapons dating from
the 5th century BCE. The appeal of the mercenary life
may explain the presence of these artefacts.

As already mentioned, Celtic mercenaries definitely
participated in the Syracusan expedition to Greece in
369/8 BCE. They were probably recruited, through the
Ancona trading-post, from the Senones. Mercenary
service was one of the chief activities of this Celtic tribe,
as Senonian burial-grounds indicate. About half of the
graves that have been excavated are those of armed
men. These also contain a great deal of wealth, such as
could only really have been acquired as booty. In 307
Syracuse again recruited 3,000 Celts; they fought
alongside Samnites and Etruscans in the expeditionary
army of Agathocles in Africa.

The golden age of the Celtic mercenary, though, began
with the onset of the bitter struggles between the heirs
of Alexander the Great. Celtic Mercenaries who had
previously fought in Macedonian service probably
returned to Central Europe as informers for their
kinsfolk while the Great Expedition of 280 BCE was
being planned. This meant that many thousands of
courageous, well-trained and experienced soldiers
were available to the Celtic generals. As a bonus they
were also cheaper than Greek equivalents. One gold
Macedonian stater would buy the fighting skill of a
Celtic mercenary for a campaign lasting several
months; a Greek would expect the same amount for
a month's service.

After the Great Expedition, Celtic mercenaries fought
and died on all the battlefields of the Mediterranean
area, in the service of Greece, Carthage or anyone who
had the means but not the military might to match
their ambition.

Mercenary service certainly played a very important role
in the transformation of the Celtic world of the 3rd
century BCE, most obviously in the adoption of coinage.
The designs of their first coins were inspired by those
most often used to pay mercenaries, notably the stater,
the 'Philip' and the coins issued by Alexander the Great.
A large settlement of this period was recently discovered
in Moravia, on the ancient north–south 'amber route'.
It yielded an extraordinary range of coins from Greece
and Carthage that are difficult to put down to trading
exchanges. Only mercenary activity can explain this
exceptional concentration in a location that was
particularly well placed for the recruitment of armies
that may have included Germanic tribes from further
north in addition to Celts.

Left

Pedestal vase with slip decoration, from the burial at Montfercaut à Marson (Marne).
Derived from Hellenic kantharoi, but here without the handles, this shape is particularly common in the Danubian region where this decorating style is also widespread. Its ubiquity is one of the most obvious repercussions of the events of 280 BCE and of the 'returning wave' of the Great Expedition.
Second quarter of the 3rd century BCE. Height: 240 mm. London, British Museum.

Opposite

Chariot axle-pin in iron with bronze head, from the 'La Courte' burial-ground, Leval-Trahegnies (Belgium).
This image, whether a human face or the head of a horned animal (a ram), surmounted with two leaves that might equally be ears, is playfully ambiguous. It's up to the spectator to decide, change his mind, perhaps return to his first impression. There is no definite interpretation, only forms to inspire the imagination …
First half of the 3rd century BCE. Length: 50 mm.
Brussels, Musées Royaux d'Art et d'Histoire.

Movements of armed bands and formation of new tribes

Further north, all of our documentary information on the names and locations of different tribes dates from the Gallic Wars. However, archaeology can amplify it, at least where there are enough artefacts to enable us to follow the vicissitudes of settlement and to identify possible cross-fertilization. The situation is particularly clear in Champagne, where the areas that became depopulated around the end of the 5th century BCE were gradually reoccupied, starting in the south, the Senones' historic territory. Small groups began to arrive around 270 BCE, and founded new necropolises or reused the burial-sites that had lain abandoned for two centuries. They can be differentiated from indigenous inhabitants – the Remi to the north and the Senones in the south – by typically Danubian female jewellery, which is quite unusual in the region: ankle rings with hollow ovals, no torcs, bracelets arranged asymmetrically. However, these non-indigenous groups quickly assimilated some local customs. Interred men are always buried with full equipment, such as that found throughout the La Tène area, including: a sword in its scabbard, often decorated, with its suspension loop of a heavy metal chain; a spear, generally fortified with a spur; a shield, its metal *umbo* (conical boss) sometimes enriched with ornamental appliqués; possibly a broadsword; and often a razor. Some parts of this equipment, notably the sword suspension system, evolved rapidly in this period.

Military inventions and innovations tended to spread very quickly, reflecting the great mobility of an increasingly specialized soldiery. Even the La Tène sword, which was much prized as a weapon, was progressively modified: it was lengthened to serve the needs of the cavalry, who used it primarily for cutting, but became a short, less cumbersome, double-edged sword for the infantry.

In general, the situation seems to have evolved towards a new stability, with the formation of territorial communities that remained in continuous settlement until the Gallic Wars. Perhaps the Danubians who went west gave impetus to the formation of new, stronger tribes by assimilating local groups who had hitherto been too few in number to achieve autonomy. This may explain the emergence of the Belgic tribes alongside the established Remi and Senones. The process continued over several generations, which may be explained by the lack of ethnic homogeneity in the Danubian groups, who had previously been united primarily as warring bands.

The Galatians of Asia Minor

From Bithynia they [the Gauls] went further into Asia. Out of the 20,000 men not more than 10,000 were carrying arms, yet so great was the terror they inspired in all the nations west of the Taurus, that those who had no experience of them, as well as those who had come into contact with them, the most remote as well as their next neighbours, all alike submitted to them. They were made up of three tribes, the Tolostobogii, the Trocmi and the Tectosagi, and in the end they divided the conquered territory of Asia into three parts, each tribe retaining its own tributary cities. The coast of the Hellespont was given to the Trocmi, the Tolostobogii took Aeolis and Ionia, and the Tectosagi received the inland districts. They levied tribute on the whole of Asia west of the Taurus, but fixed their own settlement on both sides of the Halys. Such was the terror of their name and the growth of their numbers that at last even the kings of Syria did not dare to refuse the payment of tribute. The first man in Asia to refuse was Attalus the father of Eumenes, and contrary to universal expectation, fortune favoured his courageous action; he proved himself superior in a pitched battle. The Gauls, however, were not so far disheartened as to renounce their supremacy in Asia; their power remained unimpaired down to the war between Antiochus and Rome. Even then, after the defeat of Antiochus, they quite expected that owing to their distance from the sea the Romans would not advance so far.
TITUS LIVIUS, *The History of Rome*, XXXVIII, 16.

Opposite
Bronze openwork mounting, probably for the cover of a wooden ceremonial vessel, found in one of the two chariot-burials recently discovered at Roissy-en-France (Val-d'Oise, France).
The design of this superb object follows a ternary principle: a central triskele, itself composed of hemispherical triskeles, is surrounded by three monsters with serpentine bodies and the heads of mammals with pointed ears whose tips curve around other hemispherical elements, this time in a binary pattern. The whole is ringed with a swarm of chained monsters that emphasize and amplify the rotary movement of the group.
Second quarter of the 3rd century BCE. Diameter: approx. 200 mm.
Saint-Germain-en-Laye (Yvelines), Musée des Antiquités Nationales.

The birth of a Gaulish people: the Parisii

The small Celtic tribe that gave its name to Paris entered recorded history in 53 BCE, when Julius Caesar called together a Gaulish council. The Parisii were frequently mentioned thereafter, but there is no documentary evidence about their origin. Similarly, until recently archaeology had not shed much light on the matter. The few proto-historic traces suggested an abrupt decline – perhaps even a break – of occupation in their historic territory between the Bronze Age (end of the third millennium to the 8th century BCE) and the 3rd century BCE. The first artefacts that could be certainly attributed to Celtic settlements dated from the latter era. These comprised items unearthed from a few cemeteries and isolated graves – the burial-ground of Saint-Maur-des-Fossés and the chariot-tomb of Nanterre.

Recent research, though, has helped to illuminate the Parisii's history. Excavations at Bercy have revealed Bronze Age and Iron Age settlements, and the area seems to have been abandoned suddenly some time before the end of the 5th century BCE. This could have been due to climatic change, the diversion of a river, or a host of other factors. Settlement might have continued to some degree, but the abandonment undoubtedly signals a major environmental reorganization of the Parisii site.

Many more 3rd-century BCE graves and cemeteries have recently been found, too, at Rungis, Bouqueval, Le Plessis-Gassot and Roissy. Large-scale excavations of these sites have demonstrated that there is no connection between them and preceding settlements, which were generally Neolithic and therefore several millennia earlier. The artefacts are exceptionally interesting and remarkably consistent, with the oldest dated to around 275 BCE.

One convincing theory links the establishment of these cemeteries with the activities of the highly mobile warrior groups that criss-crossed Europe from the Atlantic seaboard to the Balkans (and Asia Minor), and from the Danubian region to the Mediterranean. The grave-goods found at Rungis exhibit similarities with those found in different regions of Celtic Europe where these military groups halted or settled between 280 and 250 BCE. A type of articulated metal chain for attaching a sword (of the short-lived 'ladder' design that was soon replaced by sturdier models) has been found in the Paris region (at Saint-Maur-des-Fossés) and in newly discovered cemeteries in Champagne, in Volcae territories in the Languedoc (at Ensérune) and in the Danube region (at Belgrade-Karaburma). These chains are generally associated with scabbards decorated with the distinctive 'dragon-pair' insignia of a particularly mobile and dynamic military elite. Among the Parisian warrior graves that contained a scabbard with this emblem, one in the recently excavated little burial-ground at Plessis-Gassot stands out. It also included two black-varnished Etruscan goblets, indicating that the deceased had spent time in Italy. However, the bronze appliqués on the shield display unmistakable links with the Danubian region, too. This is a striking testimony to the mobility and the multiplicity of contacts of the military elite that finally settled in the Paris region. The presence of a ternary torc, the typical female ornament of the Senones, in another grave on the same site obviously signals the presence of at least one woman of that tribe. So it seems that Julius Caesar was correct when he described the friendliness and the long-standing ties between the Parisii and the Senones.

Left
Detail of the Roissy-en-France cover-mounting.
This remarkable creation displays all the skills of Celtic art at its peak. Full picture p. 89.

Opposite
Chariot axle-pin in iron with bronze head, from the burial with the openwork cover at Roissy-en-France (Val-d'Oise).
The face suggested by an assembly of geometric volumes – the central one inverted – results from the transformation of a chain of palmettes; the swirls of the base become the bulbous eyes, and the central leaf, the only one unchanged, the nose …
See pp. 88–89.
Second quarter of the 3rd century BCE. Length: 50 mm.
Saint-Germain-en-Laye (Yvelines, France), Musée des Antiquités Nationales.

Suggestions of links with Danubian settlements are particularly persuasive because of the remarkable bronze panels that decorate some of the chariot burials in the Parisian tombs, notably one of the graves at Roissy and those now in the National Museum of Antiquities. The Central European links of the Parisii are as obvious as those of the Mezek chariot in Bulgaria, which arrived in that region with the Great Expedition. Furthermore, the very name Parisii seems to confirm their origin, whether it derives from a traditional formulation, Quarisii ('those who have [become] settled'), or, as a new theory suggests, from the word for a type of lance, as did the name of the Gaesatae (from gae, spear) and probably also that of the Belgae. There are, intriguingly, a number of lance-shaped military standards that probably came from this warrior elite milieu of *c.* 280 BCE. One is from the Fère-Champenoise grave of a man from one of the immigrant groups that settled in the region at that time.

While the Parisii were establishing themselves in the 3rd century, their namesakes – the Parisi – were doing the same thing much further north. These were a Yorkshire tribe, and evidence for them has been found in Iron Age cemeteries. They certainly retained indigenous practices, such as the foetal position of the skeletons, but their burials also had elements found in the regions known to have been affected by the migrations of 280–250 BCE. Rectangular enclosures surrounded the tombs and two-wheeled war chariots, typical of the Parisii but very unusual elsewhere at that time, were buried along with their Parisi owners.

Probably some time later, around 150 BCE, the Parisii developed a network of *oppida*, hill-forts with an urban character. These sites seem to have been developed in order to control waterways, the axes of the traffic from which this tribe derived its wealth, which is illustrated by one of the most handsome coinages created by any Celts.

Left
Chariot burial SP 1002 from the 'La Fosse Cotheret' burial-ground at Roissy-en-France (Val-d'Oise, France) during excavation.
At the left side, half-buried in the earth, the remains of the wheel bindings. To the right, in front of the transverse brace, is the openwork cover. The other uncovered pieces are the metal parts of the chariot.

Left
Detail of the terminals of a bronze torc from the burial-ground at Jogasses à Chouilly (Marne).
Palmettes, here transformed into the expressive outlines of big-nosed, large-eyed faces, are one of the most popular themes of this golden age of Celtic art; in this example, the S-scroll has been added, along with residual leaves of the foliage swirls. (see p. 134 and 136).
Early 3rd century BCE. Height of the detail: approx. 80 mm.
Châlons-en-Champagne (Marne, France), Musée Municipal.

A world in full expansion

During the 3rd century BCE, then, the Transalpine Celts spread over a large part of Europe. The world they inhabited was becoming increasingly prosperous, and trade was growing on a scale and with an intensity hitherto unknown. Major routes continued to develop at a pace, as is indicated by several bridges found in Switzerland that were constructed in this period. However, the military impact of the Celts on the Mediterranean world has overshadowed the spread of La Tène culture to the north, west and east, with La Tène elements thriving in the Iberian Peninsula, the British Isles, towards Scandinavia and even on the edges of the Russian steppes. La Tène weapons and certain ornamental styles were adopted by peoples who had until then been impervious to this culture. Such imitation undoubtedly reflects the great prestige achieved by the Celts, through their military reputation but probably also through their appealing belief system. The only direct evidence we have of this is in works of art whose images suggest continuous movement. Anthropomorphic, zoomorphic or vegetal shapes and forms link in an endless metamorphosis designed to evoke the progress and continuity of the universe.

Opposite
**Bronze belt-hook,
Loisy-sur-Marne (Marne).**
Animal ears are added to the impression of a face resulting from the transformation of the palmette; even the working part, the ring, participates in the image by forming a pair of horns. This successful realisation is an excellent illustration of the virtuosity and the creative ability of Celtic artists at the height of their powers: functional aspects, symbols and different natural elements merge in the same image, strikingly and perfectly harmonized.
First half of the 3rd century BCE. Height: 55 mm.
Châlons-en-Champagne (Marne, France),
Musée Municipal.

The development, expansion and decline of the Celtic urban centres (2nd–1st century BCE)

The turbulent events of the 3rd century BCE culminated when, at the very height of its territorial expansion and cultural influence, the La Tène Celtic world stabilized and even partially retreated. In Italy, not even the presence of Gaesatae mercenaries from the Rhône Valley could prevent a Roman victory over a coalition of Insubres and Boii at the Battle of Telamon (225 BCE). Between 218 and 207 the Cisalpine Celts enjoyed some respite from Roman aggression because of Hannibal's expedition into Italy, which many of them joined, but in 191 the Boii were finally, unequivocally defeated, and some of them returned to their native regions. The Roman occupation of all Cispadane Gaul was followed by the foundation of the colony of Bononia (Bologna) – which took the place of the Felsina, the old capital of Etruria south of the Po – and by the construction of the Via Aemilia that passed by that town and facilitated the rapid dispatch of troops from Ariminum (Rimini) on the Adriatic coast to Placentia (Plaisance) on the Po. The Insubres and Cenomani, the great Celtic peoples of Transpadane Gaul, meaning 'located to the north of the river Po', retained a superficial autonomy, but their power was greatly reduced by Roman support for the independence of smaller tribes that had been their dependants, particularly those who controlled access to the Alpine passes. In 186 the tentative settlement of a contingent of 12,000 Celts in Venetia prompted a vigorous Roman reaction, followed by the foundation of a colony at Aquilia five years later. Rome soon pressed home its advantage in the region with the conquest of Istria, thus ensuring control of the eastern gateways to Italy and free access to the 'amber route'.

Fear of Transalpine attack, revived by the short-lived success of Hannibal's expedition, led Rome to take an interest in the Western Mediterranean, especially the Iberian Peninsula, which since the first Punic War (264–241 BCE) had become a source of precious metals and troops for Carthage. In 238 Hamilcar Barca had landed at Cadiz and set about the Carthaginian conquest of the peninsula. This was achieved, apart from a coastline that had been colonized by the Phoenicians for many centuries, under the leadership of Hamilcar's son Hannibal. On the eve of his expedition into Italy, Hannibal controlled almost the entire region south of the Douro, much prized for its rich deposits of gold and silver. His allies at the time were the powerful Celtiberians of the Meseta, an almost inexhaustible reserve of mercenaries famed for their courage and endurance.

Above

Bronze ritual chariot from Merida (Spain).
It shows a rider accompanied by a dog chasing a boar, which, after the horse, is the animal most often depicted by the Celts. They are frequently associated, notably on coins, where the boar often serves as a military emblem.
This is therefore the evocation of an important mythological scene connected with the solar deity.

4th–5th century BCE. Height: 120 mm.

Saint-Germain-en-Laye (Yvelines, France), Musée des Antiquités nationales.

Below

Silver fibula from Cañete de los Torres (Spain).
The shape is inspired by La Tène examples of the 3rd century BCE but is distinguished by the presence of figurative elements: a hunting scene, also found on other peninsular fibulas. In antiquity, the Iberian Peninsula was famed for its extraordinary richness in precious metals.

2nd century BCE. Length: 90 mm.

Madrid, Museo Arqueológico Nacional.

The Iberian Celts

The Celts of the Iberian Peninsula are rarely mentioned in general works on the Celtic populations of Europe, apart from in linguistic studies. Evidence of ancient Celtic dialects has been found there in inscriptions written in an alphabet borrowed from the Phoenicians via Iberians of the Mediterranean coast, as well as in many names of places and people. The place names are often similar to those found in Gaul and other ancient Celtic regions, notably those ending in -briga (height, fortress). Among the tribal names we even find the Celtici (Keltikoi in Greek), located by classical writers to two areas hundreds of kilometres apart: in Galicia, near Cape Finisterre; and in southern Portugal, around Cape St Vincent. It was to the latter that Herodotus referred (Histories, II, 33 and IV, 49) when he described the Celts as 'the most westerly, after the Cynetes, of all European nations'. The Cynetes hailed from modern south-western Portugal, situated between the 'sacred promontory' (Cape St Vincent) and the mouth of the Anas (Guadiana). Therefore, as has already been stated, around the end of the 6th century BCE Celtic settlements extended almost to the extreme south-western corner of Europe. But it is so difficult to explain this long-established presence – which seems to have no cultural connection with Hallstatt–La Tène settlements – that the Celts of the Iberian Peninsula tend to be divorced from the traditional picture, based since the end of 19th century on the link between the spread of La Tène culture (or its Hallstatt predecessor) and the expansion of Celtic populations from an original Central European nucleus. Even had there been late migrations of small groups, it is now clear that we must look to a much earlier arrival (2nd or even 3rd millennium BCE) for the primary origin of the Celtic presence in the peninsula, which is west of an imaginary line running from the mouth of the Guadiana to the middle of the Ebro Valley.

Here, as with the Golasecca culture in northern Italy, the existence of a culture that developed independently of any Hallstatt–La Tène influence may explain the limited receptivity to La Tène culture found in Celtic groups who are distinct from the central group. Only a faint echo is found in the 3rd century BCE, the period of the central group's greatest influence. Certainly the cultural autonomy cannot be attributed to any lack of contact. The presence of a late 6th-century belt-hook of Iberian origin in a burial in the Hallstatt princely tumulus at Magdalenenberg in the Black Forest proves that long-distance contact occurred. And, of course, Herodotus linked the Celts of the Iberian Peninsula with those who lived close to the sources of the Danube.

The obvious singularity of the Hispanic Celtic culture, wrongly considered to be marginal, actually masks many underlying relationships with their Trans-Pyrenean cousins, especially in religion and artistic expression, where they show the same tendency to use images for complex and allusive messages. Similarities can also be discerned in the organization and general evolution of their social structures. These began as tribal communities, attached to castros (fortified places), which controlled, often from the Bronze Age onwards, the activities of a small region. In the 3rd and 2nd centuries BCE these in turn developed into powerful confederations, city-states with urban centres akin to the oppida of La Tène Celts, who put up fierce resistance against both Carthage and Rome.

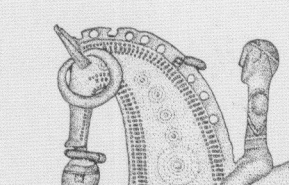
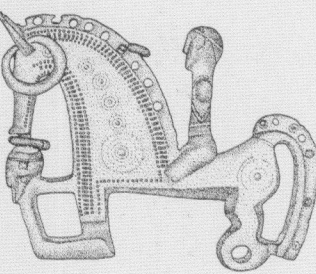
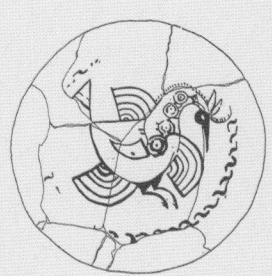
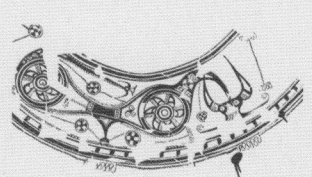

Below, left
Bronze fibula, unknown Spanish provenance.
It shows a rider with, in front, a human head with pierced ears that originally served as rings, as in those of the mounting. This detail and the open eyes indicate that this is not a trophy, a 'severed head', but rather an image of the warriors' tutelary god. This type of ornament, typical of the Celtiberian region, was probably the insignia of the equestrian military elite.
2nd century BCE. Width: 90 mm. Madrid, Museo Arqueológico Nacional.

Below, centre
Inner design of a stemmed goblet from Numantia with polychrome painted decoration.
The subject is a crane, a mythological bird associated in Gaul with the divine Tarvos Trigaranus ('Bull with the three cranes'), of which various representations are known in different Celtic regions. The essential and effective image also recalls the gyratory movement of a triskele, thanks to the shape and the arrangement of the wings.
1st century BCE. Diameter: 170 mm.
Soria (Spain), Museo Numantino.

Below, right
Evolved design of a painted Numantian pot called the 'bull vase'.
The integration of abstract symbols (solar wheels, triskele, etc.) into the image of the animal probably indicates its celestial character (the 'divine bull'), known in other Celtic regions. This is a specifically Celtic treatment, unknown in the Iberian painted pottery that inspired Numantian production. The development covers at least half the circumference
1st century BCE. Height of the painted band: around 200 mm.
Soria (Spain), Museo Numantino.

Left
Gold coin of Cunobelinos, Shakespeare's Cymbeline, king of the powerful Catuvellauni and Trinovantes, from the Thames estuary.
The picture of a sprouting ear of corn, which together with the vine is the only cultivated plant identifiable on the images, reflects the important role played by crops in the economy of the Celtic peoples. The inscription CA MV refers to the agglomeration of Camulodunum (Colchester), where Cunobelinos's gold coinage was minted.
Diameter: 20 mm. London, British Museum.

The Iberian wars, the bane of Rome

When the second Punic War ended in 201, Rome seized the former Carthaginian territories in the peninsula as trophies of war. This opened an almost continual series of conflicts with the native inhabitants, especially with the bellicose and powerful Celtiberians of the central plains, and with other peoples of Celtic origin. Resistance to Rome was fierce, but after almost half a century of combat between armies of many thousands, Celtiberia was finally subdued. Nevertheless, the Celtiberians revolted again in 154, and the powerful Arevacii inflicted a crushing defeat on a Roman army at Numantia. Peace was re-established two years later after a bitter struggle, but by then the wars against the Celtiberians, who were fierce and indefatigable opponents, had become a nightmare for and led to serious difficulty in recruiting troops. The hard-won peace was brutally broken yet again in 147 by Viriatos, leader of the Lusitanii of the lower Douro Valley. He seized a large part of the southern peninsula, inflicting severe defeats on the Romans, and incited to rebellion the powerful Vascones of the western side of the Meseta, as well as the Numantians. Viriatos' assassination in 139 brought the Lusitanian Wars to an end, but the Celtiberians continued the struggle. Two years later they routed the Roman army at Numantia, the hill-fortress that was seen as the centre of their resistance, later being described by Cicero as the 'terror of the Empire'. In 134, led by Scipio Aemilianus, the legions laid siege to the fortress, but it was a year before they took it. After twelve months outside the walls, Roman reprisals were savage: the starving survivors inside the fortress were sold into slavery and the city was razed. Sporadic uprisings continued and were generally easily repressed, but the wild mountain tribes in Cantabria and the Asturias in the north-west of the peninsula remained thorns in the side of Rome until much later. Finally, in 26 and 25 BCE, the Emperor Augustus himself led an army of 70,000 men against the last independent Celtic territories of that part of Europe.

After his death, the Helvetii nevertheless attempted to do that which they had resolved on, namely, to go forth from their territories. When they thought that they were at length prepared for this undertaking, they set fire to all their towns, in number about twelve – to their villages about four hundred – and to the private dwellings that remained ...

Julius Caesar, *The Gallic War*, I, 5.

But that was far in the future. Having crossed the Pyrenees in 218 BCE, Hannibal travelled through southern Gaul, where he was greeted by warlike tribes with varying degrees of hostility. These were the Volcae, the Arverni, the Allobroges, and the Gaesatae of the Rhône Valley, who rose to prominence in the region around the middle of the 3rd century BCE. While the evidence is slight, everything indicates that from around that time this part of Gaul underwent a process of stabilization, with the formation of new and powerful tribal confederations accompanied by the development of new-style settlements. These resembled the urban centres of the Mediterranean world to such an extent that Polybius, the earliest writer to describe these societies, termed each of them *polis* (town). The only site of this kind that has been identified in the region is an apparently open-plains settlement, at Aulnat (near Clermont-Ferrand). Founded at the latest around the middle of the 3rd century BCE, it was probably one of the principal centres of the Arverni. In function it represented the equivalent of the fortified urban centre described by the Latin word *oppidum* that is typical of the last two centuries of Continental Celtic independence. Modern scholarship has established a distinction between open agglomerations and fortified settlements. The presence or absence of fortifications does not necessarily reflect the particular role of a settlement; there are other criteria to consider.

Opposite
View of the valley of the river Vltava (Bohemia), from the site of the Třísov *oppidum*.

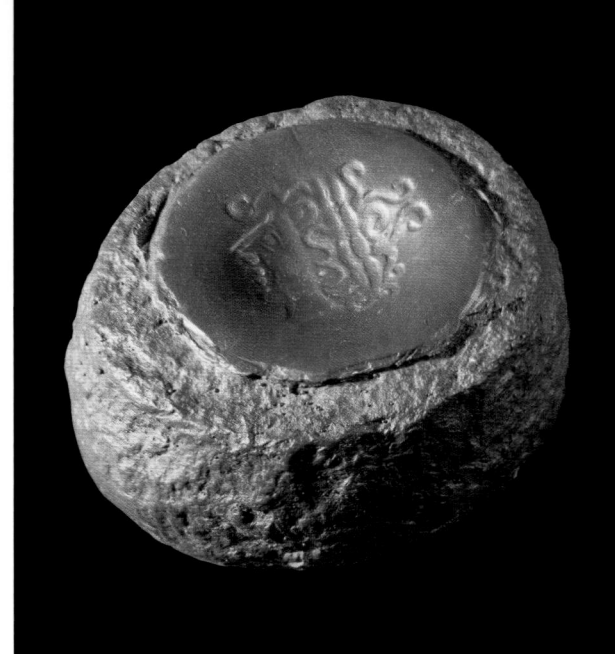

Coinage and urban centres: the emergence of city-states

From the 3rd century BCE onwards, one of the most obvious indications that Celtic society evolved into urban-type centres is the appearance and distribution of coinage. For the Celts, this was initially a convenient way of quantifying the worth of precious metal for important transactions. As the designs adopted during this early phase (chiefly Macedonian or Hellenstic) indicate, coinage was originally introduced to pay mercenaries. Contracts were drawn up and chieftains were paid in gold pieces (staters) or silver pieces (generally multiples of the drachma). It is therefore no coincidence that local coinages first appeared in the Rhône Valley at the same time as Gaesatae mercenaries in the first half of the 3rd century BCE. Thereafter, monetary images became more distinctive, and from the 2nd century became identifying marks of regional communities, reflecting the growing assertiveness of the city-states. From then on, coins were used in everyday transactions, thanks to the introduction of fractions of the original values and, later, of low-value bronze pieces.

It is likely that the development of urban centres, like that of coinage, came from increasing Celtic familiarity with the Mediterranean world. The change of attitude among the Celts is best illustrated by two events that occurred a little less than a century apart, in 280 and 186 BCE. The armies of the Great Expedition searched for loot and destroyed towns, as recent excavations in Bulgaria testify. When they did settle, as in the case of the Galatians, they did not found their own towns but established themselves on the fringes of a pre-existing urban structure. By contrast, in 186 Transalpine Celts migrated to eastern Venetia and established control of the territory by founding an *oppidum*. This was a colonizing expedition, comparable to the Mediterranean approach. We do not know precisely where these Celts originated, nor do we know any of their previous history or have archaeological evidence for this foundation. But we do have some information about another case: the birth and development of the network of *oppida* in Bohemia, which was a consequence of the return to their homelands of the Boii who had previously settled in Italy, after their defeat in 191.

Celtic coinage

The use of coinage, universal among the Celts from the end of the 3rd century BCE, is one of the most significant symptoms of the economic mutation of the Celtic world: the practice of barter was replaced, at least in part, by trading based on currency. The power to issue coinage was supervised by the magistrates, known to the Celts south of the Po Valley as *argantocomaterecus* and to the Transalpines as *arcantodannos*. It was not simply a question of prestige but also a source of profits, since, as a rule,

each striking led to a slight depreciation in the precious metal content by comparison to the previous one, while the nominal value was supposed to remain the same. Coinage therefore inevitably reflected not only the realities of economic life but also of political events.
The requirement to distinguish between successive issues from the same city, while maintaining a general resemblance, led the coin engravers to develop a remarkable capacity for variation in the depiction of images.

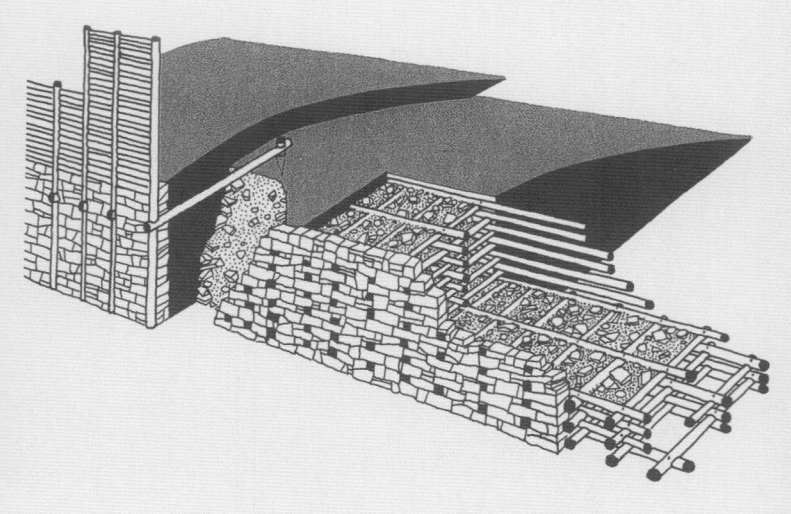

Diagram showing two successive phases of the rampart of the *oppidum* of Manching, near Ingolstadt (Bavaria). End 2nd or 1st century BCE.
First (right), the murus gallicus (Gaulish wall) type, with the ends of the horizontal frame of beams held in the drystone facing; next (left), the type most common in Central Europe, with vertical stakes embedded in the walls.

Reconstruction of the lower part of the wall of the entrance to the *oppidum* of Finsterlohr (Baden-Württemberg, Germany), 1st century BCE.
Vertical stakes were embedded in the outer facing every 2 metres (6¹/₂ ft).

The *oppidum*, cornerstone of the city-states

Classical writers used the term *oppidum* to designate a fortified place and also a 'township' of a region. Modern usage is based on descriptions of large agglomerations in Julius Caesar's *Gallic Wars*, and on the findings of excavations undertaken since the 19th century on a number of such sites in various European countries. The term is generally reserved for a large fortified concentration dating from the 2nd–1st century BCE that may be considered a tribal stronghold because of: its size; the density of its population; the structured nature of its occupation; the variety and quality of its artisan activity; and indications of a particular commercial, administrative or religious function, notably the existence of public spaces and of buildings of unusual size or design. The *oppidum* was therefore part of a system or network that included lesser habitats as well as other, smaller *oppida*, and was integrated in its turn in a wider network formed by the axes of long-distance trade.

These *oppida* were not simply improvised as immediate reactions to exterior danger, because they never seemed to be sited on the basis of purely strategic considerations.

They were located on important communication routes, and acted as staging-posts and market places near river crossings, at the mouths of valleys and at the confluence of rivers. They then made the most of the natural defences that were to hand, building on a hill or an isolated plateau, on a spur, or at the mouth of a river where it was possible to control the waterway efficiently. However, there were also *oppida* on the plains, where the defences were entirely manmade, such as the *oppidum* of Manching near Ingolstadt (Bavaria), which was surrounded by a circular enclosure, an arrangement conceptually different to the rectangular layout familiar in the Mediterranean world.

The excellent locations of these regional meeting-places and the way they fitted into the Continental network of long-distance trade are best appreciated by the fact that many *oppida* are now large modern cities. This is the case in northern Italy (Milan, Bergamo, Brescia, Como, Turin), in the descendants of the capitals of almost all the tribes of Gaul (Amiens, Besançon, Bourges, Paris, Poitiers, Reims) as well as in Basel, Berne, Geneva, Bratislava and Budapest.

Great conurbations also sprang up near *oppida*, such as Autun and Prague, which took the place of Bibracte and Závist, respectively. In Spain Avila, Salamanca and many other cities grew from Celtic foundations.

Undoubtedly, the Celtic development of *oppida*, a framework of coherent territorial ensembles that has stood the test of time, has been one of the cornerstones of Europe.

Opposite, left
In situ reconstruction of a section of the rampart of the Donnersberg *oppidum* (Rheinland-Pfalz, Germany).

Opposite, right
Aerial view of the excavation of the *oppidum* of Manching (Bavaria, Germany).
The subdivisions marked by ditches or rows of stake-holes and the tracks crossing them are clearly visible.

Diagram of the eastern gateway of the *oppidum* of Manching near Ingolstadt (Bavaria, Germany), second half of the 2nd century BCE.
The arrangement of graduating wings, typical of Celtic oppida, facilitated better defence of access to the gateway, surmounted by a wooden tower.

Model reconstruction of a section of the inner layout of the Manching *oppidum* near Ingolstadt (Bavaria).
The regularity of the layout, complete with public highway and communal spaces, together with the permanent subdivision into buildings, confirms the urban character of this type of settlement.

Small bronze head from the *oppidum* of Stradonice (Bohemia).
This formed the pommel of the anthropomorphic handle of a short sword, apparently the weapon of a chieftain.
It is probably an image of the principal deity venerated by the military class. An identical head has been found in the
Moravian oppidum of Staré Hradisko; very similar ones have been discovered in France and even in Ireland.

First half of the 1st century BCE. Height: 38 mm. Prague, Národní Muzeum.

The Boii: the turbulent history of a great tribe at the heart of Europe

To this day, the name of the Boii lives on in the heart of Europe, in Bohemia, the Boiohaemum (country of the Boii) of classical writers. Bavaria may also come from this root. This powerful tribal confederation, which at the height of its power probably also occupied part of the central Danube Valley, seems to have sprung from a long-established indigenous population whose roots can be traced back to the second half of the 3rd millennium BCE. From the second half of the following millennium, tribes who settled south of the Elbe were distinct from their northern neighbours, who practised the Lusatian Urnfield type of culture. This parallel development, which occurs only a few kilometres apart, can be explained solely by the juxtaposition of two great ethnic groupings: Germanic to the north and Celtic to the south. In the first half of the 6th century BCE a large territorial grouping developed, centred on the previously mentioned fortress of Závist. This probably coincided with the emergence of the confederation of Boii, ancestors of those members of the same tribe who invaded Italy 150 years later. The Závist site was abandoned when the Italian invasion took place, as were the fertile plains in the west and centre of the region. Only small settlements in southern Bohemia continued the funerary customs typical of La Tène culture: cremation followed by direct interment of the ashes, sometimes with pottery. Some features of these customs appeared among the Boii of Italy, such as ritual breaking of the swords deposited in graves.

These Italian Boii settled in Etruria, between the Po Valley and the Apennines in what is now Emilia-Romagna. Recent research indicates that they did not destroy existing urban structures but integrated well into a local society composed of Etruscans, Umbrians and Ligurians. Their confederation of 112 tribes was a significant military force: in 191 BCE, after several years of heavy defeat in battle, they still managed to raise an army of 50,000 men for one last stand against Rome. Boii wealth is illustrated by the loot displayed at the Roman triumph after that final battle: apart from the military spoils, chariots laden with arms and standards, there were bronze vases, 1,471 gold torcs, 79 kilos (247 [Roman] pounds) of gold, 749 kilos (2,340 [Roman] pounds) of raw or beaten silver, and 234,000 silver coins (Livy, XXXVI, 40).

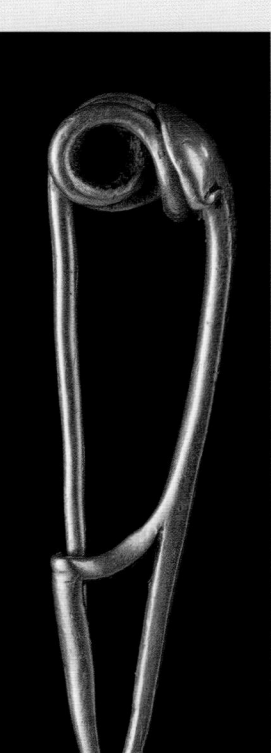

Left
Gold fibula from the *oppidum* of Stradonice (Bohemia).
An exceptional jewel demonstrating the riches of the Boii elite.
Mid-1st century BCE.
Length: 60 mm.
Prague, Národní Muzeum.

Some of the Boii who had lived for two centuries in close contact with the urban environment of central Italy subsequently returned over the Alps to resettle in Central Europe, and they set about developing a network of *oppida*. Around 114 BCE they fought a victorious resistance against the Cimbri and the Teutons. However, at the beginning of the 1st century BCE, they established an *oppidum* on the site of Bratislava, designed to ensure control of one of the principal trade routes between Northern and Southern Europe, which probably led to a consequent weakening of their power in Bohemia. There followed a cessation of the development of the *oppida* network and a retreat to the central sites.

According to classical sources, confirmed by archaeological evidence of the violent end of the Bratislava *oppidum*, Boii power in that region was annihilated by a Dacian offensive under King Burebista in the middle of the 1st century BCE. Their former territory, around Lake Neusiedl, was thereafter called 'the desert of the Boii'.

Around 60 BCE – whether before or after the Dacian victory has not yet been resolved satisfactorily – a group of Boii laid siege to the town of Noreia, capital of the kingdom of Noricum (now Styria, Austria). There they met a delegation of Helvetii, who invited them to join a westward migration to south-western Gaul in 58 BCE. The Helvetian coalition was defeated at Bibracte, leaving the 32,000 Boii as the only remaining Celtic force in Gaul. They became clients of the Aedui and settled in the Sancerre region on the left bank of the Loire, then one of the smallest cities in Gaul. Their Bohemian cousins, enfeebled and sheltering in the central *oppida*, were overrun several decades later by the Germanic influx of the Marcomanni.

Obverse and reverse of a heavy silver piece of coin of the Boii who settled on the site of Bratislava.
It was equal in value to 6 drachmas (around 16 grammes). This is an uninscribed variant of a coin struck with the name of COVIOMARVS, found at Reca (Slovakia).
First half of the 1st century BCE.
Diameter: 25 mm.
Budapest, Magyar Nemzéti Múzeum.

**A range of communal pottery from the *oppidum*
of Stradonice (Bohemia).**
1st century BCE. Height: 165–330 mm.
Prague, Národní Muzeum.

Opposite
**Some fine pottery from the *oppidum* of Stradonice
(Bohemia).**
*Made on a fast wheel and cooked in very advanced ovens,
these vases illustrate the level achieved by the specialist craft
production of the oppida.*
1st century BCE. Height: 275–335 mm.
Prague, Národní Muzeum.

Excavations carried out in Bohemia on the sites of *oppida* give us a complete picture of how this urban network was established. Závist, which had been abandoned over two centuries earlier, was reoccupied around 180 BCE by a wealthy community who had devised an elaborate urban plan. They undertook its gradual restoration. The first extension, of about 100 hectares (250 acres), was completed some time after 150 BCE, when Závist was at the head of a network of *oppida* on the principal trade routes. The first to be founded was at Hrazany, followed by one at Nevězice, upstream on the River Vltava, and Stradonice, which was to be about the same size as Závist, on the Berounka, a tributary of the Vltava. České Lhotice in eastern Bohemia was halfway from Závist to Staré Hradisko, a hillside outpost on the 'amber route'. The plan was probably eventually to join up with the *oppida* system of the Danube Valley, although this was never achieved (save for the *oppidum* of Třísov that dominated the upper reaches of the Vltava towards Linz). Clearly reflecting a desire to control the great trade routes, the network was a colonial enterprise, and was carefully planned. With the exception of Závist, all of the *oppida* were built on new sites.

Outside of Bohemia, different models of urban development were apparently adopted by the Celts. In Switzerland and Gaul they seem to have extended or replaced existing large open-field settlements with *oppida*, probably around 50 BCE. However, these *oppida*, just like those in Bohemia, were generally on strategic points along the great trade routes. This evolution culminated in the establishment of city-states, which was the last metamorphosis of the powerful tribal confederations of earlier times.

Clearly, then, we can discount the theory that associates Celtic urbanization with the Roman conquest of Narbonne and Rome's resulting influence on neighbouring regions of Gaul. Similarly, this urbanization occurred too early to have been a defensive reaction against the incursions of the Cimbri and the Teutons. The *oppida* had already been in existence, certainly in Central Europe and probably elsewhere, for more than fifty years by the time these Germanic tribes started to make their presence felt.

Classical writers like to wax lyrical about the devastating effect of these Germanic hordes. However, they probably had far less impact on the Celts than the Roman authors would have us believe. Their nucleus was the Cimbri, a tribe originating in Jutland (Denmark). They were driven out of their homeland by a catastrophic 'tidal-wave' in about 125 BCE, and their ultimate aim seems to have been migration to Italy. However, having been checked in the north-east of the peninsula, despite a victory over a Roman army at Noreia in 113, they turned west. This new stage of their migration precipitated an uprising against Rome among the locals: in 107 the Volcae allies of the Tugurni, a branch of the Helvetii who belonged to a coalition that formed around the Cimbri and the Teutons, defeated a Roman army at Tolosa (Toulouse). Many other alliances seem to have been struck between Celtic and German peoples, who were united against a common enemy, Rome. Particularly interesting is the name of the leader of the Cimbri who died in 101 at Vercellae. He was called Boiorix ('king of the Boii), which suggested a last attempt to return to Italy on the part of some Boii.

The political situation in Europe, however, was no longer favourable to roaming adventures of this kind. While the Celtic world had evolved in the 3rd century as a direct result of the activities of mobile military bands, standing armies of elite warriors in city-states were now the norm. These forces notably included well-trained cavalry regiments recruited from the ranks of the nobility. By 100 BCE, massive troop levies were no longer necessary, except during major conflicts. Paradoxically, though, concentration of power through urbanization actually weakened Celtic society and made it increasingly vulnerable to enemy attack. If an enemy could breach the *oppida*, the nerve-centres of the system, they could seize the whole territory.

Small and large silver phalerae from the hoard discovered around 1927 at
Manerbio sul Mella (Lombardy, Italy).
*This group of harness fittings comprised: two large phalerae, like that on the right, decorated with a central triskele
(see p.145) and twenty moustached heads on the rim; 12 small phalerae, like that on the left; fragments of four
longitudinal ornaments decorated with a moustached head surmounting a stylised ram's head. It formed the
ceremonial harness fitments for two horses, probably the 'horse with all its trappings' that Titus Livius (The History
of Rome, XLIV, 14) mentions as being among the diplomatic gifts to the Celtic princes of Noricum.*
Early 1st century BCE. Diameter: 100 and 190 mm. Brescia (Italy), Museo Civico dell'Età Romana.

The cavalry, crack troops of the cities

Recruited from the ranks of the warrior
nobility, from about 250 BCE onwards the
cavalry totally replaced the war-chariots that
had previously constituted the shock troops
of Celtic armies. They became the elite
permanent corps of the city-states, formed
and maintained by the aristocrats who
governed them. The cavalry's essential role
in battle is especially well illustrated in
Julius Caesar's *Gallic Wars*. Thus, the chief
responsibility of the cavalry, particularly
among the Aedui, was the equivalent of
military command of the city's troops.
The efficacy of these mounted attack units
resulted from progressive development of
their equipment and techniques. In the
2nd century BCE, the cavalry sword became
considerably longer, to facilitate cutting
rather than thrusting, and the sharp point
was gradually eliminated. The La Tène
sword was thereby transformed into the
cavalry sword, perfectly adapted to a charge
in formation.

Celtic cavalry by the beginning of the
1st century BCE, as shown on a panel of the
Gundestrup Cauldron and several other
illustrations, had saddled horses with full
harness, ridden by cavalrymen wearing
spurs. The frequency with which these spurs
are found when excavating *oppida* may
reflect a proportionate concentration of
cavalry troops. Their equipment consisted of
the long sword, but also a spear, helmet and
shield, sometimes also a coat of mail or a
light breastplate.
Trained in formation manoeuvres, the cavalry
became the Celtic armies' strike force; the
effectiveness of its charge could determine
the outcome of a battle. It was also crucial
to the prestige of the cities, and the image
of an attacking, spear-carrying rider
frequently features on coinage from 100 to
50 BCE, such as Boii 'BIATEC' coins. These
were probably minted at the *oppidum* that
stood on the site of modern Bratislava: they
show a rider charging at the gallop, upright

on his saddle, spurs on his heels, brandishing
his long sword, with a large oval shield on
his left arm.
These elite troops were well trained and
drilled, but, engaged as they were in all the
battles of a Celtic world on the defensive,
their numbers eventually dwindled. As they
did so, they lost their effectiveness. Caesar
makes it clear that the enfeeblement of these
elite units was the key to the defeat of the
Gaulish cities.

Opposite
**Bronze and iron spurs from the
oppidum of Stradonice (Bohemia).**
*The quantity of spurs discovered in the
oppida of Stradonice and Staré Hradisko
(Moravia) indicates the number of elite
cavalry contingents based there.*
1st century BCE. Length of the right example: approx. 55 mm.
Prague, Národní Muzeum.

Top left
Reverse of a silver coin of the Boii from Bratislava, showing the name BIATEC.
A rider with a large shield on the left arm charges, brandishing his sword. He is wearing spurs and his saddled horse wears full harness with a round phalera on the haunch at the junction of the straps. See pp. 106 and 110.
Diameter: approx. 25 mm.

Bottom left
Reverse of a silver piece of the Pictones of Gaul, bearing the name VEPOTALOS.
The figure wears a helmet with cheek-flaps, a coat of mail or a light cuirasse, a belt with a long sword on the right; in his left hand he holds a shield, in his right a spear and a boar-emblem. It is the full equipment of the attack cavalry, the Celtic military elite at the beginning of the 1st century BCE.
Diameter: approx. 15 mm.

Panel of the military procession (E) from the Gundestrup cauldron (Denmark).
The detail (above, left) shows the carynx blowers and the figure with a boar-crested helmet that follow the infantrymen on the lower level. See p. 112 and 225.

Following pages
Panel showing the military procession (E) from the Gundestrup cauldron (Denmark).
It is undoubtedly a mythological scene, possibly the same as that represented on the Hallstatt scabbard (whose content is much debated). It gives an excellent idea of the equipment and marching order of a Celtic army at the beginning of the 1st century BCE. See p. 224.
First half of the 1st century BCE. Height: 200 mm. Copenhagen, Nationalmuseet.

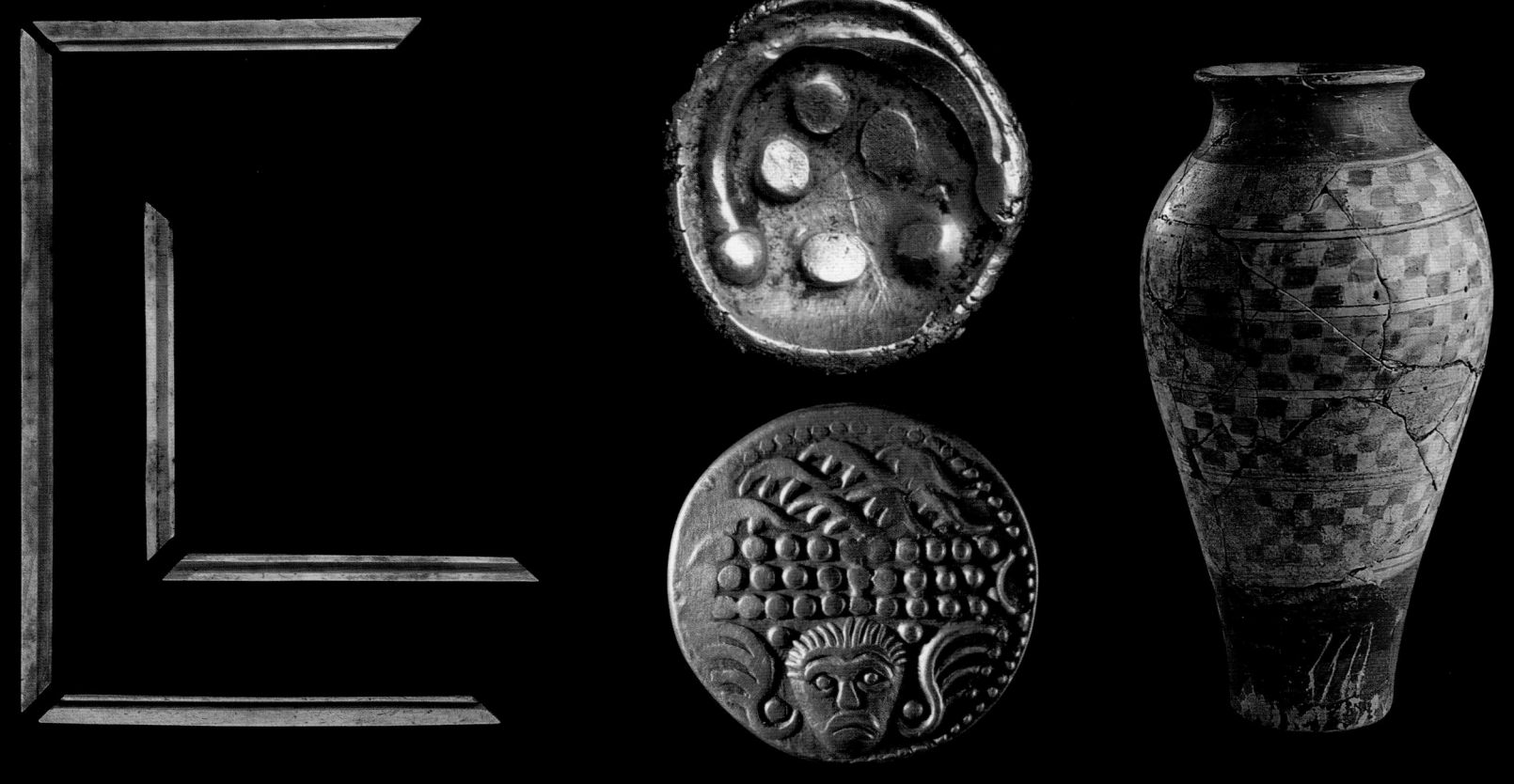

Ivory frames for wooden tablets that were covered in wax and used for writing with a stylus.
This instrument had a point at one end and a flat spatula for erasing at the other; many examples have been found in the oppida of Central Europe, where the practice of writing is not otherwise attested except by alphabetical signs incised on pottery or rare monetary inscriptions (see p. 106 and 111).

Above, top
Central European Celtic gold coin of the type called *Regenbogenschüsselchen* ('rainbow cup'), found at Erkenbrechtsweiler (Swabia, Germany).
Late 2nd–1st century BCE. Diameter: 18 mm.

Above, bottom
Celtic silver coin from Noricum (modern Styria and Carinthia).
First half of the 1st century BCE. Diameter: 20 mm.

Painted vase from Roanne.
First half of the 1st century BCE.
Height: 285 mm.
Roanne (France), Musée J. Déchelette.

This was clearly understood by Caesar, who wrote of his determination to lay siege to Avaricum (Bourges), the township of the Bituriges: 'He confidently expected that on taking that town, he would reduce beneath his dominion the state of the Bituriges' (*Gallic Wars*, VII, 13). In fact, at the beginning of the 1st century BCE, behind the prosperous façade and apparent might of the great Celtic city-states lay a system that was vulnerable. It was entirely dominated by a small number of aristocrats who sought to control everything by concentrating all activities in its central point, the *oppidum*.

The Roman conquest of Gaul was certainly made more likely by the existence of cities organized in a network of *oppida*: Rome had never been inclined to seize territories that were not to some extent urbanized, and therefore did not have a rudimentary centralized organization. As is well known thanks to the writings of its conqueror, Gaul was prosperous, furnished with a network of *oppida* linked by well-defined routes and had an effective political and administrative organization that was in some cases equal to that of Rome itself. Its conquest was long and difficult, but Caesar skilfully took advantage of internal disputes between the tribes, tension between the large city coalitions and the frailty of local bonds of patronage and alliances.

Once Roman domination over Gaul was achieved in 50 BCE, it undeniably helped to stabilize the Gaulish cities, which retained in most respects their territorial integrity. However, Rome simultaneously supported, as it had in Cisalpine Gaul, the independence of small tribes hitherto subject by the bonds of clientship to the great states whose power Caesar wished to restrict. This probably explains the emergence of small, previously unknown cities at this time.

To the east, the Roman conquest of Pannonia in 12 BCE and the occupation of Noricum three years later pushed the Roman frontier as far as the Danube. The Celtic populations of the Transdanubian region thereafter enjoyed the prosperity of the *Pax Romana*. They were organized into a structure of *civitates peregrinæ* (foreign cities), perpetuating those of the local Boii, Taurini, Eravisci, Latovici and Scordistae. They continued to worship their divinities and to wear their traditional garb, as is well attested on the funerary steles of women native to both Pannonia and Noricum.

The Cotini, established in the Carpathian Mountains near the upper reaches of the Vah (in modern Slovakia), were the only major Celtic tribe of that region to retain their independence. And they managed to remain autonomous for another two centuries, thus becoming probably the last independent Celtic enclave on the Continent. Because elsewhere, in those regions where the Celts had not been integrated into the Roman Empire, they were submerged by the Germanic wave.

Opposite
A range of bronze toilet objects from the *oppidum* of Stradonice (Bohemia).
1st century BCE. Prague, Národní Muzeum.

Left
Detail of one of the extremites of the central appliqué of the bronze facing of a ceremonial shield found in the river Witham (UK).
It shows an array of palmettes modified to suggest the head of an animal with a prominent muzzle, bulbous eyes and big pointed ears … This is a popular approach in Celtic art of the 4th and 3rd centuries BCE, as is the presence of finely engraved designs, invisible when viewing the object at a normal distance
3rd century BCE. Height of the detail: approx. 250 mm. London, British Museum.

Preceding pages
Gaming dice from the *oppidum* of Stradonice (Bohemia).
The very large number found on the site reveals one of the favourite pastimes of the Boii elite. It is interesting to note that dice and chess pieces featured in the Italian tombs of Boii aristocrats from the 3rd century BCE.
1st century BCE. Length: 10–30 mm. Prague, Národní Muzeum.

The Celts in pre-Christian Britain and Ireland
(1st century BCE–5th century CE)

In 55 BCE, when Julius Caesar disembarked on the island of Britain around 20 kilometres (12 miles) north of Dover, he described the tribes he found as follows: 'The interior portion of Britain is inhabited by those of whom they say that it is handed down by tradition that they were born in the island itself; the maritime portion by those who had passed over from the country of the Belgae for the purpose of plunder and making war, almost all of whom are called by the names of those states from which being sprung they went thither, and having waged war, continued there and began to cultivate the lands' (*Gallic Wars*, V, 12). He concluded: 'The most civilized of all these nations are they who inhabit *Cantium* [modern Kent], which is entirely a maritime district, nor do they differ much from the Gallic customs. Most of the inland inhabitants do not sow corn, but live on milk and flesh.'

Caesar oversimplifies the truth of settlement in a region that he knew only briefly and partially. However, he was probably correct to divide the island into two major groupings that were differentiated as much by their origins as by their ways of life: on the one hand, Celts of indigenous, and therefore ancient, origin; on the other, tribes that had emigrated from the Continent much more recently. In relation to the latter, other writings mention two examples that confirm Caesar's text: the Atrebates, established in the west of Kent, were kin to those who gave their name to Artois; and the Parisi of Yorkshire have already been mentioned in connection with their Gaulish namesakes, the Parisii. However, other tribes of the coast and the lower reaches of the Thames, whose names have no equivalent on the Continent, have been proved, through both documentary and archaeological evidence, to have direct links with the north of Gaul.

This complex of insular peoples, traditionally defined as 'Belgae' or 'Gallo-Belgae' because of their Continental links, has long been considered to have resulted from a migration that took place between about 150 and 70 BCE; that is, shortly before Caesar arrived. Increasingly well-documented traffic between the island and the Continent undoubtedly did involve groups of migrants at this time, but this would hardly result in the situation described by Caesar, in which two large culturally, commercially and agriculturally distinct groups existed in Britain.

Caesar was particularly struck by a military technique of the Kentish warriors. It relates to the use of war-chariots, which had been abandoned in warfare on the Continent two centuries earlier, to be replaced by regiments of cavalry. They continued to be used only as ceremonial vehicles, in competitions or parades, as in Rome during the triumphs accorded to victorious generals. However, they were still used in battle in Britain when Caesar arrived, and presumably had been for the previous 200 years. They probably arrived with some of the mobile groups of warriors who crossed Europe after the Great Expedition. Fellow-travellers in this mass movement of people settled in northern Gaul, where they became the initial nucleus of the Belgae.

Opposite
The fort of Dun Aengus, brooding on a cliff-top on the west coast of the island of Inishmore (Galway, Ireland).
It hangs nearly 70 metres (230 ft) above the Atlantic. The triple fortifications are composed of thick drystone walls; those remaining in the centre are six metres (20 ft) high. These mighty defences were further reinforced by a large barrier of thousands of angular rocks, a 'chevaux-de-frise' designed to slow the progress of assailants at a distance where slings might be used effectively. According to tradition, this fortress was constructed by the fourth mytical race of Irish settlers, the Fir Bolg, who took refuge there after their defeat by the Tuatha Dé Danann.

Left
Maiden Castle, the imposing fort of the Durotriges (Dorset, UK).
This developed from the 3rd century BCE on the site of an ancient Neolithic enclosure. Excavations have revealed that the impressive double line of enormous earth ramparts behind ditches, with an exterior sloping barrier, is the last of four stages of construction going back to the Iron Age. The complexity of the defensive system protecting an area of some 20 hectares (50 acres) is probably linked with the development of the sling for military usage from the 3rd century BCE.

Continental migrations and the insular substratum

The extension to the British Isles of this last great Celtic migration is further confirmed by the excavation of artefacts with obvious Continental connections – in some cases Danubian, as in the north of Gaul – that can be dated accurately to the first half of the 3rd century BCE. Many brooches have been found in Britain that are similar to Continental designs of the period. Similarly, a pair of 3rd-century flat spoons that were found in a tomb at Pogny match some unearthed from a burial-site in Britain. Several annular hairpins, a type of ornament particularly common in the British Isles, have also recently been found on the Continent. Other finds belong indisputably to the period when La Tène art reached its height. Among La Tène-type objects found in Ireland, the oldest so far is a tubular golden torc with false terminals, decorated with the 'knot of Hercules' motif introduced to existing Celtic communities from those of their number who settled in Italy. Discovered around the middle of the 19th century in a bog at Knock (County Mayo), this jewel is undoubtedly a Continental import, datable to the early decades of the 3rd century BCE. It seems likely that it was brought to Ireland by a band of immigrant warriors.

However, this was not a large-scale invasion. The new arrivals probably became intermingled with the existing local society rather than landing *en masse* and proceeding to eliminate or displace the indigenous population. The case of the Parisi of Yorkshire is indicative. As has been mentioned, although their graves contain Continental-type objects (notably brooches and pins) and two-wheeled chariots, the skeletons generally lie in the foetal position, as was the local custom. There is also no evidence of a rapid decline in population in the fortified settlements of the British Isles. So it seems that fairly small, mobile and dynamic groups, imbued with a powerful warrior ideology (as is reflected in the art of the objects that accompanied them), integrated with the local communities. This migration and subsequent settlement of armed men may explain some aspects of ancient Irish literary tradition, such as the tribal hero who defends his territory, and the *Fianna*, an independent band of warriors who remain resolutely on the margins of communities.

Unfortunately, this theory of Continental warriors' immigration into the British Isles in the aftermath of the Great Expedition cannot be proved. However, it is indisputable that Britain was Celtic long before then; the first documents that discuss the Atlantic regions clearly indicate this fact. None of these texts has come down to us in full, but we know them through quotations from more recent writers.

Opposite
Top of the central mount of a bronze shield found in the Thames at Wandsworth (UK).
This human mask in high relief, composed of several geometric forms, illustrates not only the Continental roots of insular art but also a similar concept of the role of the image.
3rd century BCE. Height of the mask: 50 mm.
London, British Museum.

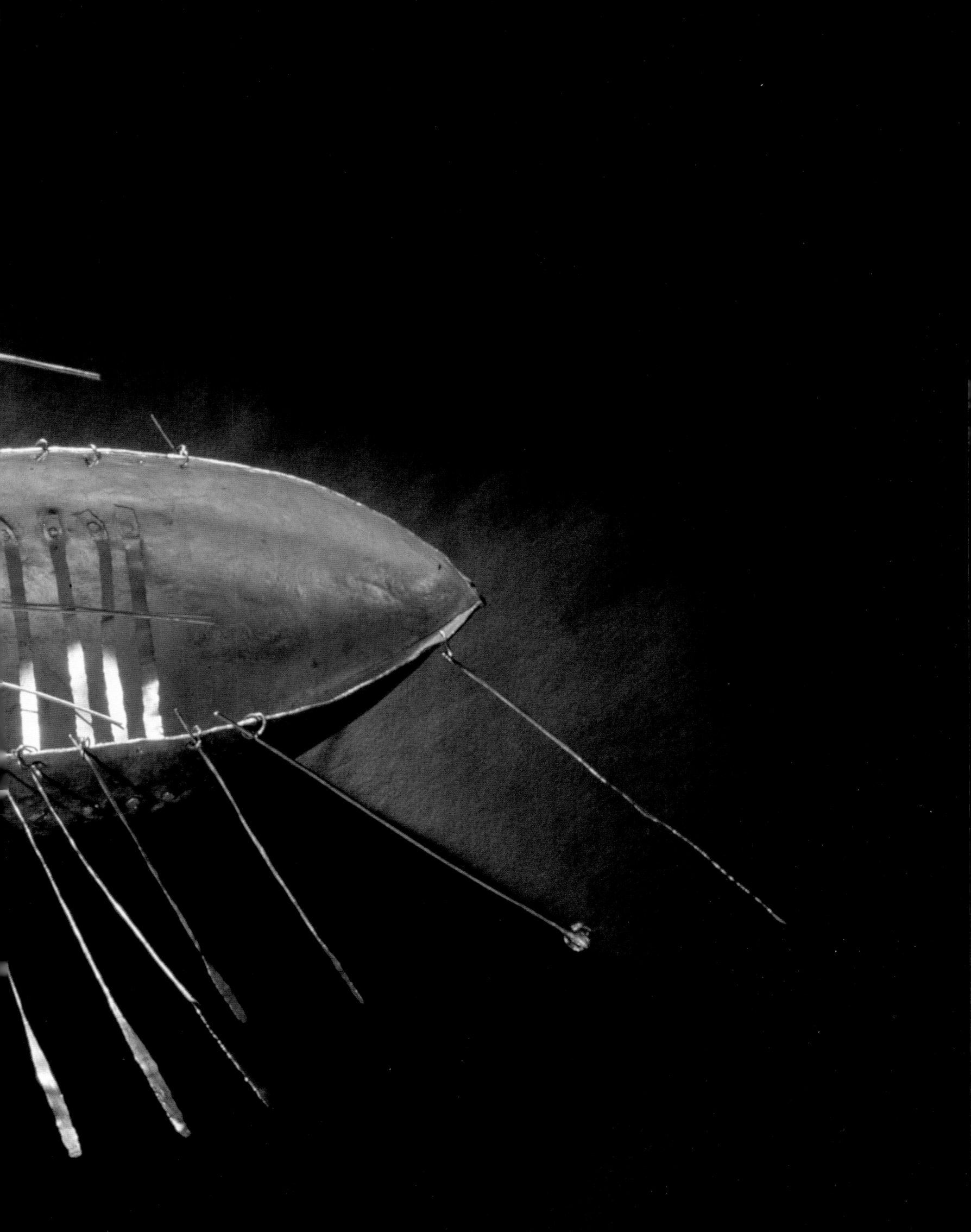

Detail of the sheet bronze mountings of a bucket found in Aylesford (Kent, UK).
Pairs of stylized horses, possibly monstrous (one has a double tail and a sort of aigrette instead of an ear), are flanked by rosettes enclosing a six-branched gyratory motif, surrounded by four birds' heads wrapped around concentric circles and groups of S-scrolls that form four circles arranged squarely around a larger circle; the tips of the S-scrolls divide the circles into two overlapping halves like the yin-yang symbol. These undoubtedly symbolic images confirm the ceremonial nature of the receptacle. See p. 125.

The discovery of the Atlantic islands by early navigators

A faint echo of early Phoenician navigation of the Atlantic, now confirmed by the discovery of trading-posts on the Portuguese coast north of Lisbon, has survived thanks to several passages in the *Ora Maritima* (a description of the coast from Brittany to Massalia) of Avienus, a Latin poet of the 4th century BCE. This poem recounts the voyage of Himilco, a Carthaginian who sailed north up the Portuguese Atlantic coast at the end of the 6th century. According to the fragments we have, he seems to have navigated his way through a misty ocean filled with seaweed and sea-monsters before arriving at islands called the Oestrymnides, probably near the southern coast of Armorica (Brittany). The Oestrymnians traded with two large islands: Ierné and Albion (Ireland and Britain). The principal trading merchandise was probably metal, which had from earliest times been exported by sea to the Tartessian or Phoenician trading-posts of the Atlantic coast (as is attested by a collection of bronzes found in a shipwreck at the mouth of the Odiel near Huelva, which had been collected from a variety of places as far afield as Ireland) and overland to the northern shores of the Mediterranean.

Other information on these islands probably came to light as a result of the tin trade but remained shrouded in myths. In a lost work on the Hyperboreans, Hecataeus of Miletus (writing in the second half of the 6th century BCE), who was possibly the first author to mention the Celts, referred to the existence over the sea from the land of the Celts of an island as big as Sicily. Hecataeus related that Apollo was especially venerated there, the inhabitants having dedicated a magnificent enclosure to him with a circular temple where even Greeks, both Athenians and Delians, came to worship. Diodorus Siculus reported this information but clearly thought it was a fable. However, it could well have been a garbled version of the tales of travellers who had visited the island of Britain.

Two centuries after the time of Himilco, when Alexander the Great was conquering an immense empire, the Greek Pytheas of Massilia (Marseille) undertook a long navigation towards the legendary lands of the north, the source of amber and tin. He wrote an account of an astonishing voyage that apparently took him as far as Iceland (Thule) in a work called *On the Ocean*, now sadly lost and known only through sceptical mentions in other classical works. In fact, the record of the latitudes attained by

Preceding pages
Small gold model of an ocean-going vessel, found with six other gold objects at Broighter (Derry, Northern Ireland), on an ancient beach.
The Broighter boat is similar to those of the Armorican Veneti, described by Caesar: rowers' benches, large square sail rigged on a horizontal yardarm, eight oars on each side, rudder from stern to port. The average dimensions of such boats would have been 30 metres (98 ft) in length and 12 metres (39 ft) in width.
1st century BCE. Length: 196 mm. Dublin, National Museum of Ireland.

Wooden bucket with metal fittings found in an inhumation grave at Aylesford (Kent, UK).
This is one of a series that now amounts to some 50 utensils of this type, found from southeast England to the Pyrenees and the Carpathian borders. This sort of receptacle, with a capacity from 3 to 5 litres (6 to 9 pints) formed part of a drinking service for wine, which was imported in quantity and drunk during the feasts that were one of the most important events of Celtic social life, probably also linked to religious ceremonies. This may explain the symbolic nature of the decoration and the fact that the few staves that have survived seem to have come from wood of the yew, a sacred tree according to Irish texts.
1st century BCE. Diameter: 267 mm. London, British Museum.

Detail of the handle-mount of the Aylesford bucket.
The head is probably a representation of the chief Celtic god, the solar and sovereign deity associated with the tree of life (here reduced to the symbolic palmette surmounting the headdress) and with mistletoe.

this intrepid navigator (who was an astronomer and a skilled mathematician well acquainted with all the scientific knowledge of his time) corresponds perfectly with the places that he claimed to have visited.

He sailed past Gibraltar and navigated along the Atlantic coast to arrive at the peninsula of the Ostimioi (Armorica), passed Cape Kabaïon (Pointe du Raz or Pointe de Penmarch), the island of Ouximasa (Ouessant) or Uxisama and turned towards the large islands that he was the first to describe as Prettanikai (Britannic). He then sailed twice around the coast of Britain, which he drew as a triangle with a perimeter remarkably close to the reality. If we take marine currents into account, he probably first sailed along the west coast, from Belerion (either Lizard's Point or Land's End) to the Orkas (Orkneys), then down the eastern coast as far as a promontory he called Kantion (Kent), almost opposite the mouth of a great Continental river (the Rhine or the Escaut), where the coastline abruptly changed direction to lead to the tin mines of Cornwall, back near Belerion.

Pytheas must have had direct contact with the natives to learn of the currents, tides and winds, essential for navigation in

these waters, as well as information on the principal geographical landmarks, which he recorded under their local names. The place (and people's) names that he noted in Armorica and the islands are for the most part similar or even identical to those still in use several centuries later; their Celtic origin seems indisputable. The names Ierné and Albion, already known from Himilco, correspond to the Old Irish words Eriu and Albu for these lands.

As for the Ostimioi of Armorica, they must surely be the Osismii who, in Caesar's time, occupied what is now the French *département* of Finistère and the western side of the Côtes-d'Armor. In Celtic their name means 'the furthest'; in other words, they were 'the people at the end of the world', which perfectly describes their geographical location. The fact that these place names are Celtic implies a Celticization that was already deep-seated.

By the 1st century BCE, when Julius Caesar set foot on the island of Britain, causing it to enter the historical record of Europe, the western Celtic islands already had a long history of Continental contact, migration and trade, as is proved by a few names and many archaeological artefacts.

Reverse of a gold coin of the Trinovantes-Catuvellauni that bears on the obverse the name of king Tasciovanus (25–10 BCE).
It shows a rider brandishing the carnyx, the Celtic war trumpet, and the inscription SEGO, indicating the unknown location of the mint or possibly a concept directly linked with the image; this Celtic root word means 'endowed with force' or 'victorious'
Diameter: approx. 20 mm. London, British Museum.

Opposite
The ring-fort of Staigue (Kerry, Ireland).
Situated above the northern bank of the Kenmare Estuary, this is one of the best-preserved examples of this type of habitat, typical of the Irish Iron Age. It was probably built during the centuries preceding the introduction of Christianity as the residence of one of the dynasties that ruled the country at that time.

The conquest of the island of Britain

These archaeological artefacts show that, in the preceding decades, there was a continual influx of men, objects and ideas to the south coast of England and the Thames Estuary, indicating flourishing commercial exchanges with the Continent. Consequently, this region developed more rapidly than others on the island. City-states, such as those that had existed in Gaul since the 2nd century, were starting to develop. Large fortified complexes such as Camulodunum (Colchester) and Verulamium (St Albans) sprang up and became centres of power comparable to the great Continental *oppida*. Even more indicatively, coinage was adapted from Continental designs from the beginning of the 2nd century BCE. The first writing left by the insular Celts may be found on coins dating from about 50 BCE. They carry short inscriptions in Latin characters, generally the abbreviated names of people, perpetuating the memory of members of great local dynasties who are known from the writings of classical historians. These include: Commios, king of the Atrebates, who came from Gaul; his sons Tincommios and Verica; Tasciovanos, king of the powerful Catuvellauni of Essex; and his son Cunobelinos (later immortalized as Shakespeare's Cymbeline), whose coinage also bears the first four letters of his capital, Camulodunum.

The first tribes to strike their own coinage were probably the Catuvellauni and Trinovantes, who lived north of the Thames and, under the leadership of Cassivelaunos, rose against Caesar in 54 BCE. They were able to assemble an elite corps, 4,000 chariots strong, against him. This figure has historically been scorned, but recently at least its plausibility seems to have been asserted by the discovery of a metal foundry to equip this type of vehicle, as used by the military aristocracy, on the site of Gussage All Saints (Dorset).

Caesar's two expeditions successfully subdued such uprisings, and almost a century of peaceful exchange between the island and the Continent followed. Writing in the time of the Emperor Augustus, Strabo noted that the British chieftains,

> after procuring the friendship of Caesar Augustus by sending embassies and by paying court to him, have not only dedicated offerings in the Capitol, but have also managed to make the whole of the island virtually Roman property. Further, they submit so easily to heavy duties, both on the exports from there to Celtica and on the imports from Celtica (these latter are ivory chains and necklaces, and amber-gems and glass vessels and other petty wares of that sort), that there is no need of garrisoning the island; for one legion, at the least, and some cavalry would be required in order to carry off tribute from them, and the expense of the army would offset the tribute-money; in fact, the duties must necessarily be lessened if tribute is imposed, and, at the same time, dangers be encountered, if force is applied.
> (*Geography*, IV, 5, 3)

Right
Chariot axle-pin in iron and enamelled bronze, from King's Langley (Hertfordshire, UK).
1st century BCE. Height: 130 mm.
London, British Museum.

Far right
Horse bits in bronze with enamel inlay, from Rise near Hull (Yorkshire, UK).
1st century BCE. Length: 135 mm.
London, British Museum.

Above and opposite
Details of a ceremonial shield in bronze enhanced with inlays of red enamel, found in the Thames at Battersea (UK).
The very formal decorative plan maintains the tradition of allusive figuration and the possibility of multiple readings. See p.198.
2nd century BCE. London, British Museum.

That final phrase, much more ominous than the preceding passage, was shown to be prophetic in 43 CE when the army of the Emperor Claudius, commanded by Aulus Plautius, invaded. The conquest of south-eastern Britain, the richest part of the island, was difficult, as is shown by evidence of Roman military assaults on many indigenous fortified sites. The difficulty of countering the actions of hostile tribes and the uprisings of ancient allies, such as the Iceni of Norfolk, obliged the Roman army to push further north, where resistance gathered around Caratacos, son of Cunobelinos and the last king of the Atrebates. Following his defeat in 49, fighting with the Ordovices of north Wales, his wife, daughter and brothers were all captured. Caratacos himself took refuge with Cartimandua, queen of the powerful Brigantes, but she handed him over to the Romans. Brought to Rome to feature in a triumph, he appealed directly to Claudius, who was impressed by his discourse (reproduced by Tacitus in his *Annals*, XII, 36–7) and pardoned him. Caratacos' mastery of

Latin shows the degree to which even hostile, distant aristocrats were imbued with Roman culture.

Peace in the new province lasted only about a dozen years. The demands of Roman bureaucrats provoked Rome's traditional allies, the Iceni, to rebel in 61 while the Roman governor Suetonius Paulinus was engaged in suppressing the druidic sanctuary of the Isle of Mona (Anglesey), thought to be the principal centre of resistance to Rome. Led by Queen Boudicca, the rebels, who had been joined by other discontented tribes, attacked the colonial capital of Camulodunum and the trading centres of Londinium (London) and Verulamium, massacring the Roman garrisons. Nevertheless, the uprisings were soon quashed and Boudicca committed suicide by taking poison on the battlefield.

The advance of the Roman armies was continued during the reign of the Emperor Vespasian, especially after 77, under the command of Cnaeus Julius Agricola, father-in-law of the historian Tacitus, who left a detailed account of these

campaigns. Following an expedition against the Ordovices of Wales, in 80 the governor established the northern frontier of the province by building a series of fortifications between the Clyde and the Firth of Forth. He then advanced even further north, and planned to invade Ireland, although this was never put into practice. His army penetrated as far as the territory of the Celts of Caledonia, whom Agricola defeated in 83 on the slopes of Mons Graupius (the Grampians), while his fleet sailed around Scotland. In 122 a new line of defence, designed to contain the attacks of the belligerent Picts of Scotland, was constructed by the Emperor Hadrian. Situated more than 100 kilometres (60 miles) south of Agricola's earlier frontier and linking the mouth of the Tyne and the Solway Firth, this imposing wall, 100 kilometres long, was equipped with forts and watchtowers.

When Rome abandoned Britain to her destiny three centuries later, the distant province was largely Romanized and Christianized but it had managed to retain its Celtic dialects.

Moreover, part of the island had remained independent. The resurgence of the old Celtic kingdoms was therefore led by a Christian aristocracy imbued with Roman culture, and in the 5th century they spearheaded the defence of the island against Germanic invaders, the Angles and Saxons. From this troubled and obscure period, evocatively termed the Dark Ages, originates one of the great sagas of European literature. Its central hero, King Arthur, was the mythical representation of a war chieftain called Artorius from either the south-west or the north of the island.

Around 516 he inflicted his first heavy defeat on his enemies at Mons Badonicus (generally identified as the fortress of Badbury Rings in Dorset), but after decades of struggle he was finally defeated and killed around 539 at the Battle of Camlann. (Camlann may be a later form of Camboglanna, the name of a Roman fort on Hadrian's Wall.) Artorius undoubtedly existed but he remains obscure, and of course he has been completely overwritten by the legend.

As in Irish legends, hints of actual events remain elusive, shrouded in a web of mythology. The Arthurian cycle is saturated with a heritage that has turned its protagonists into heroes of mystical age, and any attempt to record the events of that time and place with precision is doomed to failure. Only one substantial Celtic region remained entirely independent until the advent of Christianity: Ireland. However, this island was neither isolated nor entirely unknown in the ancient world. Writing of Agricola's military exploits, Tacitus reported:

> Ireland, being between Britain and Spain and conveniently situated for the seas round Gaul, might have been the means of connecting with great mutual benefit the most powerful parts of the empire. Its extent is small when compared with Britain, but exceeds the islands of our seas. In soil and climate, in the disposition, temper, and habits of its population, it differs but little from Britain. We know most of its harbours and approaches, and that through the intercourse of commerce. (*Life of Agricola*, 24)

Archaeology fully confirms this, as Roman trade with the island has been attested by numerous discoveries. Furthermore, the maps of the geographer Ptolemy, drawn in the 2nd century CE, included significant features of the Irish coastline – ports, promontories, estuaries of the principal rivers – as well as the names of tribes and large settlements of the interior, so the country must have been well known. While several names are easily recognizable today – the rivers Senos and Buvinda are the Shannon and the Boyne – sadly, it is impossible to pinpoint with certainty the majority of the sites that Ptolemy recorded. It is tempting to see in the northern 'Regia' or 'King's town' (there is another 'Regia' further south) the royal site of Emain Macha (modern Navan Fort), but there is no way of knowing for certain.

Particularly interesting is the fact that the names of tribes established in the south-west of the island include the Brigantes, namesakes of a powerful British tribe, and the Manapii, whose name is almost identical to that of the Menapii, a Belgic tribe who settled along the coast between the estuaries of the Escaut, the Meuse and the Rhine. It is therefore probable that, like Britain, Ireland experienced, either directly or indirectly, the effects of the great Continental population migrations of the first half of the 3rd century BCE.

The history of ancient Ireland was considerably enriched following excavation of several sites hitherto known only in legend. Fortunately, unlike the Celtic Continent, Ireland was able to preserve both its language and the teachings of an intellectual elite that facilitated accurate oral transmission of literary works. Thus, when the proscription against recording them in writing was raised, following the adoption of Christianity around 440, the monks who were the direct heirs of the druids transcribed coherent and quite pure versions of the vernacular literature. Despite some retouching that they deemed necessary, these writings, together with some Gaulish texts, have come down to us as close approximations of the oral literature of the ancient Celts. Constructed locally but based on a foundation that was probably common to all the ancient Celtic people, they constitute a mythological oeuvre of unquestionable antiquity and authenticity. Their successive creators wove into them the geographical setting and certain historic events that were inseparable from them in the collective memory. Therefore, Ireland is alone among the ancient Celtic countries in having preserved, like Greece or Italy, the connection between her territory and her mythology. We can compare the setting where the gods and heroes of mythical times flourished with archaeological data obtained from the same sites. The significance of this approach reaches well beyond Ireland, since a chapter in the history of the whole of ancient Europe is thus opened to research.

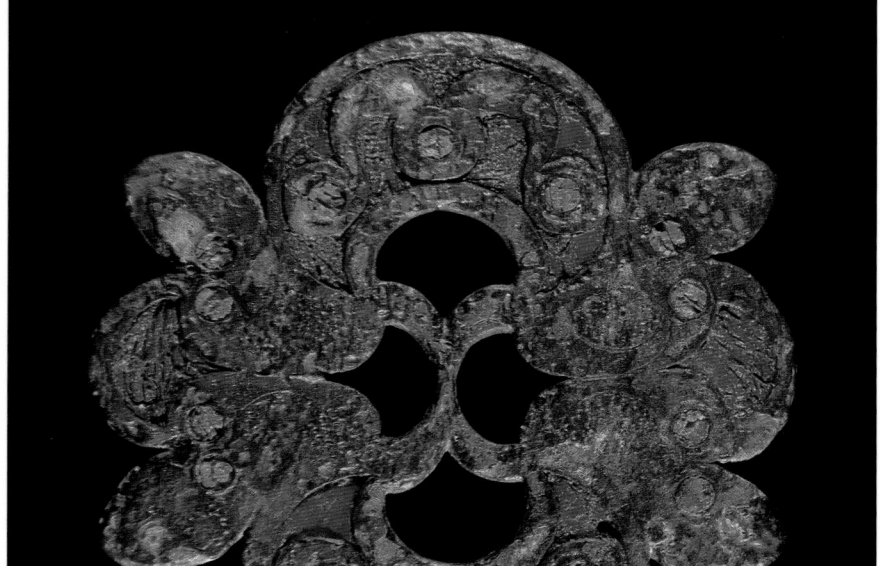

Left

Bronze harness-piece decorated with red and orange champlevé enamel, found in London (UK).

1st century. Total height: 85 mm.

London, British Museum.

Opposite

The coast of Finistère, at Crozon.

The first Mediterranean navigators to venture on the ocean must have been struck by the amplitude of the Atlantic tides. Probably informed by the native Armoricans, the Marseillais Pytheas (4th century BCE) linked them with the moon. He was well in advance of the writer Timaeus, his contemporary, who believed the tides were produced by the great rivers descending from the Celtic mountains.

Myths and archaeology

The first results obtained from mythical royal sites are indicative of the potential of this approach. At Navan Fort, the legendary Emain Macha of the kingdom of Ulster, excavation of the great mound that crowns the summit of the hill has revealed a complex network of circular ditches and structures, and artefacts from the end of the Bronze Age and the beginning of the Iron Age (around 700 BCE), such as the guard of a Hallstatt-type scabbard, the accessory of a prestigious weapon, rare even on the Continent. Emain Macha seems to have been the residence of high-ranking people, and, interestingly, medieval annals pinpoint 668 BCE as when this seat of the kings of Ulster was founded by the warrior queen Macha (actually a goddess). This date is as close as makes no difference to the founding date proposed by archaeologists. From a later phase, the 3rd century BCE, the skull of a North African monkey (*Macaca sylvanus*) was discovered, proof of the contact with the Iberian Peninsula that Tacitus' writings imply.

The most astonishing result of the excavations is the temple corresponding to the final phase, dated with precision to 94 BCE through dendrochronology. A circular edifice 43 metres (47 yards) in diameter, it consisted of 275 oak posts disposed in concentric circles around an enormous oak trunk. This monumental construction was probably little used, as it was filled with lime to a height of 2.5 metres (3 yards) and set alight, then covered with a layer of grass sods. This odd practice suggests a religious act, a kind of definitive consecration of the sacred nature of the place.

Similar excavations at the royal site of Dún Ailinne (Leinster) have also revealed ancient Neolithic occupation, followed by a succession of circular enclosures, probably with a religious function, extending over more than 500 years from the 3rd century BCE.

Far from mirroring the situation at the time of the introduction of Christianity, then, it seems that the myths connected with these places reflect deep-rooted memories of historical facts, preserved with uncanny precision. Of all the Celtic countries, pre-Christian Ireland is the only one whose historical events are known solely from very vague echoes, but it is also the only one to have preserved an authentic commentary on its most ancient history.

Left

Decorative crescent-shaped harness-fitting in bronze with champlevé red enamel, from Westhall (Suffolk, UK).

1st century. Width: 103 mm.

London, British Museum.

CIVILIZATION

The colourful and orderly

world of the Celtic millennium:

daily life, beliefs

and ideals

Left
Detail of a bronze torc from Jogasses à Chouilly (Marne).
See p. 92 and 134.
Early 3rd century BCE. Height of the detail: approx. 60 mm.
Châlons-en-Champagne (Marne), Musée Municipal.

A world-view centred on a distant past

Like all peoples of antiquity, the ancient Celts lived by a set of general principles that defined the world, its origins and its structure. Unfortunately, no Celtic written records exist to clarify this world-view for us; Caesar tells us that the druids, as custodians of wisdom, believed that sacred doctrines could be transmitted only orally. However, a few brief snippets of information are mentioned by classical writers, while others can be gleaned from Irish legends, although, as was discussed in the previous chapter, these were written at a late stage and were somewhat modified by the Christian monks who recorded them. Finally, analysis of Celtic art highlights the frequent use of a number of symbolic elements related to fundamental principles governing the division of time and space.

Unfortunately, we do not know the myths that would have explained and illustrated how these principles were established. And it is equally difficult to distinguish specifically Celtic concepts from those that may have evolved from an earlier, more general Indo-European basis, or from an even older heritage. The establishment of a stable and coherent spatial–temporal framework is inextricably linked with the emergence of the first sedentary, agricultural societies in the 5th millennium BCE, as is shown by community monuments that were set up according to significant astronomical orientations. These include not only the impressive megalithic complexes of Western Europe but the vast circular enclosures of Central Europe, which were formerly thought to be fortified dwellings. The absence of internal construction, the presence of openings towards the cardinal points and the concentration of particular objects, notably terracotta female statuettes, indicate these enclosures' cultural utilization, apparently during ceremonies linked to specific points in the agricultural year.

It is undoubtedly during this era that the first European calendars, essential for efficient agriculture in a temperate zone, were devised. Later, the growing discrepancy between a sequence of years composed of twelve *lunar* months with the cycle of *solar* years gradually led to the use of calendars of different levels of complexity. There is evidence that such time-measurement systems were adopted in Europe at least from the 2nd millennium BCE onwards.

However, there is a much more recent, exceptional and explicit illustration of the general principles that the Celtic intellectual elite applied to the cyclical passing of time, the fundamental component in their belief system. It is a five-year calendar, incised around the end of the 2nd century CE on a bronze tablet discovered in 1897 at Coligny (Ain, France). Several fragments with similar inscriptions were then found on another site about 30 kilometres (18 miles) west of Coligny at Villards-d'Héria (Jura). This calendar, inscribed in an age when time was generally measured using the Julian Calendar of the Roman administration, was obviously used only for liturgical purposes in a local sanctuary where traditional Gaulish worship persisted. It shows over a five-year period – a lustrum – the annual cycle of twelve lunar months, with the corrections necessary to adjust them to the solar rhythm. It was thus possible to perform the rituals of the yearly cycle at the times specified by ancestral usage, something that would have been impossible to determine with a Roman calendar.

Opposite
**Detail of the terminals of a bronze torc
from Pogny (Marne).**
*This simple motif of paired S-scrolls could be either
a human or animal face.*
Second half of the 3rd century BCE. Height of the mask: 12 mm.
Châlons-en-Champagne (Marne, France), Musée Municipal.

Detail of the decoration of a bronze torc from grave No. 2, Villeseneux (Marne).
Palmettes transform into three groups of three faces twisting around the body of the torc.
Early 3rd century BCE. Height of the detail: approx. 15 mm.
Épernay (Marne, France), Musée Municipal d'Archéologie et du Vin de Champagne.

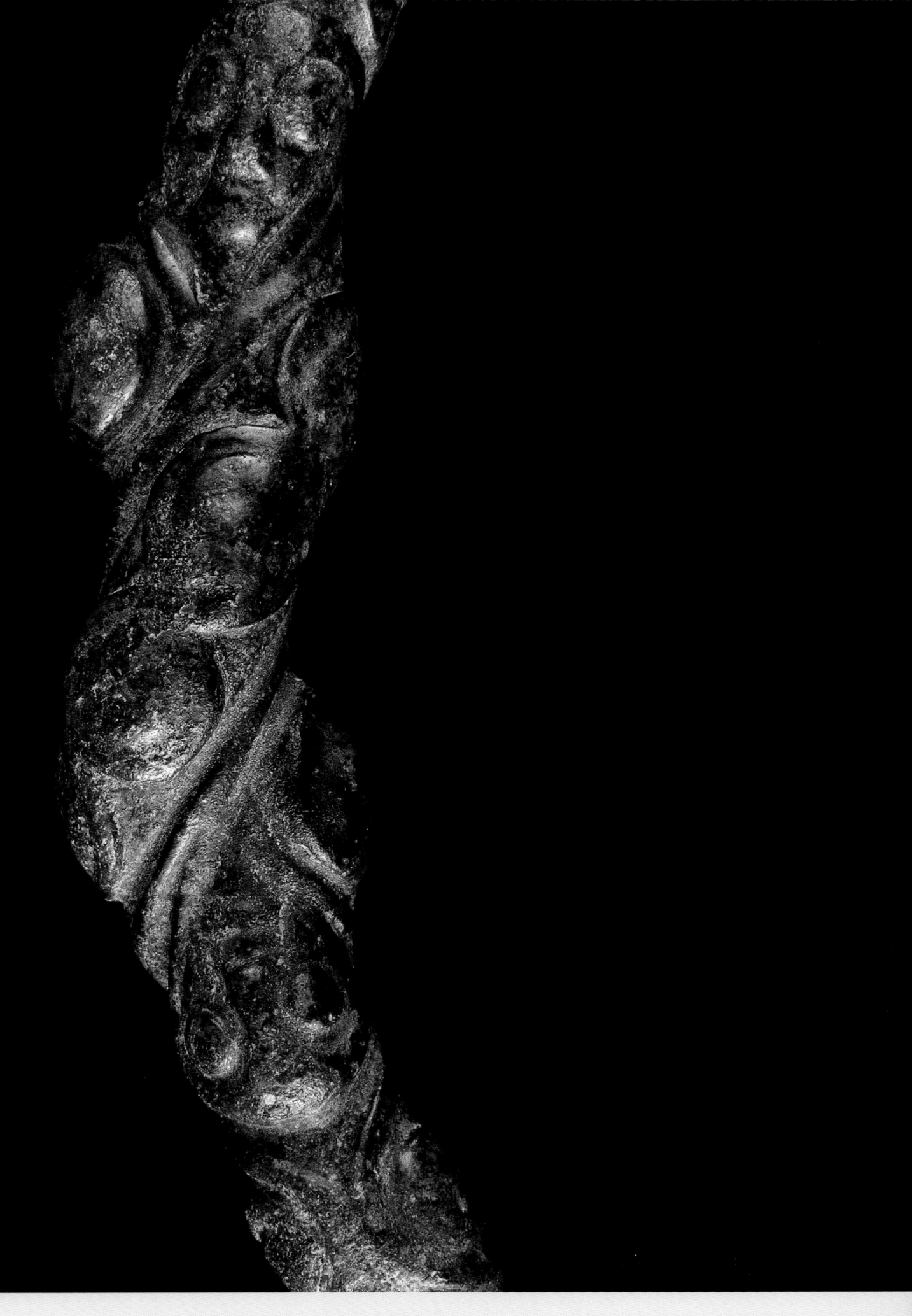

Detail of the decoration of a bronze torc from grave No. 3, Villeseneux (Marne).
The body is decorated with three pairs of faces linked by S's.
Early 3rd century BCE. Height of the detail: approx. 30 mm.
Épernay (Marne, France), Musée Municipal d'Archéologie et du Vin de Champagne.

The Celtic calendar according to the Coligny inscription

The Coligny Calendar consists of 2,021 lines laid out in tabular form in 16 columns. These illustrate the 62 months of a five-year period, including two supplementary months inserted in the middle to correct for the difference between the lunar and the solar years. The solar year, one complete orbit of the sun by the earth, takes 365.25 days. The lunar year, twelve full moons, occurs over either 354 or 355 days.

The Celtic month is generally made up of two 15-day periods, separated on the calendar by the word 'ATENOUX' (possibly 'return of the dark time'), which designates the night of the new moon. However, the second period might be less than 15 days long, to maintain a balance between a lunation – the interval of time (about 29.5 days) from one new moon to the next – and the duration of the month. In that case, the month was annotated with the letters 'AN[ATM]' (literally, 'not good', meaning 'incomplete'), with the exception of the month Equos – the ninth of the calendar, approximately equivalent to our month of July – which is the only 30-day month followed by such an annotation. The names of the other 30-day months are followed by the letters 'MAT[V]' ('good'). The last day of the second 15-day period in the 29-day months is replaced by the word 'DIVERTOMV' ('valueless', or 'pass' to the following month).

The first month of the year was Samonios (approximately equivalent to our November) and the last Cantlos (October). The new year was therefore on about 1 November. The annotation 'TRIN[OX] SAM[ONI] SINDIV' ('the three nights of Samonios today') that appears on the calendar on the second day of the second 15-day period of Samonios, corresponds to the 'three nights of Samain' that marks the first day of the year in the Irish calendar. It is the only feast indicated on the calendar.

The discrepancy between the lunar year of either 354 or 355 days and the solar year was reconciled by the introduction of two intercalary months, indicated on the Coligny table: the first, inserted at the beginning of the lustrum, was the 30-day month of Mid, placed at the head of the first column before the Samonios of the first year; the second, inserted after two and a half years, was the month of Ciallos, also of 30 days, placed between the months of Cutios and Giamonios, at the passage from the dark half to the light half of the year. The days of these two intercalary months are accompanied by annotations linking them to chosen days in various months of the year. This feature has not yet been wholly clarified, but it may indicate a staggered distribution of the insertion of days, subsequently regrouped into complete months. It would thus have been possible to avoid an over-long lag by comparison with the solar year. This sophisticated transfer system for notation of the days of the intercalary months, borrowed from the 30-month period for which it adjusts the lag, is what distinguishes the Coligny Calendar from all other calendars of antiquity. It is thought that at the end of an 'age' – thirty years – an intercalary month was removed, which would have established a satisfactory average duration of 365.2 (in comparison with the solar year of 365.25) days for a year over that period.

The Coligny Calendar undoubtedly developed precise measurements and calculations over many centuries of astronomical observation. Only the druids possessed the necessary knowledge to perform such tasks. The fact that the calendar was committed to writing is eloquent testimony to the decline in druidic learning after the Roman conquest of Gaul, a consequence of its abandonment by the scions of the aristocracy in favour of Greek and Latin studies, the only route to careers in the Roman administration.

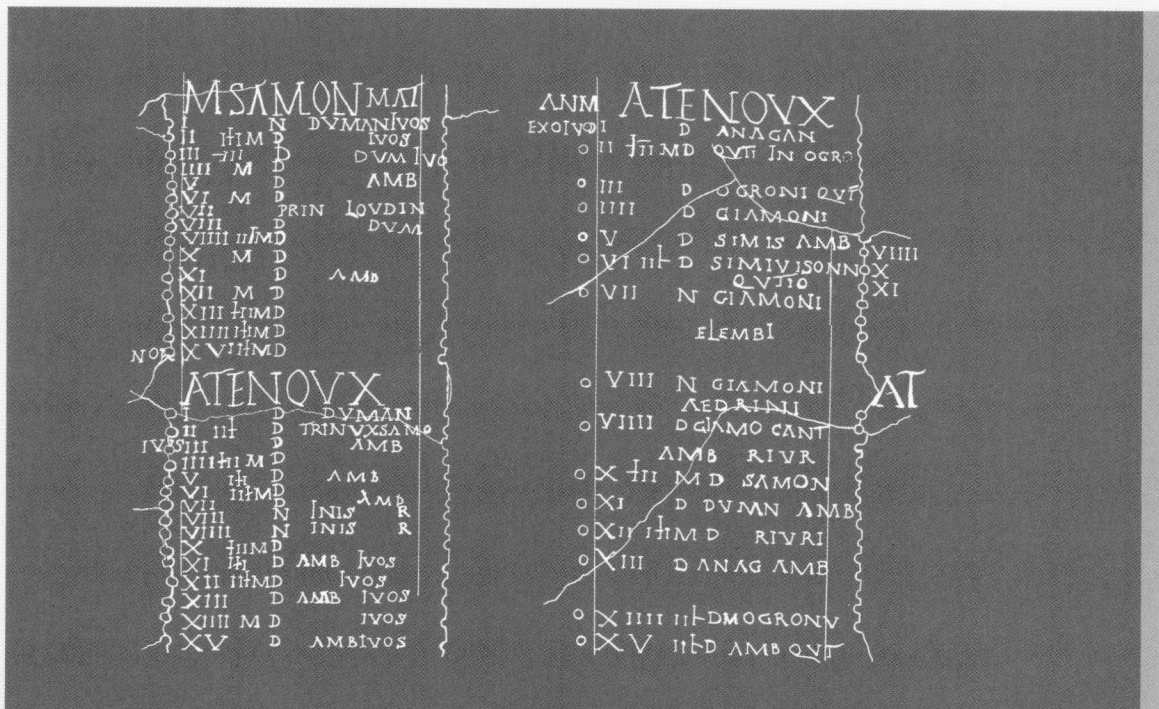

Detail of the Coligny bronze tablet.
Left, the two 15-day periods of the month Samonios, first of the 12 months of the second year. At the beginning of the second 15-day period, after ATENOUX and the word DUMAN, referring to the month Dumannios (the second month, corresponding to our December), there is a notation TRINVXSAMO[NI], *approximately equivalent to All Saints' Day or the French Toussaint.*
Right, two 15-day periods of the second intercalary month, with references to the months to which the days that they include are allocated.
End 2nd century. Lyon (Rhône, France),
Musée de la Civilisation Gallo-romaine.

The festivals of the Celtic year

Thanks to their preservation in Irish tradition, we know the four great festivals of the Celtic year: Samain, Imbolc, Belteine and Lugnasad. Samain, around the end of our month of October, marked the new year, a time when the barriers between the underground world of the dead and that of the living were broken down. It lives on today in the form of Halloween. In February Imbolc, a festival associated with the goddess Brigit, equivalent to the Roman Lupercalia and modern-day Mardi Gras, marked the end of winter's icy grip, the renewal of vegetation and life, and the birth of lambs. Belteine in May heralded the start of the warm season. In August Lugnasad, a festival marked by great gatherings, was associated with the god Lug, the chief solar god of the Celts. Under the Roman Empire, this festival became that of Augustus on the date of the reunion of the Gaulish council at Lyon; it was the equivalent of the Christian Feast of the Assumption or the Italian Ferragosto.

Of these four festivals, only the first is indicated on the Coligny Calendar, probably because their dates were determined by non-lunar and non-solar astronomical indicators. Considering the obvious absence of any relationship with either the solstices or the equinoxes, it seems likely that the dates of the festivals were fixed by observation of particularly bright stars. According to a recent theory, Samain and Belteine, the festivals at the beginning of the two chief seasons of the year, may have been associated with the heliacal rising of Antares (in the constellation of Scorpio) and Aldebaran (in Taurus), respectively. These two large, bright stars are located at 180° to the ecliptic (the sun's apparent orbit) so that, at the heliacal rising of one, the nocturnal sky is dominated by the other. The year is thus divided in two, with a winter of 179 days and a summer of 186 days, corresponding well with the climatic calendar of temperate Europe. Confirmation of this concept of the Celtic year can be found in the Gallo-Roman zodiac inscribed on a pair of tablets discovered on the site of the sanctuary of Grand (in Lorraine). It is divided in two, one part placed under the sign of the Moon and the other under that of

the Sun; the former begins with the zodiac sign of Scorpio, the latter with that of Taurus. The dates of Imbolc and Lugnasad may have been determined respectively by the heliacal rising of Capella and Sirius. As the date of the heliacal rising of all of these stars varies over time, any calendars that the Celts transcribed must have given only approximations of when the festivals would actually take place.

According to Julius Caesar, the Gauls 'compute the divisions of every season, not by the number of days, but of nights; they keep birthdays and the beginnings of months and years in such an order that the day follows the night' (*Gallic Wars,* VI, 18). Pliny the Elder observed, 'the sixth day of the moon . . . marks the beginning of the months, years and centuries, which last for thirty years; this day is chosen because the moon is already strong without being a half-course' (*Natural History,* XVI, 249). This nocturnal priority is obviously a consequence of the lunar origin of the Celtic calendar, with the twelve-month year subdivided into a first half that is dark and wintry, from Samonios to Cutios (around the beginning of November to the end of April), followed by a light, summery half, from Giamonios Cantlos (beginning of May to end of October).

This dynamic binary principle is symbolically expressed by the swirling 'S's that indicate the supposed passage of the sun during both halves of the year. The sun's east–west journey from rising to setting is presumed to be followed by a parallel nocturnal journey from west to east, made below the horizon and thus describing a spiral that increases from the winter to the summer solstice, the median point of the 'S', then decreases to its lowest point, which corresponds to the return to the winter solstice. Omnipresent in Celtic art, the 'S' expresses the fundamental binary principle that regulates the dynamic of universal order. Inscribed on a circle, it divides the surface into two interlinked halves, like the Chinese yin–yang symbol. It is also one of many possible evocations of the double mistletoe leaf, a plant that grows in the dead of winter, symbolizing the cycle of perpetual movement in which life and death, darkness and light, are inseparable from each other and interlinked.

Detail of a bronze torc from grave No.4, Villeseneux (Marne),
with three nodules decorated with S's in relief.

Early 3rd century BCE. Height of the detail on the left: 25 mm.

Épernay (Marne, France), Musée Municipal d'Archéologie et du Vin de Champagne.

The triskele, a Celtic emblem then and now

The three-branched gyratory motif most familiar from the insignia of the Isle of Man might be a very ancient Celtic design, but it is not uniquely Celtic. It is likely that it was highly significant for many other ethnicities in antiquity, too. The various versions of the term itself – including the Breton *triskell* – come from an Ancient Greek root, *triskelês* ('three-legged'). This first designated a tripod, then the familiar turning motif formed by three human legs turning at right angles; the latter appears on some Greek coins, sometimes as a hallmark, as well as on the

flag of the Isle of Man. In particular, like its Latin equivalent *triquetrum* ('three-angled'), the term recalls the triangular shape of Sicily and, later, for some writers, Britain.
The first representations of the triskele that can be attributed with certainty to the Celts are themselves ancient, dating back to the 6th century BCE. The motif is featured on Central European painted pottery, and a terracotta version is known, probably made to hang with other objects, such as oak-leaves or rings, on the branches of a sacred tree in a Bohemian shrine.

In the 5th or 4th century BCE, with the development of a highly original non-geometric Celtic art, the triskele became, after the 'S', one of the major symbols of the repertory. It is sometimes associated with the 'S' in complex compositions whose subtlety we are only just beginning to appreciate. When used to accompany a figurative theme, it is generally linked with the horse, the divine metamorphosis of the sun. Some theories suggest that the triskele represents an abstract form of the sun in movement, threefold because the number

Detail of a bronze ankle ring from Kšely (Bohemia).
Knobs decorated with triskeles in high relief.
3rd century BCE. Height of the knobs: 36 mm.
Prague, Národní Muzeum.

Detail of a bronze ankle ring from Plaňany (Bohemia).
Knobs decorated with two S's in relief, overlapping around a central medaillon, itself decorated with an S.
3rd century BCE. Height of the knobs: 42 mm.
Prague, Národní Muzeum.

three is the expression of divine perfection, of movement without end or beginning, and because it evokes the three points of the sun's daily orbit: rising, zenith, setting. In this case, the association of the 'S' with the triskele, especially triskeles integrated into a series of 'S's (a design that was particularly common in the 4th and 3rd centuries BCE), represents the annual sequence of the movement of the sun.

Left
Central motif of the large silver phalera from Manerbio sul Mella (Lombardy, Italy).
Three S's form a triskele. See p. 110.
Early 1st century BCE.
Diameter: approx. 80 mm.
Brescia (Italy), Museo Civico dell'Età Romana.

Design of a buffer bracelet, Prague-Žižkov

Triskeles frame a central S. At each end, triskeles with a contrary movement to those of the centre.

Beginning of the 3rd century BCE.

Maximum depth of the body: 12 mm.

Prague, Národní Muzeum.

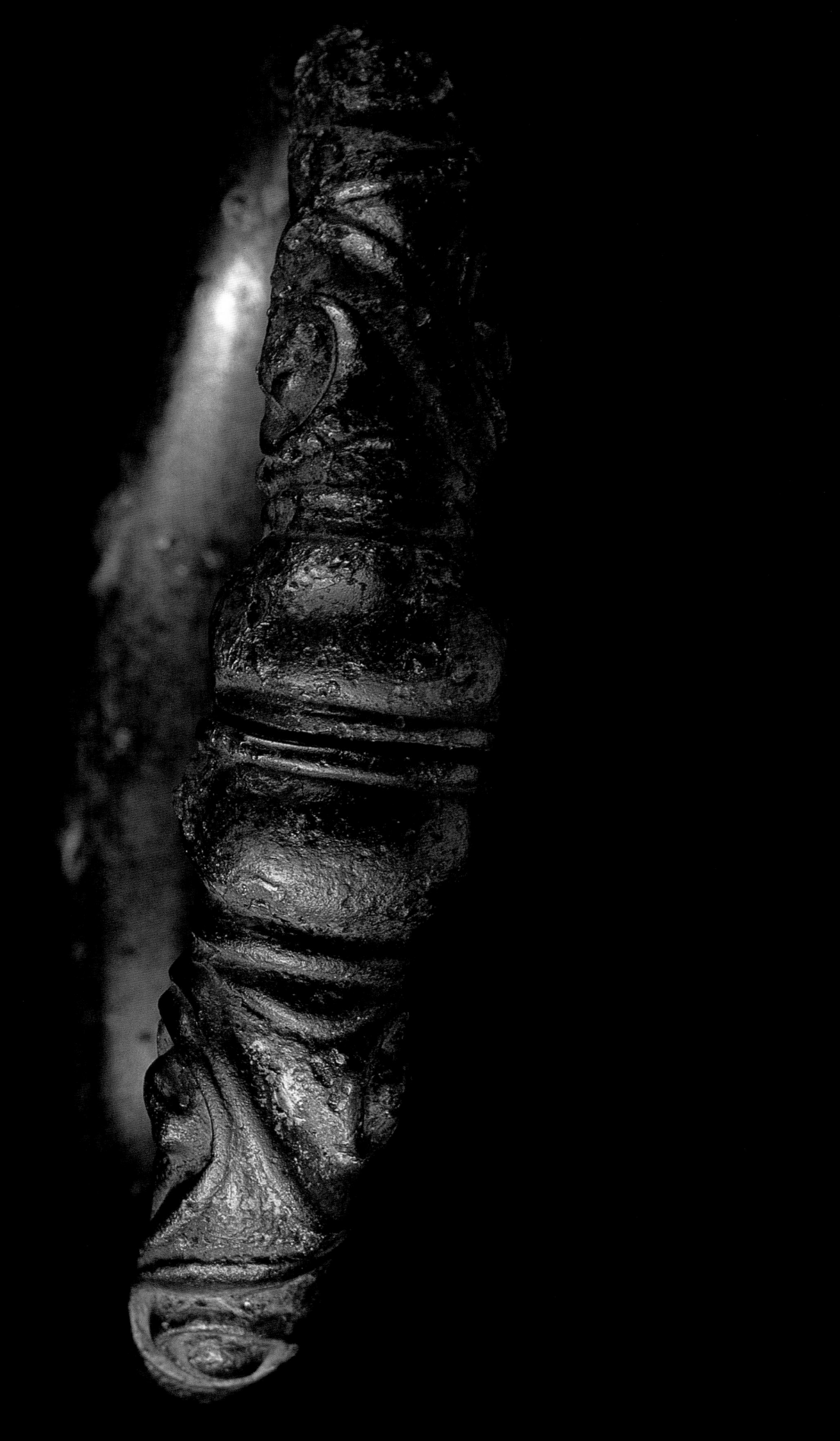

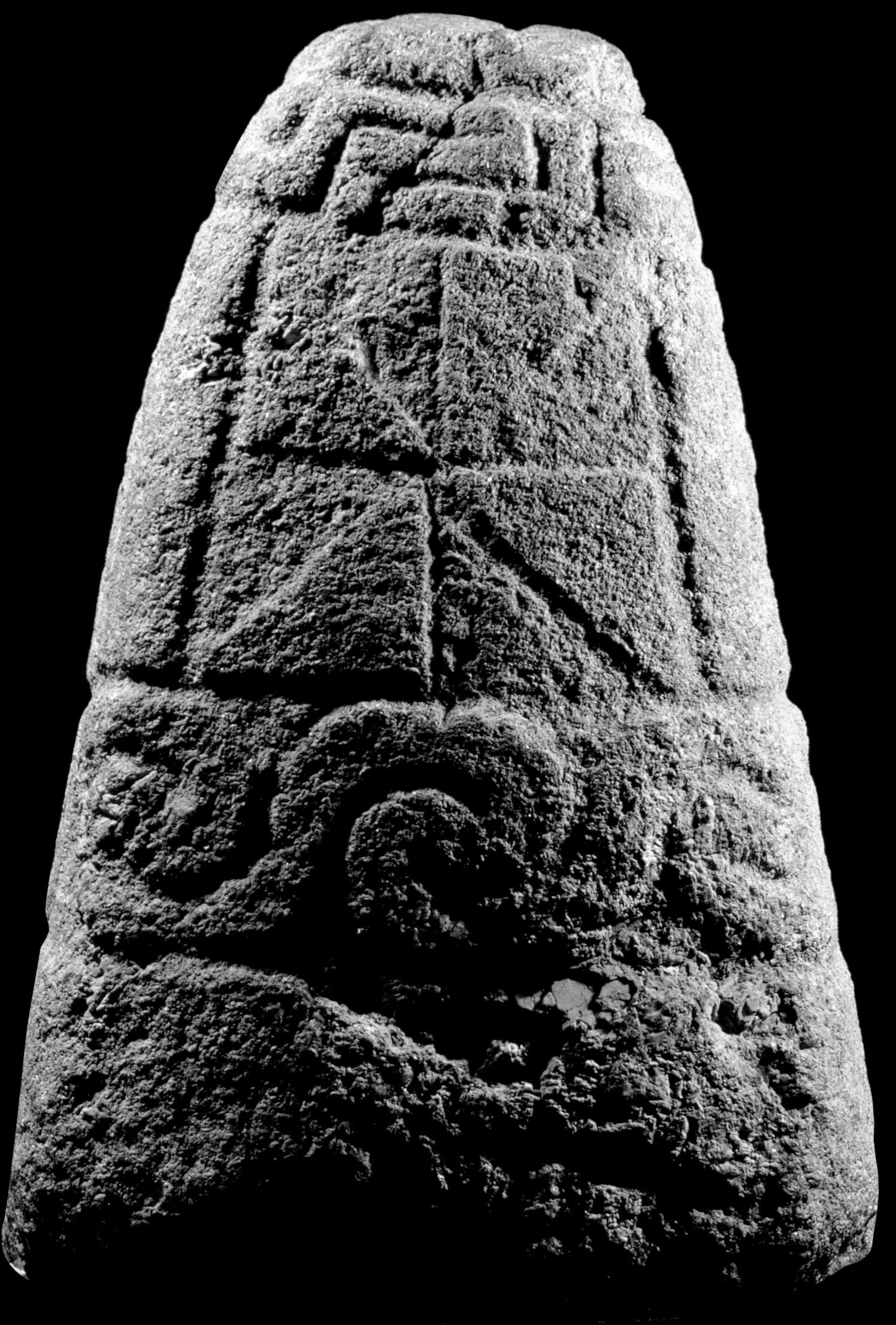

Plan of the designs on the four sides and top of the pyramidal stele at Kermaria-en-Pont-l'Abbé (Finistère, France).
The flat summit has two diagonal lines that link the corners; each corresponding panel has a different, though always quaternary, motif; meanders, angular at the top and curvilinear at the bottom, run around the stele, forming a unifying motif with all panels. See p. 148.

Sculpted stone from Turoe (Galway, Ireland).
Another example of a Celtic omphalos, *sadly displaced from its original site, the Iron Age fort of Feerwore.*
Left, sketch showing the way the decoration is divided into four panels; the narrow ones, joined by a wavy line, probably correspond to the axis of the sun's course from east to west.
Height of the part above ground: approx. 1,200 mm.

The sun's progress was also the basis for the Celts' spatial perception of the world, which they conceived as divided into four parts on two perpendicular axes, east–west and north–south. This is represented diagrammatically by a solar wheel with four rays. From the 2nd millennium BCE these are often associated with aquatic birds said to be hitched to the sun's chariot, or with the birds of prey that, according to Greek mythology, were sent by Zeus from the ends of the world to cross above its centre, Delphi, the sanctuary of the sun god Apollo. The Celts seem to have been deeply imbued with this notion of the symbolic centre, and they have been credited with several stone monuments that symbolize it in the same manner as the celebrated *omphalos* of Delphi.

Two of the most impressive of these 'world navels' come from Kermaria-en-Pont-l'Abbé (in Finistère, France), probably the site of an ancient sanctuary close to the headland of Penmarch, and from Turoe (in Galway, Ireland), which has always been associated with an Iron Age fortification.

In both cases there is a lower band of motifs – meanders or Greek keys – that may symbolize the ocean that surrounds and sustains the Earth, while the upper part is divided into four panels.

A universe in four parts

On the truncated tip of the pyramidal stone in Kermaria there are two diagonals that cross in the centre, each panel thus corresponding to one of the four cardinal directions. They carry various quaternary motifs – swastikas, leaves, cruciforms – indicating that the space is divided into four parts, at once equal and different, which share a common centre. The rounded top of the Turoe monolith, like that of the Greek *omphalos*, is completely covered with a tangle of linked motifs sculpted in light relief, this time dispersed over four unequal triangular panels joined by a wavy line. The two narrower panels may correspond to the rising and setting of the sun, linked by its progress, which is suggested by triskeles; the two large panels may correspond to south and north. If this is the case, the carved designs may symbolize the principal stars and constellations associated with these parts of the heavens.

Opposite
Pyramidal stone stele from Kermaria-en-Pont-l'Abbé (Finistère).
One of the best-known examples of the Celtic omphalos, *the crossing point of two great perpendicular axes around which the universe is ordered.*
4th century BCE. Height: approx. 850 mm.
Saint-Germain-en-Laye (Yvelines, France), Musée des Antiquités Nationales.

Left

Flat bronze spoons found in Ireland, probably used in ritual libations.

These are generally found as attached pairs, one spoon being engraved with two perpendicular lines whose intersection is marked by a circle or a round hole; there may also be a round hole near the rim of the other spoon, which remains smooth.

1st century. Height: approx. 120-140 mm.

London, British Museum.

They assembled together at the same place, the fortress of the kings at Tara. 'We thank the gods', they said, 'that we have returned, O Ireland. Let Ireland be divided among us', they said, 'as is fitting. Let the sage Fintan come before us and may Ireland be divided as he decrees.' And so Fintan divided Ireland into five parts.

The First Battle of Mag Tured, Irish mythological text.

The symbolic centre

This concept of a quadripartite space organized around a centre is the origin of the geographical subdivision of Ireland as attested by medieval texts: four provinces, each symbolically lending a part of its territory to a fifth, the province of Midhe (the Middle Kingdom), the location of Tara, where the high kings of Ireland were crowned, and Uisnech, its sacred centre. This concept of a space divided by two orthogonal axes into four sectors arranged around a circular centre is the basis for many Celtic art compositions. Its symbolic value probably explains its presence on the concave part of the previously mentioned ritual bronze spoons found in Pogny. Interestingly, the combination of the cross and the central circle is still typical of the Irish Christian cross.

This design was also used for the organization of Celtic communities in the three Galatian tribes of Asia Minor, who were inspired by this ideal model to divide themselves into tetrarchies. The Greek term corresponds with the Latin *pagi*, a word designating the 'cantons' mentioned by Caesar, notably among the Helvetii where they were four in number. This organization of the common space of ethnic groupings was geographically designated as *mediolanon*, meaning 'centre of the territory', to be understood in the symbolic rather than the topographical context. It was used in many *oppida* in Gaul and other regions of Celtic Europe. The first to be documented is the best known and one of the oldest, and has given its name to the modern city of Milan. This layout was also used for what are now the modern towns of Saintes (which owes its name to the Gaulish tribe of Santonae), Evreux (named for the township of the Aulerci Eburovices), Châteaumeillant, and for many places, such as Miolan, Meilhan, Meillan and Montmeillan, that existed in the territory of ancient Gaul. In the 2nd century BCE the Greek geographer Ptolemy recorded several sites with similar names in Central Europe, and one among the Ordovices of what is now Wales.

It can be confidently asserted that Celtic concepts of time and space have left a sufficiently deep impression to be perceptible even now, despite their dilution over the centuries.

Opposite

A range of different types of votive wheels from the *oppidum* of Stradonice (Bohemia).

1st century BCE. Diameter: 15–55 mm. Prague, Národní Muzeum.

Left
**Reconstitution of a *crannóg*
at Cragganowen (Clare, Ireland).**
*A raised platform on piles above a
body of water, the* crannóg, *from the
Irish* crann *(tree), is a type of Irish
Bronze Age habitat that survived
until the Middle Ages. These artificial
islands, sometimes linked to the bank
by a bridge, bore one or several
constructions. By their size and
function as a protected dwelling of
a noble family, they were the
equivalent, in low-lying regions where
stone was scarce, of the ring-forts
(raths) whose traces are scattered all
over the Irish countryside.*

Peasants and artisans

The economic foundation of the Celtic world in the Iron Age
was agriculture, carried out efficiently, rationally and in a much
more sophisticated manner than is generally considered to be
the case. Without the capacity to produce such abundant
surpluses, it would have been impossible to develop specialist
craftsmanship or to establish a trading system based on an
urban network of *oppida*.

Throughout the age, the most common rural unit in the Celtic
world seems to have been a small group of families, probably
blood relations. They lived chiefly in hamlets, small villages or
the large farms of the nobility, each comprising at most half
a dozen dwellings. These were typically surrounded by a
territory of between 50 and 100 square kilometres (19 and 38
square miles), only part-cultivated, the remainder being left
in woodland or as pasture. The rectangular fields, still
recognizable in some parts of Great Britain, were not very large.
Their area was usually between 10 and 15 ares (a quarter and
a third of an acre), the average amount of land that could be
worked by the ard, or swing-plough, in one day. The fields were
probably defined by banks and hedges that protected them
from wind and the depredations of wild or domestic animals.
The landscape of Iron Age Celtic Europe must have closely
resembled the countryside of western France, or Britain before
the changes caused by the lifting of enclosures.

Both pastoral and arable agriculture were practised. Extensive
experiments based on archaeological data have shown that
ancient wheat varieties – einkorn (*Triticum monococcum*),
spelt (*Triticum spelta*) and emmer wheat (*Triticum dicoccum*)
– which were known from the dawn of agriculture in the
temperate zone (in the 6th millennium BCE) and cultivated by
Iron Age Celts, were well suited to the soils and techniques of
the time. They seem to have provided very large harvests.

As they required less added nitrogen than modern hybrids,
with an application of natural fertilizer three times a year
they could yield an average harvest of 3 tonnes per hectare
(7 tons per acre). This yield is markedly superior to those
considered exceptional in the Middle Ages, and larger even
than those achieved under the same conditions from modern
varieties, which are also poorer in protein and have lower
nutritional value.

The Celts also cultivated barley (used especially to make a
beer whose name, *cervesia*, while supplanted in English by
the word derived from the German *bier*, survives in the Spanish
cerveza), rye, oats, millet and buckwheat or black wheat
(*Fagopyrum*). The last of these was particularly suited to poor
ground and to cultivation at high altitudes. The grain was stored
in lofts surrounded by stakes to keep out rodents, or in
underground silos. Experiments have shown that the silos are
especially effective: the grain will keep without deterioration
or loss of germination capacity for several years, provided the
pit is lined with straw, completely filled with well-packed grain,
and is airtight, watertight and emptied completely when
needed. This conservation method was therefore suitable for
surpluses to be used for sowing and trading but not for daily
consumption. Grain was ground by hand or, later, milled using
stone querns, and the flour was used to make bread, flat cakes
and gruel. According to the Greek historian Diodorus Siculus,
the Celts simply harvested the ears of corn and stored them
in covered granaries, withdrawing daily what they needed to
prepare their meals.

Opposite
**Bronze statuette of a boar, from
Prague-Šárka, Bohemia (detail).**
*Originally this was probably fixed to
a military standard or a helmet.*
2nd–1st century BCE. Height: 65 mm. Prague, Národní Muzeum.

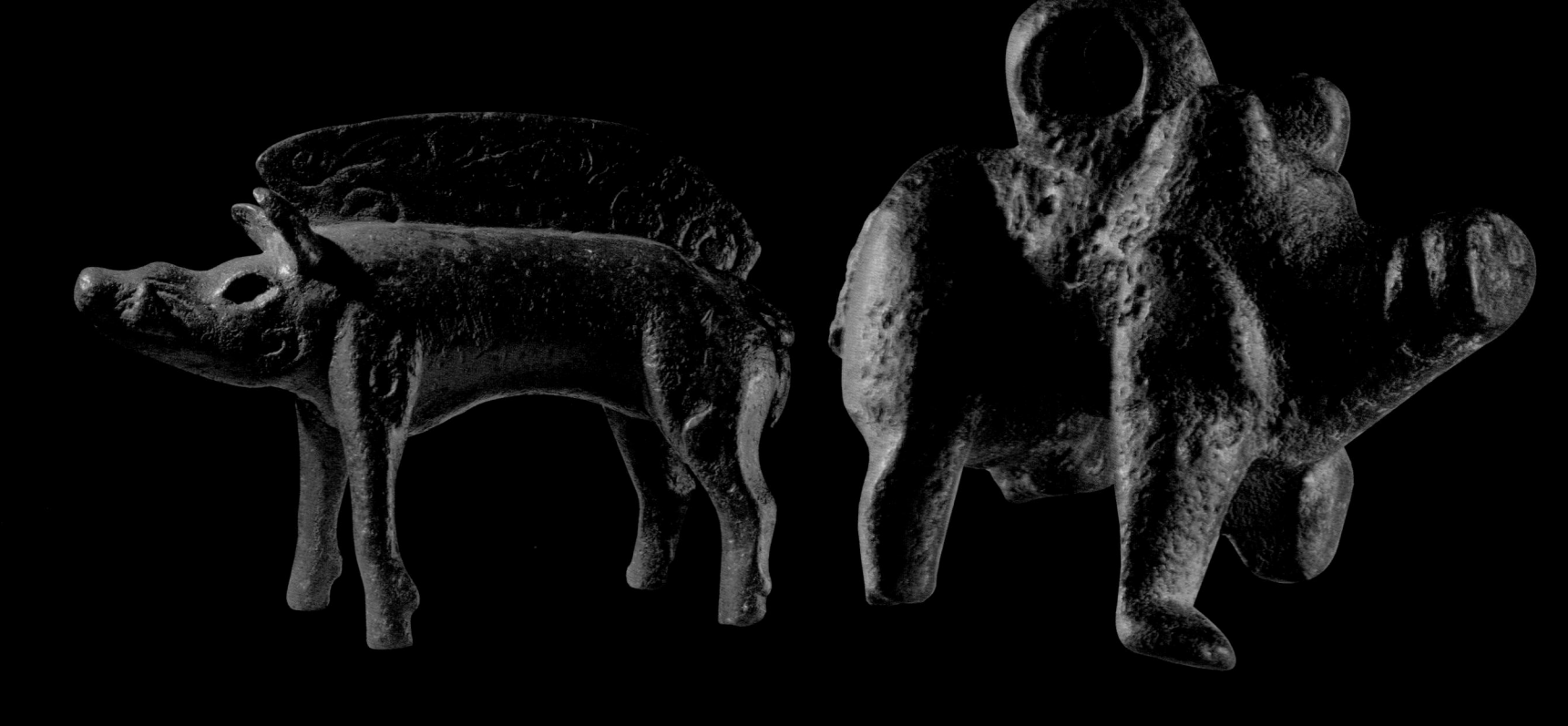

Bronze statuette of a boar from Báta (Hungary).
3rd–2nd century BCE. Length: 109 mm.
Budapest, Magyar Nemzéti Múzeum.

Bronze pendant in the shape of a boar, from Přisnotice (Moravia).
2nd–1st century BCE. Length: 35 mm.
Brno (Czech Republic), Moravské Muzeum.

Legumes were other important components of the Celtic diet, especially as they could be dried and stored. Probably grown in rotation with grains, they included peas, lentils and, above all, the broad bean (*Vicia faba minor*) or 'Celtic bean', a very nutritious plant that could be used as fodder. Vegetables of European origin that had long been cultivated, such as cabbage, turnips and carrots, as well as onions and garlic (introduced into the rest of Europe from the Mediterranean in the 3rd millennium BCE), were usually eaten fresh but could be stored under certain conditions.

Wild plants supplemented the diets of humans and animals. The forests were heavily exploited for wood used in construction and as fuel, and they were therefore much less dense near Celtic settlements than they would be in later ages. They were also plundered for berries and acorns, while hedgerows probably provided nuts and sloes. Chenopodium (*Chenopodium album*) or wild spinach, a plant that self-seeded near settlements, was probably consumed, like other wild plants, as much for its medicinal properties as for its nutritional value. Apple and pear trees were pruned to improve their yields, and they may even have been grafted in a style similar to that used today, as distinctive knives that would fit this purpose have been found. Flax and hemp were grown to make cloth, which was then dyed with woad (blue), or madder-root (red), still in use as late as the 19th century CE. Finally, willow, hazel, brambles and rushes provided, as they still do, the raw materials for basketwork.

With the exception of a few plants, chiefly those of American origin (notably the potato), the vegetables grown on an Iron Age Celtic farm therefore differed little from those grown in temperate-zone Europe right until the development of monocultures and intensive agriculture. Similarly, their tools – hoes, spades, rakes, billhooks, sickles and scythes (used in haymaking from the 5th century BCE) – were very similar to those used until the 20th century CE. Only the ard was supplanted, by the plough. However, ancient implements – which became lighter and easier to handle after the iron ploughshare was developed in the 5th century BCE – were still well designed for tilling either light or heavy soil. Draught work was done by cattle whose milk, according to the geographer Strabo, was a dietary staple. It was made into cheese, as the existence of cheese-drainers that pre-date even the Iron Age prove.

Bronze statuette of a boar from Neuvy-en-Sullias (Loiret).

1st century. Height: 270 mm.

Orléans (Loiret, France), Musée historique et archéologique de l'Orléanais.

Bronze fibula in the shape of a boar, from a grave at Dürrnberg bei Hallein (Austria).

Second half of the 5th century BCE. Length: 60 mm.

Hallein (Austria), Keltenmuseum.

Livestock, which provided most of the meat consumed, played an important role in the life of ancient Celts, as is shown by the battles for its possession as described in Irish literature. The standing of minor Celtic nobles depended less on the acreage of land they exploited than on the number of cattle they owned. These animals were a small, short-horned breed (*Bos longifrons*), now extinct, but similar to the modern Dexter.

Raised in an environment that would now be described as 'free range', strong, fast and even dangerous (if Strabo is to be believed), the Celts' traditional domestic pig was much smaller than the wild boar, modern pigs or even those breeds that were introduced into Gaul following the Roman conquest. Its flesh was particularly appreciated by the Celts, especially at feasts. Celtic salted pork was famous and was exported even to Italy. This innovation in preserving food, which probably explains the expansion in salt mining around the beginning of the 1st millennium BCE, contributed greatly towards the mobility of Celtic populations.

Sheep were generally very different to those we know today, too (although the modern Soay breed from St Kilda in Scotland is virtually identical). They were extraordinarily agile animals and provided wool of excellent quality. Goats were raised chiefly for their milk. The farmyard also included domestic varieties of hens, geese and ducks, with cats and dogs completing a familiar picture. Celtic horses, similar in size to large modern ponies, were ridden or harnessed to war- or ceremonial chariots; their flesh was also eaten.

Game does not seem to have featured prominently in the Celts' diet, with deer and boar hunted chiefly as a means to keep weapons skills polished in times of peace. Fishing was carried out in rivers, lakes and the sea. A large quantity of shells found among culinary debris unearthed in Armorica featured varieties still eaten today, evidence that seafood was also consumed.

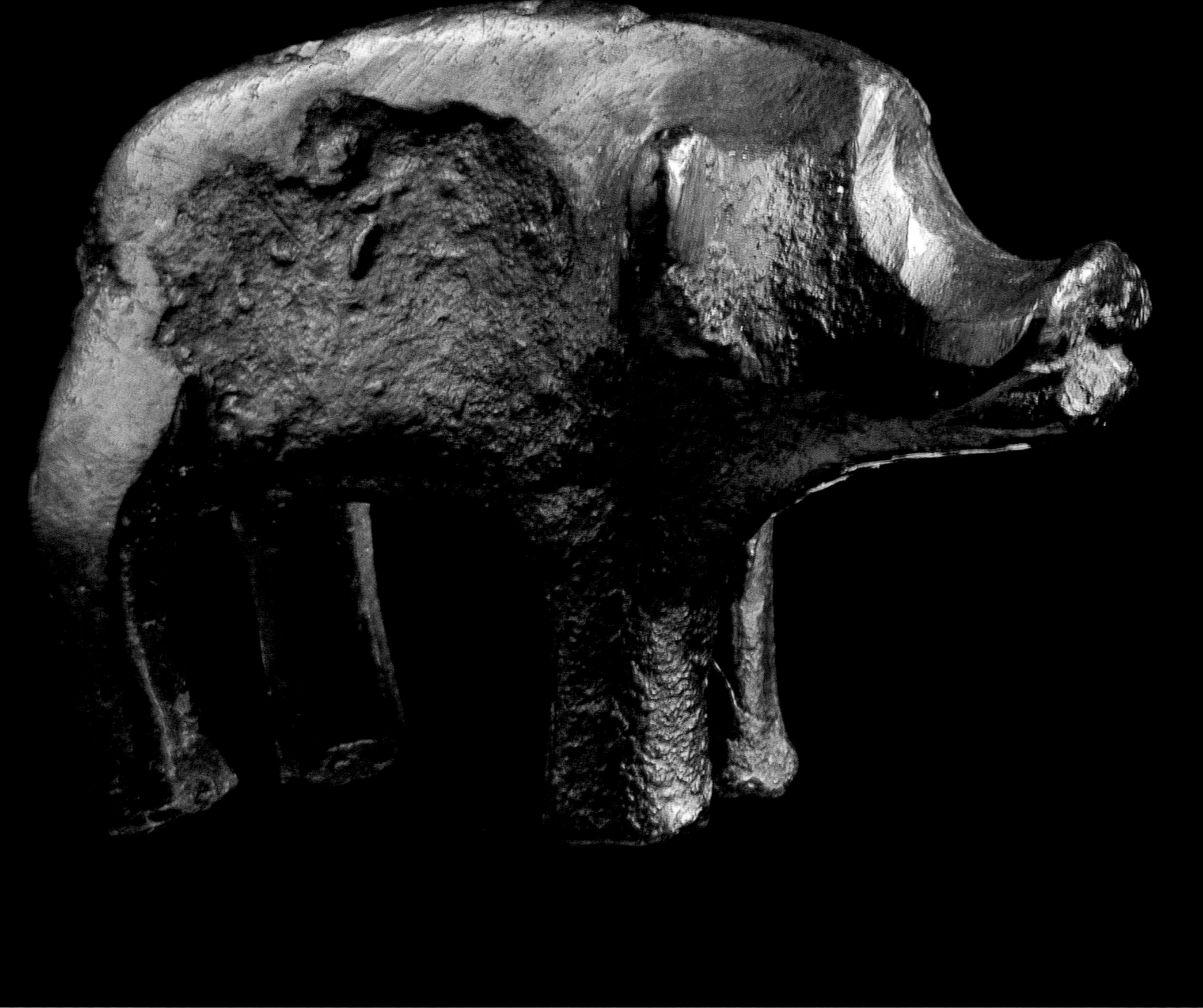

Small bronze statuette of a boar, from the Stradonice
oppidum (Bohemia).

1st century BCE. Height: 25 mm. Prague, Národní Muzeum.

Opposite
Terminal of a bronze fibula from Panenský Týnec
(Bohemia), featuring the head of a sheep
surmounted with a type of diadem.

Second half of the 5th century BCE. Height of the detail: approx. 25 mm.

Prague, Národní Muzeum.

Left
Detail of a gold double armring from Molesme (Côte-d'Or).
3rd century BCE. Width of the double band: 17 mm.
Troyes (Aube, France), Musée des Beaux-Arts et d'Archéologie.

Opposite
The Otava river.
*In the Middle Ages this tributary of the Vltava in southern
Bohemia was still renowned for the richness of its gold-bearing
sand. Many gold-mining sites from the La Tène era have been
identified there. .*

Agricultural surpluses facilitated the development of a class of high-quality craftspeople, which constitutes one of the most remarkable aspects of Celtic civilization from 500 BCE onwards. The areas where their skill is nowadays most evident are undoubtedly metalworking, forging, smelting and jewellery. Extracted from readily available pig iron using small furnaces, iron was originally forged and distributed in the form of ingots, of which the oldest, weighing between 1 and 6 kg (2 and 13 pounds), were bi-pyramidal in shape. A deposit dating from the 5th century BCE, discovered in Armorica near St-Connan, contained 50 ingots with a total weight of around 3 quintals (300 kg; 660 pounds). Ingots of this type were later replaced by long flat bars, worked at one end to form a paddle, which made them look rather like a sword-blade. Some 1,500 of these bars have been found in Britain, where, according to Caesar, iron ingots of a set weight were used as currency, along with copper and gold coinage.

> Silver is lacking in Celtic lands, but there is much gold [...]. The rivers, in their course [...] butt up against the foothills of the mountains [...] and fill up with gold particles
>
> DIODORUS SICULUS, *Bibliotheca Historica*, V, 27.

Apart from this bullion, the smiths also produced weapons – swords and spears that were often of remarkable quality thanks to skilful mixing and soldering of various grades of iron – well-designed and well-crafted utensils, and various objects essential to other trades: hoops for casks, wheel-bindings and other fittings for wagons. Ornamentation was the province of master bronze-workers and jewellers who, like the smiths, were skilled in various techniques. They were also adept in the difficult art of designing and executing, following complex guidelines, the subtle decoration that would endow an object with supposedly magical power. This bestowed special prestige: they were masters of their material but also of the symbolic language that was addressed to the gods.

The trades of the god Lug

The doorkeeper asked Samíldánach [Lug] 'What art do you practise. No one without art comes to Tara.' 'Question me', he said, 'I am a carpenter.' The doorkeeper replied 'We need thee not. We have a carpenter already.' [Then Lug declares that he is, in turn, a smith, champion, harpist, hero, poet and historian, sorcerer, leech, cupbearer, brazier, each time to the same response from the porter.] Then he said 'Ask the king if there is a single man who possesses all these arts and if he has I will not enter Tara.'[...] The doorkeeper recounted all this to Nuada, who said 'Let him come in, for never before has a man like him entered the fortress.' *The Second Battle of Mag Tured*, Irish mythological text.

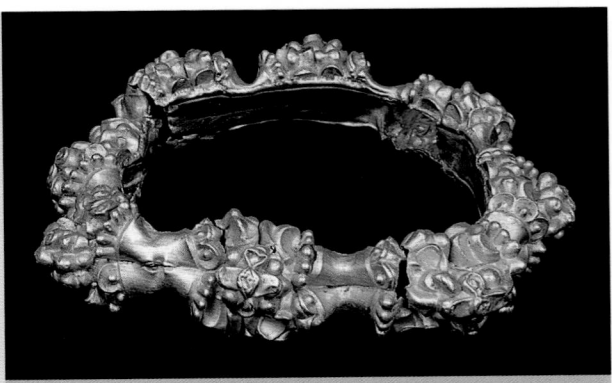

Gold armband from Lasgraïsses (Tarn).
See p. 79.
3rd century BCE. Diameter: 130 mm.
Toulouse (Haute-Garonne, France), Musée Saint-Raymond.

Detail of a bronze armband from Podlešín (Bohemia).
It illustrates a bronze-decoration technique called 'pastillage' that was inspired by jewellery techniques; the object is cast using the cire perdue ('lost wax') method.
3rd century BCE. Height of the decoration: approx. 5 mm.
Prague, Národní Muzeum.

Detail of the decoration of the bow of one of the iron fibulas (a) from Conflans-sur-Seine (Marne).
See the drawing below, left.

A

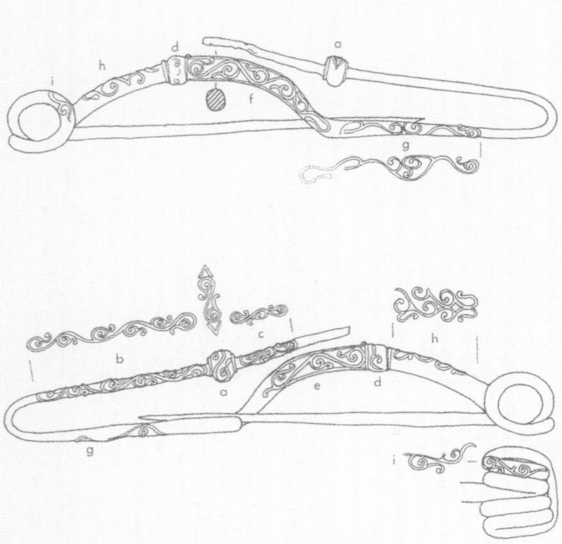

Fibulas in worked iron from Conflans-sur-Seine (Marne).
They were exceptionally well preserved, probably in an incineration burial. On one, (b), monsters like those of the Cernon scabbard (see p. 10 and 191) merge on the bow in a foliage scroll. The other example, (a), is decorated with an exclusively vegetal motif. These remarkable pieces illustrate the astonishing mastery of the Celtic smiths; no tool marks can be seen, even though this is not malleable wax but iron.
Second third of the 3rd century BCE.
Length: 170 and 116 mm.
Troyes (Aube, France), Musée des Beaux-Arts et d'Archéologie.

B

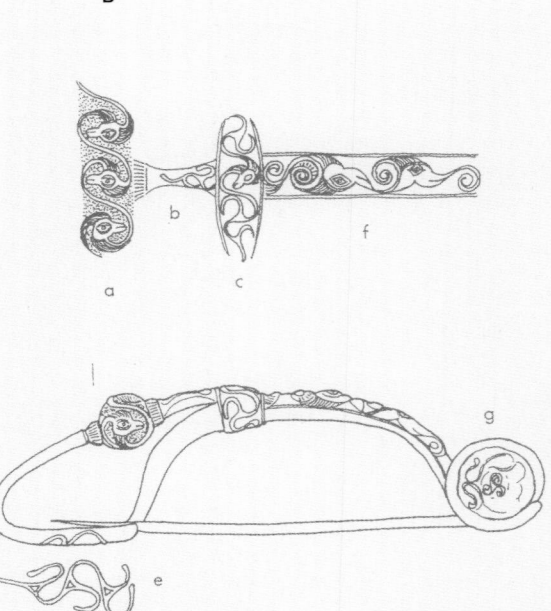

Detail of a worked iron armband from Ponětovice (Moravia).
Iron objects, although generally poorly preserved, were often worked with great skill.
3rd century BCE. Height of the decorative motif: 10 mm.
Brno (Czech Republic), Moravské Muzeum.

Detail of the bow decoration of an iron fibula (b) from Conflans-sur-Seine (Marne).
See the drawing on the opposite page.

Magicians of the forge and the furnace

Celtic art at its most brilliant, during the 4th and 3rd centuries BCE, corresponded closely with the craftsmen's mastery of smelting and forging, the only skills to have left traces that enable us to study them closely. Smiths and metalworkers achieved such virtuosity that some of their creations remain inimitable, even using the latest modern techniques.

The ornamentation of iron by engraving, chiselling, stamping and other, more obscure, methods was formerly known only through a few well-preserved artefacts: for example,

the finely engraved scabbard found at Cernon-sur-Coole and some astonishing brooches from Conflans (both in France). However, considerable progress in the restoration of excavated metal objects has recently revealed that such high artistic and technical standards were by no means rare in the Celtic world of the 3rd century BCE, especially wherever a concentration of clients from the military elite could be found.

The bronze-workers had perfected the ancient lost-wax process. This involved

making a wax model of the desired object, coating it in a fine refractory clay to make a mould, then melting the wax to enable the mould to be baked and refilled with molten bronze. A special alloy with a high lead content was used, enabling the production of complex pieces that displayed a high level of delicate craftsmanship. Sets of rings found among the Danubian Celts are spectacular advertisements for this skill, especially anklets decorated with either complex volutes or large, slender, supple and perfectly rendered scallops.

Opposite
Detail of a girdle-chain in bronze inlaid with red enamel, from Telce (Bohemia).
The hook features the head of an animal, probably a horse.
3rd century BCE. Length of the hook: 70 mm. Prague, Národní Muzeum.

Enamel: colours borne of fire

The oldest evidence of vitreous material being fused directly on to an object comes from the end of the 5th or beginning of the 4th century BCE. It can be seen, together with coral inlays and appliqués, on pieces such as the circular plaque found at Auvers-sur-Oise (France) and the pair of ceremonial flagons from Basse-Yutz (now in the British Museum). In the 4th century BCE, the most frequently used method was still the inlay of oval cabochons, fixed to the object by a central rivet; these are chiefly found in Switzerland, on brooches, torcs and bracelets. On the Amfreville ceremonial helmet (now in the Musée des Antiquités nationales, Saint-Germain-en-Laye), red glass inlays were supplemented with enamelling that seems to have been fused on to a fine iron mesh placed directly on the headpiece. The parallel use of this red enamel alongside coral – the idea that it was used as a substitute does not seem to fit the evidence – shows that each material was accorded magical properties: the petrified blood of the sea and the blood that came from fire.

The 3rd century BCE, when the manufacture of coloured glass bracelets developed, was also when the technique of fusion directly on to an object was perfected. Thereafter, red enamel became a favourite embellishment for weapons and ornaments. New colours, notably yellow and blue, were introduced in the 2nd and 1st centuries BCE, but red remained by far the most frequently used.

The technique would later develop in a particularly spectacular fashion in Britain, where skilled craftsmen were masters in a variety of styles. Their skill was so famous that a sophisticated Greek of the Imperial era, Philostratus of Lemnos, noted, 'it is said, the barbarous neighbours of the Ocean know how to pour these colours [white, yellow, black and red] on to red-hot copper where they fuse together, become hard as stone and keep the forms that have been designed for them' (*Images*, I, 28).

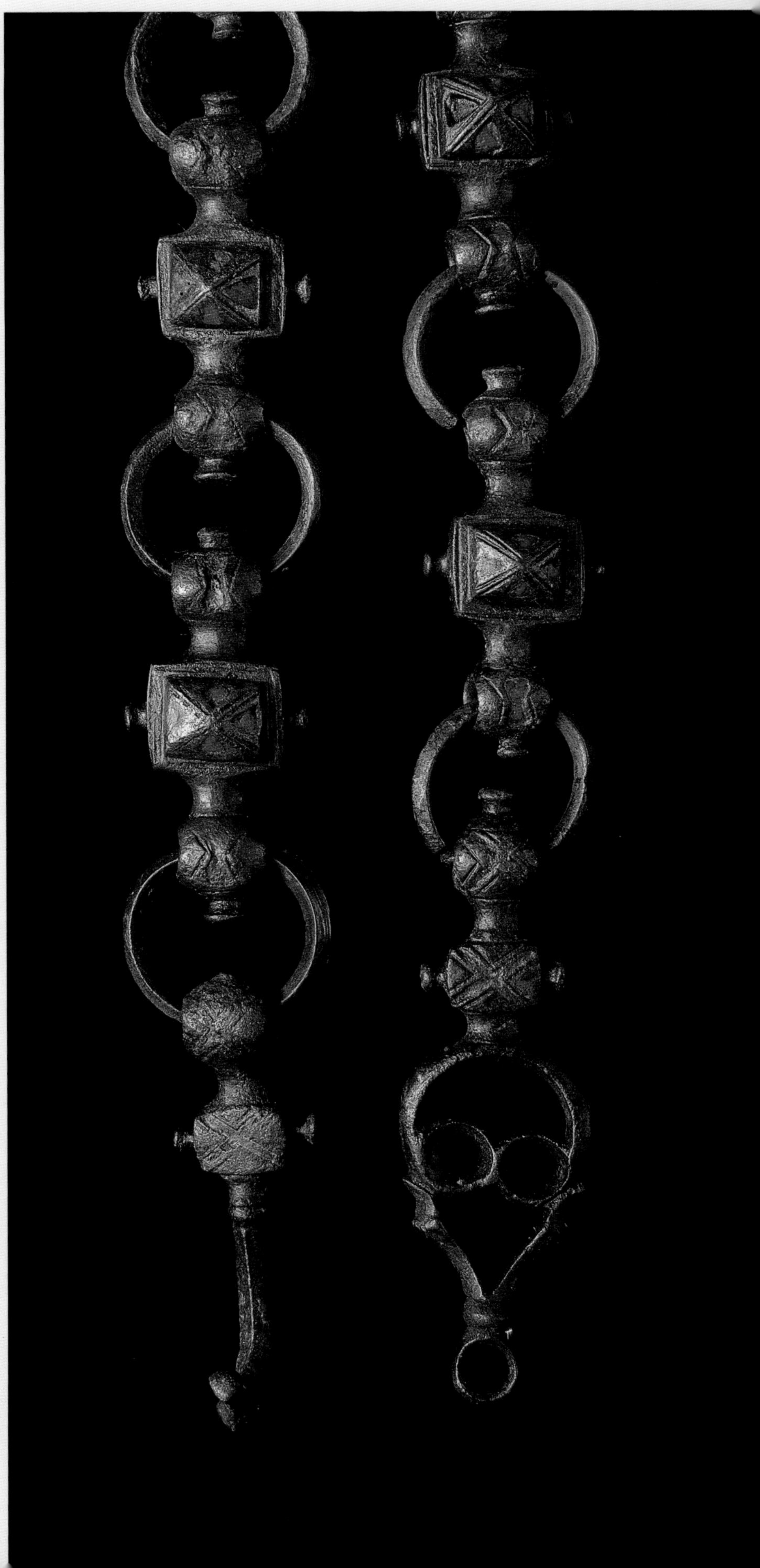

Right
Detail of a bronze girdle-chain inlaid with red enamel, from Stradonice near Louny (Bohemia).
3rd century BCE.
Length of the hook: 55 mm.
Prague, Národní Muzeum.

Streamlined terracotta vase with horizontal fluting, from Mesnil-les-Hurlus (Marne).
End 5th–early 4th century BCE. Height: 260 mm.
London, British Museum.

Terracotta bowl with painted geometric decoration, from Marson (Marne).
End 5th–early 4th century BCE. Height: 260 mm.
London, British Museum.

Metal objects – particularly in bronze but sometimes in iron – might be decorated by the application of coloured materials, especially Mediterranean coral, much sought-after and particularly appreciated for its magical virtues, or a kind of red enamel obtained from glass mosaic. At first, this was simply used in oval appliqués fixed by rivets, but Celtic craftspeople gradually perfected the process of fusing glass into prepared grooves in the metal surface. This technique, *champlevé*, reached a remarkable level of sophistication in Britain in the 2nd century BCE, well before the Roman conquest. Red, yellow and blue enamels were all used to decorate ornaments, pieces of horses' tack (bits or ornamental plaques) weapons and chariots' axle pins.

The Celts' fondness for colour was also exhibited in their preference for the multicoloured fabrics used for clothes, which were very similar to modern Scottish tartans. According to Diodorus 'the clothing they wear is striking – shirts which have been dyed and embroidered in various colours, and breeches, which they call in their tongue *bracae*; and they wear striped cloaks, fastened by a brooch on the shoulder, heavy for winter

wear and light in summer, in which are set checks, close together and of varied hues'. The woollen fabrics made in Gaul and in the British Isles were renowned and were exported to Italy. Pliny the Elder praised the skill of the Gaulish dyers who, as has been mentioned, used herbs to reproduce all shades of Phoenician purple, probably starting from a mixture of woad and madder.

As for shoes, the remarkably sophisticated examples that exist, especially from around 450 BCE, are evidence of very competent shoemakers. In general, we know little about Celtic leatherwork, but it was certainly used to make defensive armour, such as breastplates and helmets, as well as other pieces of equipment and horses' tack. The remains of a scabbard for a 5th-century BCE broadsword, found in the Belgian Ardennes, show that leather could be as finely decorated as metal.

The skill of woodworkers – wheelwrights, joiners, carpenters and coopers – developed over many years. Celtic vehicles, which were often innovative for the time, were sturdy and well designed for travelling along unpaved routes, and for military

Terracotta vase with relief decoration, from Thuizy (Marne).
3rd century BCE. Height: 220 mm.
Saint-Germain-en-Laye (Yvelines, France), Musée des Antiquités Nationales.

Pedestalled vase from Somme-Bionne (Marne).
4th century BCE. Height: 250 mm.
London, British Museum.

use, which required good manoeuvrability on uneven terrain. In the classical world cooperage was considered to be a Celtic invention. Their wooden buckets are well known, especially those in yew-wood, with beaten bronze attachments, assembled from staves in a style that is unchanged to this day. Woodworking was sophisticated, as is shown by items preserved in damp environments, notably from those settlements that once flourished on what are now bogs, which preserve organic material well. These wooden receptacles were often decorated with engraved panels, similar to those found on bronze and ceramic objects.

Recent attempts to reconstruct Celtic dwellings obviously can only guess as to how they were finished. The dwellings may have boasted sculpted elements, such as the remarkable wooden structures discovered several decades ago in a shaft in the rectangular enclosure at Fellbach-Schmiden (in Baden-Württemberg), but we cannot be sure. Nevertheless, it is certain that Iron Age houses were far from the traditional image of dingy, uncomfortable huts. The largest constructions, which were able to withstand the strongest winds, probably

had thatched roofs, and the floor area could be 100 square metres (120 square yards). Some even had an upper storey. Upkeep of these constructions appears to have been minimal. They provided good protection against cold and damp, while insects were deterred by the smoke that escaped through the thatched roof.

Fine pottery was probably manufactured from at least 450 BCE, by specialist potters who lived off the trade in their wares. Analysis of clays demonstrates that some pots ended up 100 km (60 miles) or more from where they were manufactured. However, they probably travelled so far because of what they contained, rather than because of any market for the pots themselves. For a long time, pots were hand-moulded, the wheel not coming into use until the 6th–5th century BCE, and then only in some regions, and purely for finishing. The widespread introduction of the rapidly rotating potter's wheel accompanied the expansion of the *oppida*, in the 2nd–1st century BCE. Quite sophisticated kilns from that time have been excavated, demonstrating the existence of craft centres that produced fine pottery for a sizeable market.

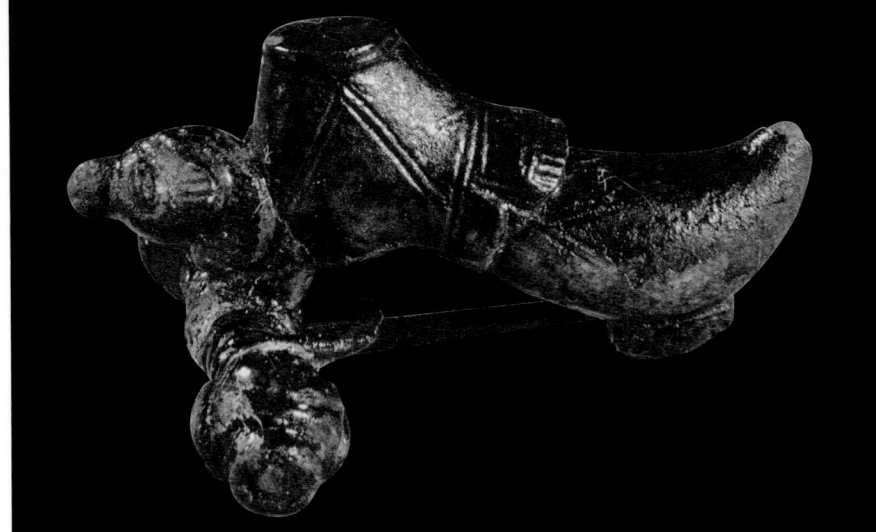

The Gallic people wear the 'sagus', let their hair grow long, and wear tight breeches; instead of tunics they wear slit tunics that have sleeves and reach as far as their private parts and the buttocks. The wool of their sheep, from which they weave the coarse 'sagi' (which they call 'laenae'), is not only rough, but also flocky at the surface.

STRABO, *Geography*, IV, 4, 3.

Celtic stone sculpture is poorly documented, compared to that of the Mediterranean world, probably because most sculptures were carved out of wood. However, some stone statues do exist, generally inspired by Mediterranean models. The oldest of these date from the 6th century BCE. Among them, the one that originally stood on a tumulus at Hirschlanden (Germany) is outstanding; it represents a naked man wearing a conical hat, a belt and a dagger. The richest 5th-century find comes from the lower Rhône Valley, from the sanctuary at Roquepertuse (in Aix-en-Provence). However, a recent discovery has unexpectedly enriched the treasury of Central European statuary from the beginning of the La Tène period. This had previously amounted to only half a dozen works, chiefly found in the Rhineland or in Baden-Württemberg, the best known being a carved stone pillar from Pfalzfeld and the fragments of a head wearing the double mistletoe-leaf motif discovered in the fortress of Závist.

But exploration of the monumental complex at Glauberg, north-east of Frankfurt, has unearthed a life-sized statue of a naked standing man equipped with a breastplate, shield and sword, along with fragments of three similar statues. Several other Central European works from subsequent centuries have been found (the Msecké Zehrovice head is the best known), but the largest group again comes from near Marseille. Excavated at Entremont (Aix-en-Provence), these sculptures date mostly from the beginning of the 2nd century BCE. However, by far the largest group of sculpted stones consists of the thousands of steles found in Armorica (Brittany). They have sometimes been associated with Iron Age burial-grounds, but generally their context is unclear, although their religious significance seems indisputable.

Information derived from classical writings and from the ever-increasing and precise data furnished by archaeology enables us to reconstruct a picture of ancient Celtic daily life and society that is vastly different to the widespread clichés. We see a diverse and prosperous agricultural economy, well-built and comfortable dwellings, a remarkable level of craftsmanship, and expanding commerce by land and sea. In sum, this was a colourful world, rustic yet somewhat refined, and not too dissimilar from our own modern way of life.

Left

Upper part of the beaked bronze flagon from Dürrnberg bei Hallein (Austria).

As with other ceremonial vessels of this kind, all the major figurative elements of the Celtic repertoire are employed here. (See pp. 178–181).

End 5th–early 4th century BCE. Total height: 458 mm.

Salzburg (Austria), Carolino Augusteum, Salzburger Museum für Kunst und Kulturgeschichte.

A society in transition

More than a thousand years elapsed between the Celts' first contact with the Mediterranean world and the arrival of Christianity in Ireland. It is hardly surprising that during such a long and eventful period, over such widespread and diverse territories, Celtic society changed. However, since available evidence is unevenly distributed chronologically and geographically, it is difficult to form a complete and detailed picture of local developments and characteristics.

The most valuable information on these aspects of the world of the ancient Celts comes from classical writings. Greek and Latin writers devoted several passages to the Celts of Italy in the 4th and 3rd centuries BCE, to the Celts of the Great Expedition (280 BCE) and to the Galatians, who were well known because they had been assimilated into a Hellenistic milieu. We also have a reasonably complete picture of Gaulish society from 100 to 50 BCE, essentially derived from Julius Caesar's *Gallic Wars*, and a colourful image of pre-Christian Irish society, largely as described in an authentically Celtic literature. In the first cases Celtic society was observed and described by outsiders; only with respect to Ireland can we say that our image of the society is drawn directly or indirectly from texts written by people living in that environment.

The Gauls described by Caesar were organized into powerful confederations of tribal communities united by common institutions, the *civitates* (cities), and with an urban network formed by the *oppida*. Ireland in the same period comprised many small tribal groups with very little interaction between them. There were no large settlements, and the only distinctive features in the sparse rural landscape were fortified enclosures (probably the residences of innumerable local dynasties) and 'royal' sites that were more places of worship than of settlement. The situation was comparable to that which probably existed in Gaul during the 6th and 5th centuries BCE, long before the formation of cities and the appearance of *oppida*.

These two systems are difficult to reconcile with a single image of the Celtic world. True, they did have features in common, indicating a certain relationship between Gaulish and Irish society, but the differences are so pronounced that one must abandon the idea of constructing a general theoretical model of ancient Celtic society. Indisputably, these were two very distinct stages in a long evolution that archaeology can help to chart and clarify, at least on the Continent. Recent excavations have given us a much better understanding of the development of these societies, with ever-increasing numbers of artefacts from burial-grounds providing precious information on the periods and regions for which written documentation is insufficient or non-existent.

Irish society embodies the more archaic of the two social systems that can be reconstructed from classical writings. The base unit is the family (*fine*), which encompasses several generations. The family taken in the wider sense (*derbfine*) – that is, five generations with a common ancestor – constitutes a clan. Several clans sharing the same territory form a tribe (*tuath*), ruled by a king. Ireland had some 150 of these petty kingdoms that in turn were grouped under the authority of regional rulers whose power generally seems to have been more ceremonial than real. The land was the collective property of the clan, so blood ties constituted the basis for both occupation of territory and the social structure. Such family bonds were of lesser importance in the urban Continental communities of the 1st century BCE, where cohesion was ensured primarily by economic and administrative imperatives.

Opposite

Sheet bronze plaque that decorated the chariot yoke above the guide-ring, from the princely burial at Waldalgesheim (Rheinland-Pfalz).

A figure with upraised arms with double mistletoe-leaf headdress, wearing a garment richly decorated with vegetal interlacings (see pp. 66–67).

4th century BCE. Height: 105 mm. Bonn (Germany), Rheinisches Landesmuseum.

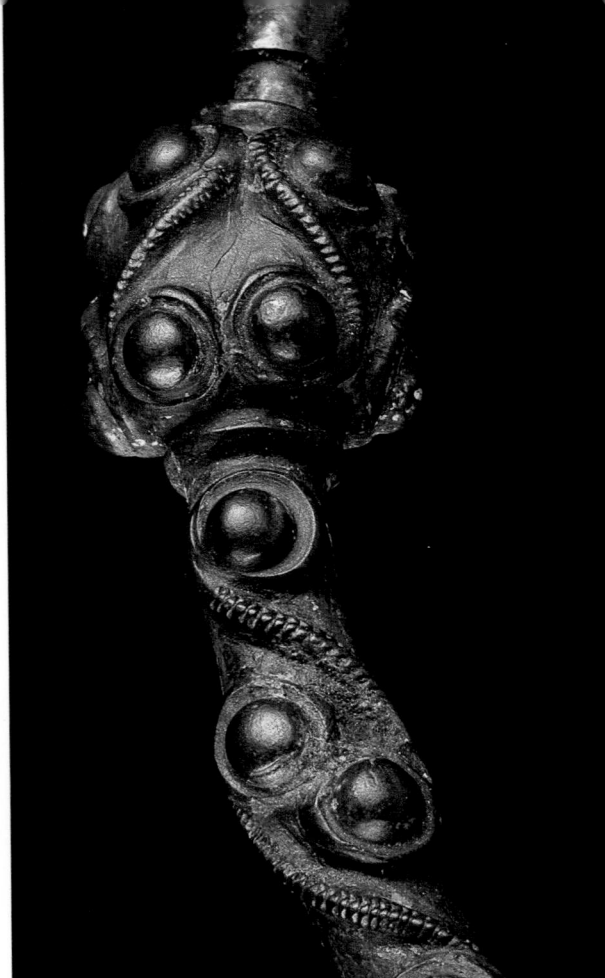

Left
Detail of a bronze torc with three cylindrical nodules decorated with S's, from grave No. 4, 'La Barbière' at Villeseneux (Marne).
See p. 144.
Early 3rd century BCE. Diameter of the nodules: 20 mm.
Épernay (Marne), Musée Municipal d'Archéologie et du Vin de Champagne.

Preceding pages
View of the elevation of the ground of the rectangular enclosure at Holzhausen (Bavaria).
Excavation of this enclosure revealed the presence of three ritual shafts and of a rectangular edifice, thought to be a temple; according to a likely interpretation of other similar enclosures, it appears to have been a sanctuary.
Dimensions of the enclosure: 90 m x 90 m (295 ft x 295 ft) approx.
Dimensions of the rectangular edifice: 6.5 m x 7 m (21.3 ft x 23 ft).
2nd–1st century BCE.

Irish women enjoyed rights little different from those of the men. The degree of independence of both related to their social standing: a noblewoman could possess goods in her own right, have a say in the choice of her husband, separate from him, accompany him to war and even fight alongside him. Some women even famously equalled the best male warriors in their combat skills. The hero CúChulainn was initiated into the secrets of martial arts by women, sorceresses who were particularly adept in this area. While this is mythology, it shows that the Irish Celts found nothing strange in the idea of warfare as an art practised by both men and women. If there was no male heir, a woman of the royal line could succeed directly to the throne; and she would rule, rather than her husband. Over the Irish Sea, similar female empowerment existed, as is indicated by the warrior-queen Boudicca, who assumed leadership of the Iceni after the death of her husband and wreaked revenge on the Romans. Meanwhile, Cartimandua, queen of the powerful Brigantes, allies of Rome, divorced her husband Venutius – who had become her political and military enemy – and took his equerry as her second husband.

Some Continental graves that feature artefacts only ever buried alongside members of regional dynasties, the 'princes' of the 6th–4th century BCE (drinking services used for community banquets, ceremonial chariots, ornaments manufactured from precious metals), are those of women, not men. The best known of these sites are those of Vix (Burgundy), Reinheim (Saar) and Waldalgesheim (Rhineland), datable to 350–300 BCE, at the very end of the period when this type of burial was practised.

The Celts had only one principal spouse. Other wives may have been taken but were considered of inferior rank, or simply used as concubines. Caesar tells us: 'The men, after due reckoning, take from their own goods a sum of money equal to the dowry they have received from their wives and place it with the dowry. Of each sum account is kept between them and the profits saved; whichever of the two survives receives the portion of both together with the profits of past years' (*Gallic Wars*, VI, 19). Although Caesar also related that the husband had the power of life and death over his spouse and children, the wife clearly was not, at least economically, in a subordinate position. In this region, therefore, general principles of society were the same as those in Ireland.

Opposite
Detail of a gold torc from the princely burial of a woman, discovered in 1954 at Reinheim (Saar).
The head of a divinity, possible female, with a headdress of a bird of prey and wearing a torc from which is suspended a trilobed palmette. See p. 183.
Second half of the 5th century BCE. Height of the detail: approx. 35 mm.
Saarbrücken, Museum für Vor- und Frühgeschichte.

Opposite
Detail of a bronze buffer torc from grave No. 3,
Hauviné 'Verboyon' (Ardennes).
Early 3rd century BCE. Diameter of the buffers: 32 mm.
Épernay (Marne, France), Musée Municipal d'Archéologie et du Vin de Champagne.

Women's jewellery, an expression of rank and ethnic identity

Until very recently, especially in rural districts, a woman's dress served as a kind of visual identity card: it signified that she belonged to a community, indicated her wealth and rank, and announced that she was single, married or widowed. The shape of the garments, their colours, the embroidered motifs, the accessories were all chosen according to strict unwritten rules, transmitted and respected down the generations. The Celts utilized a very similar system, especially before widespread urbanization. Our knowledge of these customs among Celtic society is limited, though, because it is only when the dead woman was buried with all her finery that we can examine this aspect of her garb, and this rarely happened during the *oppida* period. Unfortunately, of course, with a few rare exceptions, everything perishable – textiles, leather, human hair – remains unknown and may have played an important role. Nevertheless, metal jewellery has sometimes proved a valuable source of information, especially when it is found as it was positioned at burial. The choice and the way of wearing different ornaments – torcs, armbands, bracelets, anklets and rings – seem to follow strict rules relating to the woman's social position and her membership of a particular ethnic group, at least in some regions and chiefly from the 5th to the 3rd century BCE. Generally, certain jewellery was worn only by adult women who constituted the social elite of the community and whose number and location in burial-grounds lead us to assume they were the wives of the men buried with their weapons. Thus, women of rank among the Celts of Champagne sported, from the end of the Hallstatt period in the 5th century BCE, a torc and a pair of matching bracelets. Different shapes for the torc – open with terminals, closed with ternary decorations – would correspond in the following century to the two great ethnic groupings: the ancestors of the Remi in the north, and those of the Senones in the south. On the Swiss plateau, multiple tubular anklets were added to the torc and bracelets. Two shapes – the torc with terminals and another decorated with cabochons of coral or enamel, characteristic of the Rhineland – differentiated two geographically distinct locations. From the end of the 4th century/beginning of the 3rd century BCE, the Central–Eastern European distribution of the torc with cabochons is one of the most obvious indicators of the origin of some of the groups that settled in the Danube Valley at that time. The mingling of various sets of jewellery, a sign of new communities formed of mixed origins, was replaced by the wearing of anklets, initially with terminals, then with terrets, which became, from the beginning of the 3rd century, the chief sign of rank for women of that region. This type of jewellery, previously unknown in Champagne, is characteristic of the Danubian groups that settled there between 300 and 250 BCE. Therefore, female jewellery is a valuable resource in tracking the movements of individuals and groups during the period of Celtic expansion in the 4th and 3rd centuries BCE. It also assists in charting the formation of new ethnic groups.

Detail of a bronze anklet with nodules, from Plaňany (Bohemia).
See p. 145.
3rd century BCE.
Height of the nodules: 42 mm.
Prague, Národní Muzeum.

Left
Detail of a gold armring from Aurillac (Cantal).
Made of two overlapping rings, it was made up of fragments of two similar jewels, with reversed decoration.
3rd century BCE. Height of each body: approx. 10 mm.
Paris, Bibliothèque nationale, Cabinet des Médailles.

Within the tribe, social hierarchies were primarily established by the possession of cattle, since the land belonged to the clan and could not be privately owned. Those who owned livestock were freemen. This gave them a legal identity, with the right to bear arms and take part in the general tribal assemblies that elected the king. They could vote to depose him in the event of a serious misdemeanour, and they approved all important decisions.

Although ostensibly democratic, since it appeared to give much power to the assembly of freemen, this system was in reality controlled by a small proportion of the tribe: the great territorial chieftains on whom the rest of the community depended. The basis for this dependence was the institution of clientage, or a grant of livestock, based on contracts that established a bond between a patron and his client, designated in Ireland by the word *céle* (companion), the exact equivalent of the Gaulish *ambact*, used for those in a similar situation on the Continent. One type of contract made large interests – the equivalent of a third of the cattle – and the obligation to honour the lord and serve him in peace and war. At the beginning of the historical epoch, the contract was normally for three years, the interval between the major assemblies at which such contracts and vows of allegiance were renewed. A second form of contract was less restrictive, as the interests were less high.

It nevertheless required in return a particular surety: that the client should abandon his legal rights in favour of his patron. These were determined by his 'honour-price' or 'test-price': that is, the amount of compensation payable in damages by a third party. The client thus had no legal existence except through the mercy of his creditor; he was almost completely dependent and subject to conditions that made termination of the contract difficult if not impossible in normal circumstances.

Within this framework, a nobleman's place in the hierarchy depended on the number of clients of both types that he had. The nobles were thus divided into ranks, each of which had an honour-price proportional to its importance. This concept of the honour-price was fundamental to the pre-Christian Celtic legal code, as it specified a procedure not only for redressing wrongdoing but for every judicial action. The honour-price was the starting-point for a determination of the value of evidence, of an oath or a surety. It also dictated whether you could act as a plaintiff in a trial: it was impossible to bring an action against someone with a higher honour-price than you. Such actions required the intervention of a protector of higher rank, so it was important to seek support from the richest members of the community, those who owned enough livestock to have a large number of clients, further increasing their influence and giving still more weight to their legal standing. Julius Caesar notes a similar system of dependency in Gaul: 'The greater part, when they are pressed either by debt, or the large amount of their tributes, or the oppression of the more powerful, give themselves up in vassalage to the nobles, who possess over them the same rights without exception as masters over their slaves' (*Gallic Wars*, VI, 13).

A unique mutual dependency was therefore established between the nobles and their clients, the rank and standing of the former being determined by the latter. These links were reinforced by fosterage, a system peculiar to the Celts, in which children were educated within a family of the highest possible rank. The education ended when children reached the age at which they were considered marriageable and thus adult: fourteen for girls, seventeen for boys. We find an odd echo of this custom in the writings of Julius Caesar: 'Among the other usages of their life, they differ in this from almost all other nations, that they do not permit their children to approach them openly until they are grown up so as to be able to bear the service of war; and they regard it as indecorous for a son of boyish age to stand in public in the presence of his father' (*Gallic Wars*, VI, 18).

Opposite
Large gold torc, from the hoard discovered in 1948 at Snettisham (Norfolk, UK).
1st century BCE. Diameter of the loop terminal: 55 mm.
London, British Museum.

Beaked bronze flagon from chariot burial No.112, Dürrnberg bei Hallein (Austria).
Right, upper part.
Left, one of the monstrous animals on the rim. See p. 168.
End 5th–early 4th century BCE. Height: 458 mm.
Salzburg (Austria), Carolino Augusteum, Salzburger Museum für Kunst und Kulturgeschichte.

The child's foster family was recompensed by his or her natural parents, with the rate being fixed according to rank. The inevitable consequence of this economic levy must have been a form of self-selection according to the social hierarchy: clients sent their children to their patrons; the nobles sent theirs to the most powerful, generally royal, families; kings' sons and daughters went to other rulers who enjoyed special prestige. The advantages of this system included the direct influence and control that the highest social ranks exercised on the education of children, the establishment of bonds of loyalty between potential allies or enemies – prohibition of parricide and fratricide applied equally to foster families, with no time limit – and the security provided by the detention of hostages in the case of conflict.

The custom of fosterage certainly contributed to the fragmentation of ancient Irish society, but also to its remarkable stability. The multiple bonds that linked the different components of the social structure, as well as the role played by the extended family, helped to ease tensions and conflicts. These were raised with either the individual or the family (foster or natural) and resolved according to the legal code that applied to private affairs. This mechanism could operate even in the case of armed confrontations between tribes, which were considered to be an extension of individual disputes. Battle could thus be reduced to single combat between champions from both parties.

The king, cornerstone of the social structure, personified the tribe. He was the guarantor of harmony between the community and its land, which was considered sacred. The ideal ruler, according to ancient literature, was responsible for everything necessary to the prosperity of the community: a temperate climate, temperature and rainfall favourable to vegetation, an abundance of livestock and rich harvests, the absence of vermin and illness, peace and respect for the law. His responsibilities were therefore considerable, even if he could not presume to equal the legendary Conn, 'the best king of pre-Christian Ireland', in whose reign 'the earth was worked only a fortnight a month in springtime and gave a harvest three times a year. Cuckoos perched on cows' horns to sing. There were 100 grapes to a branch and 100 nuts to a cluster, nine furrows from every ear of corn. Calves gave milk early. The price for 12 bowls of honey and 12 bushels of wheat was an ounce of silver ... Ireland was like paradise ... with flowers full of honey' (*Airne Fíngein* [*Fíngein's Night-Watch*], 15).

Beaked bronze flagon from chariot burial No. 112, Dürrnberg bei Hallein (Austria).
Left, detail of the upper part of the handle: a monstrous animal, a kind of feline with a human head, rests its chin on a man's head on the rim of the vessel.

Right, detail of the base of the handle: a human head with animal ears, framed by S-spirals that terminate below with a trilobed palmette.
See pp. 168, 178–179.
End 5th–early 4th century BCE.
Salzburg (Austria), Carolino Augusteum, Salzburger Museum für Kunst und Kulturgeschichte.

'Handsome, amiable and prosperous' – all adjectives applied to Conn in the same text – perfectly describe the essential rules of good government. Prosperity would come through the recognition of two indispensable qualities: handsomeness, as in the integrity and physical strength needed to satisfy fully the sovereign's divine partner, the land over which he rules; and amiability, that is to say generosity towards the members of the tribe who chose the king to personify the community. So a physically disadvantaged king could constitute a danger, and had to be replaced or eliminated. Similarly, a king who kept his riches to himself also harmed the natural order. One of the sovereign's chief functions was to redistribute some of the taxes and other revenues he received, by organizing banquets and entertainments or by giving gifts to those who contributed to his glory – druids, poets, warriors and craftsmen. Not to do so was considered so reprehensible that it could lead to his dethronement. Thus, Bres, king of the mythical Tuatha Dé Danann, was deposed 'for their knives were not greased by him, and however often they visited him their breaths did not smell of ale. Moreover, they saw not their poets nor their bards nor their lampooners nor their harpers nor their pipers nor their jugglers nor their fools amusing them in the household. They did not go to the contests of their athletes. They saw not their champions proving their prowess at the king's court' (*The Second Battle of Mag Tured* [*Moytura*], 36). This story of Bres' fall sheds light on the role of poets. It is a satire – a kind of ironic verse curse declaimed before those concerned and as large an audience as possible – that would have precipitated the fall of the unworthy sovereign.

For the Celts, banquets were an essential element of social life. Given by the king or his richest nobles during great festivals, notably Samain and Lugnasad, but probably also to mark important events in the lives of the nobility – such as funerals and marriages – they brought together freemen of both sexes and different social classes and ages. Participation at the feast was obligatory, under pain of chastisement. The hierarchical order was respected in the strict division of the guests between those who sat in the hall and those who were outside (the less prosperous and the younger), and in the choice of food and drink with which they were served.

The 'Hero's Portion' recompensed those whose courage and warrior qualities were most famous; its award could give rise to debate and even lead to mortal combat. Gatherings of this kind were naturally an occasion to don the most sumptuous garb and to sport the finest jewellery, testifying to the skill of the craftsmen who had made it and to the wealth of those who had ordered it. This was also when poets, musicians, storytellers and historians could display their talent and learning. The prestige of the banquet's organizer was enhanced not only by the number and rank of those he brought together, but by the quality and variety of the entertainments presented for the guests. Those who could recount the brave deeds of ancestors and legendary heroes, who were able to compose poems or praise-songs, who could recite genealogies of noble guests were welcomed, well paid and enjoyed the privilege of expressing their discontent or disagreement by exercising the redoubtable weapon of satire.

The royal banquet, especially when it occurred during the great festivals, could certainly be called a social event, but it was primarily a religious ceremony, a sort of communion between the people and the ruler; whose responsibility it was, with the help of the druids, to ensure that nothing diverted the tribe's nurturing earth from its maternal, benevolent and generous role.

Giraldus Cambrensis, writing at the end of the 12th century CE, describes the inauguration of the king of an Ulster tribe, which illustrates particularly well the part he had to play in the perpetuation of vital forces. He first mated symbolically in public with a white mare, personifying the Earth. The animal was then slaughtered and boiled, before being eaten by the people and their king, who also bathed in the cooking broth. Of course, by this time Ireland had been Christian for many centuries, yet this ceremony has obvious parallels with pagan fertility rites. It displays the importance attached to a ruler's physical integrity: if he were mutilated or impotent, he would be unable to assume his role alongside the divinity and thus would endanger his people's harvests. The king had to be accepted by his divine companion: the Lia Fál (Stone of Destiny) at Tara was supposed to cry out, expressing on behalf of the soil of Ireland its acceptance of the new sovereign.

Left

Reverse of a debased silver coin of the Veneti of Armorica.
The horse with a human head, an evocation of the Sun in movement, replaces the pairing of the Greek prototype; it straddles a boar standard, an emblem signifying bellicose strength.
First half of the 1st century BCE. Diameter: 18 mm.
Rennes (Ille-et-Vilaine, France), Musée des Beaux-Arts et d'Archéologie.

Opposite

Statuette on the lid of a beaked flagon from the grave of the princess of Reinheim (Saar), representing a horse with a human head.
Wearing the double mistletoe-leaf headdress, the figure unites the three avatars of the sun god, corresponding to the three forms of life (see p. 173).
Second half of the 5th century BCE. Height: 52 mm.
Saarbrücken (Germany), Museum für Vor- und Frühgeschichte.

Although there are no Continental texts of equal richness and detail, archaeology enables a number of comparisons to be made between ancient Irish society and the 'princely' environment of the 6th and 5th centuries BCE. Grave-goods associated with banqueting are particularly enlightening in this respect, especially the drinking services that were sometimes designed to serve a great many people, with vessels that could hold several hundred litres of an intoxicating liquid, either wine or mead. An enormous amount of community wealth seems to be concentrated in these graves; the exceptional effort expended on burials and their monumental construction indicates the essential role these people played in the tribal community. Moreover, the imposing mounds are sometimes filled with secondary burials, as if the dead were escorting their protector to the other world. Considered in this light, these 'princes' are not simply the richest and most powerful members of tribal communities but are the representatives of a dynastic royalty with a religious foundation. Their apparent disappearance during the 4th century BCE (the grave of the 'princess' of Waldalgesheim is one of the latest to possess all the characteristic attributes) was probably due to the rise to prominence of dynamic, highly mobile communities who had broken their ancestral bonds with specific territories. For these groups, the warrior element and its own hierarchy thereafter played determining roles. The regions that seem to have been most affected by the Transalpine invasion of Italy are those where princely burials were few or poorly attested in the 5th century BCE.

The sacred aspect of kingship and its role as the symbolic link between the community and its territory seem to have disappeared completely after about 50 BCE. At this time Gaul was dominated by cities ruled by an oligarchy, powerful confederations of tribes governed collegially by the representatives of great aristocratic families.

The highest authority in the oligarchic system of government was always an assembly of freemen, those who had the right to bear arms. It seems, however, that this assembly was not regularly convoked; it met only in exceptional circumstances, such as a declaration of war. Power was retained, as least in cities like those of the Aedui, by a smaller group of prominent people – termed the *senatus* (senate) by Caesar – apparently chosen to represent the different tribes that comprised the city. This body annually elected the *vergobret* ('he who carries out sentences'), a magistrate who administered day-to-day affairs but had to submit all important decisions for approval by the senate or the full assembly of freemen. His power was limited to certain areas: taxes and duties seem to have been the province of other notables; and religious activities had, by that time, become the exclusive preserve of the druids.

The great feast at Tara

Every three years they were obliged to support the men of Ireland and to feed them for seven days and seven nights [...] No king used to go without a queen, or chieftain without a chieftainess, or warrior without ... or fop without a harlot, or hospitaller without a consort, or youth without a love, or maiden without a lover, or man without an art. The kings and ollaves [wise men] used to be placed around Diarmait son of Cerball, that is, kings and ollaves together, warriors and reavers together. The youths and maidens and the proud foolish folk in the chambers around the doors; and his proper portion was given to each one, that is, choice fruit and oxen and boars and flitches for kings and ollaves, and for the free noble elders of the men of Ireland likewise [...] red meat from spits of iron, and bragget and new ale and milk water for warriors and reavers [...] Heads-and-feet next and ... of all [kinds of] cattle to charioteers and jugglers and for the rabble and common people [...] Veal then and lamb and pork [...] for young men and maidens, because their mirth used to entertain them [...] free mercenaries and female hirelings carving and dispensing for them.
The Settling of the Manor of Tara,
Irish mythological text.

Reverse of a quarter-stater and obverse of a stater from the Gaulish city of the Parisii.
The image of the god on the right couples a headdress, seen frontally, with a face in profile. It took the advent of Cubism at the beginning of the 20th century to get back to such freedom in portrayal.
End 2nd–early1st century BCE. Diameter: 14 and 24 mm.
Brno (Czech Republic), Moravské Muzeum.

Gaulish society in the middle of the 1st century BCE, as described by Julius Caesar

'In Gaul there are factions not only in all the states [*civitates*], and in all the cantons [*pagi*] and their divisions, but almost in each family, and of these factions those are the leaders who are considered according to their judgement to possess the greatest influence, upon whose will and determination the management of all affairs and measures depends. And that seems to have been instituted in ancient times with this view, that no one of the common people should be in want of support against one more powerful; for, none [of those leaders] suffers his party to be oppressed and defrauded, and if he do otherwise, he has no influence among his party. This same policy exists throughout the whole of Gaul; for all the states are divided into two factions ...

'Throughout all Gaul there are two orders of those men who are of any rank and dignity: for the commonality is held almost in the condition of slaves, and dares to undertake nothing of itself, and is admitted to no deliberation. The greater part, when they are pressed either by debt, or the large amount of their tributes, or the oppression of the more powerful, give themselves up in vassalage to the nobles, who possess over them the same rights without exception as masters over their slaves. But of these two orders, one is that of the druids, the other that of the knights. The former are engaged in things sacred, conduct the public and the private sacrifices, and interpret all matters of religion. To these a large number of the young men resort for the purpose of instruction, and they [the druids] are in great honour among them. For they determine respecting almost all controversies, public and private; and if any crime has been perpetrated, if murder has been committed, if there be any dispute about an inheritance, if any about boundaries, these same persons decide it; they decree rewards and punishments; if any one, either in a private or public capacity, has not submitted to their decision, they interdict him from the sacrifices. This among them is the most heavy punishment. Those who have been thus interdicted are esteemed in the number of the impious and the criminal: all shun them, and avoid their society and conversation, lest they receive some evil from their contact; nor is justice administered to them when seeking it, nor is any dignity bestowed on them. Over all these druids one presides, who possesses supreme authority among them. Upon his death, if any individual among the rest is pre-eminent in dignity, he succeeds; but if there are many equal, the election is made by the suffrages of the druids; sometimes they even contend for the presidency with arms. These assemble at a fixed period of the year in a consecrated place in the territories of the Carnutes, which is reckoned the central region of the whole of Gaul. Hither all who have disputes assemble from every part, and submit to their decrees and determinations. This institution is supposed to have been devised in Britain, and to have been brought over from it into Gaul; and now those who desire to gain a more accurate knowledge of that system generally proceed thither for the purpose of studying it.

'The druids do not go to war, nor pay tribute together with the rest; they have an exemption from military service and a dispensation in all matters. Induced by such great advantages, many embrace this profession of their own accord, and [many] are sent to it by their parents and relations. They are said there to learn by heart a great number of verses; accordingly some remain in the course of training twenty years. Nor do they regard it lawful to commit these to writing, though in almost all other matters, in their public and private transactions, they use Greek characters. That practice they seem to me to have adopted for two reasons; because they neither desire their doctrines to be divulged among the mass of the people, nor those who learn, to devote themselves the less to the efforts of memory, relying on writing; since it generally occurs to most men that, in their dependence on writing, they relax their diligence in learning thoroughly, and their employment of the memory. They wish to inculcate this as one of their leading tenets, that souls do not become extinct, but pass after death from one body to another, and they think that men by this tenet are in a great degree excited to valour, the fear of death being disregarded. They likewise discuss and impart to the youth many things respecting the stars and their motion, respecting the extent of the world and of our earth, respecting the nature of things, respecting the power and the majesty of the immortal gods.

'The other order is that of the knights. These, when there is occasion and any war occurs (which before Caesar's arrival was for the most part wont to happen every year, as either they on their part were inflecting injuries or repelling those which others inflected on them), are all engaged in war. And those of them most distinguished by birth and resources have the greatest number of vassals and dependants about them. They acknowledge this sort of influence and power only'
(Julius Caesar, *Gallic Wars*, VI, 11–15).

Left
**Reverse of a gold coin attributed
to the Mediomatrices of the
northwest of Gaul.**
The solar horse surmounts a rosette
2nd century BCE. Diameter: 24 mm.
Milan (Italy), Civiche Raccolte Archeologiche e
Numismatiche.

When the Roman ambassadors arrived in
Gaul [in 218 BCE] '... a strange and appalling
sight met their eyes; the men attended
the council fully armed, such was the
custom of the country'.

TITUS LIVIUS, *The History of Rome*, XXI, 20.

There seems, therefore, to have been a division of the ancient
royal responsibilities. A number of people had specific duties,
and they generally held their positions temporarily to avoid the
development of a monopoly of power. There were severe
sanctions against those whose popularity or deeds seemed
designed to achieve personal domination, a clear sign that this
was a prime concern of those who put this system of
government in place. A few textual mentions, together with
archaeological evidence, suggest that a similar system existed
among other great tribes outside Gaul. Thus, the Boii who had
migrated into Italy comprised a confederation of 112 tribes,
governed in the 3rd century BCE by two *reguli* (petty kings),
probably elected for a limited period. They had a federal
sanctuary where the most important enemy trophies were
deposited. The Transpadane Insubres kept 'the golden
standards called immovable' (Polybius, *Histories*, II, 32) in a
similar sanctuary; these were removed only when war was
declared. When the Boii returned to Central Europe, they
retained the principle of appointing magistrates to short-term
tenures, as is attested by the fifteen or so names that feature
on coinage minted over only two or three decades in the
Bratislava *oppidum*.

The systems of government mentioned above must have had
many variants and evolutionary stages. For example, a king
in Continental Europe may have had a very different role to a
king in Ireland. This is certainly true for the pair of petty kings
of the Boii, and for Galatian royalty, which was a late form
modelled on Hellenistic sovereignty. Pre-Christian Ireland
and *oppida* Gaul represent two successive stages of Celtic
society. The Irish tribal version is older, with the king
symbolizing unity and the bond with the ancestral territory.
The later tradition of the Gaulish city maintained its cohesion
through common political and religious institutions among
the tribes that constituted it. While we know little of them,
the centralizing role of the *oppidum* is becoming increasingly
apparent. This urban agglomeration became the convergence
point for the activities of the territory and the place where
unity was manifested most clearly. The name *Mediolanon*
('middle of the country'), borne by some *oppida*, clearly
expresses this concept. It explains why, when the cohesion
and solidity of the Roman Empire were about to be
overthrown, the names of the Gaulish cities would be applied
to their principal urban centres, the direct successors of those
foci of independence, the *oppida*.

Opposite
Portico of a Celto-Ligurian sanctuary.
*This portico, with niches to display severed heads, was
found at Roquepertuse near Velaux (Bouches-du-Rhône).
Reconstituted in original stone, it is on display in the
museum of Mediterranean archaeology.*
5th century BCE. Height of the portico: approx. 3,000 mm.
Marseille (Bouches-du-Rhône, France), Musée d'Archéologie Méditerranéenne.

Following pages
Stone double-headed sculpture.
Height of the double head: approx. 230 mm.
Marseille (Bouches-du-Rhône, France), Musée d'Archéologie méditerranéenne.

The heroic ideal of the warrior

All available information on the ancient Celts confirms that the warrior element in their culture was crucial. Their military aptitude and their ability to mobilize and supply significant numbers of troops are evident from accounts of their struggles against Rome in Italy and later in Gaul. Even if this aspect of the Celtic world was somewhat overemphasized by classical writers, it undoubtedly reflects the general situation at the time, and was deeply embedded in the social system. There was a masculine, warrior elite in the Celtic world, as is indicated by the profusion of weapons that were buried alongside them. Moreover, even in Julius Caesar's time, participation in the assembly, the Celts' supreme tribunal, was reserved for men who had the right to bear arms.

Irish epics describe a society completely dominated by the heroic ideal of the warrior elite. This was a very similar world to the Greek one depicted in the Homeric epics. The sole preoccupation of those who wished to follow the example of the legendary heroes was military glory, the just reward for courage and pride, the principal virtues of those who defied death in order to conquer it. According to the Irish epic the *Táin Bó Cúailnge* ('The Cattle Raid of Cooley'; Cooley was located between modern Dundalk and Carlingford), when he was a child attending druidic school, CúChulainn, the hero of the kingdom of Ulster, overheard one day that the omens had decreed, 'the boy who today takes up arms will be brilliant and famous but his life will be short'. He immediately abandoned his games and hurried to ask the king for permission to become a warrior. After the king agreed, CúChulainn encountered the druid Cathbad, who confirmed the prediction that this hero's life would be cut short. CúChulainn's response perfectly expresses the heroic ideal: 'No matter whether I live but for a day and a night, if but my fame and my deeds live after me.'

Recounted during banquets and wakes, ancestors' glorious feats of arms – whether tribal or mythical – provided examples of proper conduct for every Celt from infancy and throughout his life. They inculcated a lively sense of honour and fame that demanded respect for certain rules: a dishonest victory was considered more degrading than a defeat inflicted by a stronger adversary, and it was inconceivable that a hero might die other than in battle. A Celtic warrior feared above all else that his reputation might be stigmatized or diminished. To be the butt of a poet's satire was the worst dishonour, as this tarnished the image that the warrior wished to leave to posterity.

Combat was not, however, solely a matter of physical strength, courage and skill in the handling of weaponry. Each warrior was conditioned by individual and sometimes contradictory constraints on his free-will, personal taboos called *geasa* that he was required to respect or defy (with whatever evil consequences this might entail). His weapons were endowed with magical virtues, and the heroes of the epics generally used supernatural resources they had learned to master during their apprenticeships. Having taken up arms and accomplished his first warrior exploits, CúChulainn moved to the island of Britain, where he spent three years perfecting his military education by learning about 'feats', powerful magical weapons. Their secrets were held by sorceresses who initiated the youth through sex. Thus educated and equipped with the mysterious and unstoppable *gae bolga* ('javelin in the bag'), CúChulainn would have been invincible were it not for his fatal *geasa*, those prohibitions that he must inevitably transgress, leading inevitably to his demise.

Opposite

Detail of the handle base of a flagon from the princely tomb of Waldalgesheim.

The head of a divinity wearing the double mistletoe-leaf is framed by a pair of serpentine monsters; inverted, they form outward-turned raptors' beaks and an undulating aigrette on top of the head. See p. 66 and 169.

4th century BCE. Height of the detail: approx. 45 mm.

Bonn (Germany), Rheinisches Landesmuseum.

Bronze fibula from Přemýšlení (Bohemia).

This figurative fibula, unique in its period, suggests a horse and a man, two avatars of the solar deity.

First half of the 3rd century BCE. Length: 70 mm.

Prague, Národní Muzeum.

Obverse of a silver coin of the Boii from the Carpathian basin, found at Esztergom (Hungary).

Early 1st century BCE. Diameter: 17 mm.

Budapest, Magyar Nemzeti Múzeum.

The magical power of the hero emerged during combat in the form of a murderous blind fury that could be turned on anyone. Thus, when the young CúChulainn returned from his first adventure, which culminated in the massacre of three warriors whose heads he brought home on his chariot, King Conchobar feared the worst: 'His hands are red with blood; he is not yet sated with fighting and if we do not take care he will kill all the warriors of Emain [the capital of the kingdom of which he was the champion].' To calm CúChulainn, the king sent a hundred naked women to meet him, but 'he hid his face ... and did not see the nakedness of the women ... To cool his rage, three barrels of fresh water were brought to him. When he was placed in the first, the water heated so much that the staves and hoops of the cask burst, like the cracking of a nut. When he entered the second vat, the water boiled with bubbles as big as a fist. When he went into the third cask, the heat was such that some men might endure it and others might not. Thus cooled, the boy's wrath diminished.'

This trance-like state that liberated the magical power of the hero could be self-induced by paroxysms, as displayed by CúChulainn before he attacked 150 sons of noble clients at the court of King Conchobar. 'It seemed as if at the blow of a hammer each of his hairs returned to his head by the place from whence it grew. It appeared as if each of his hairs threw forth a fiery spark. He closed one of his eyes until it was no larger than the eye of a needle; he opened the other until it became as big as a beaker of mead. He stretched his jaws until his mouth reached his ears. He opened his mouth so wide that the back of his throat could be seen. The hero's light sprang from his forehead.' This 'hero light', the mark of those chosen by fate, accompanied CúChulainn to the end of his life. When he was mortally wounded, he 'reached the standing stone that is on the plain and bound himself to it by his belt so that he was neither sitting nor lying, that he might die standing. Then his enemies stood around him, but they did not dare approach him; he seemed as if he were still living ... then the Grey of Macha [survivor of the two horses that drew his chariot] drew close to CúChulainn to protect him while his soul was still in his body and the hero light still shone from his brow.' Only later could the hero's corpse be decapitated, his head being taken for a trophy, following a custom attested also on the Continent by classical writers and much archaeological evidence.

Following page

Openwork iron spearhead, from grave No.3 of 'La fin d'Écury' at Fère-Champenoise (Marne).

Second third of the 3rd century BCE. Length: 620 mm.

Épernay (Marne, France), Musée Municipal d'Archéologie et du Vin de Champagne.

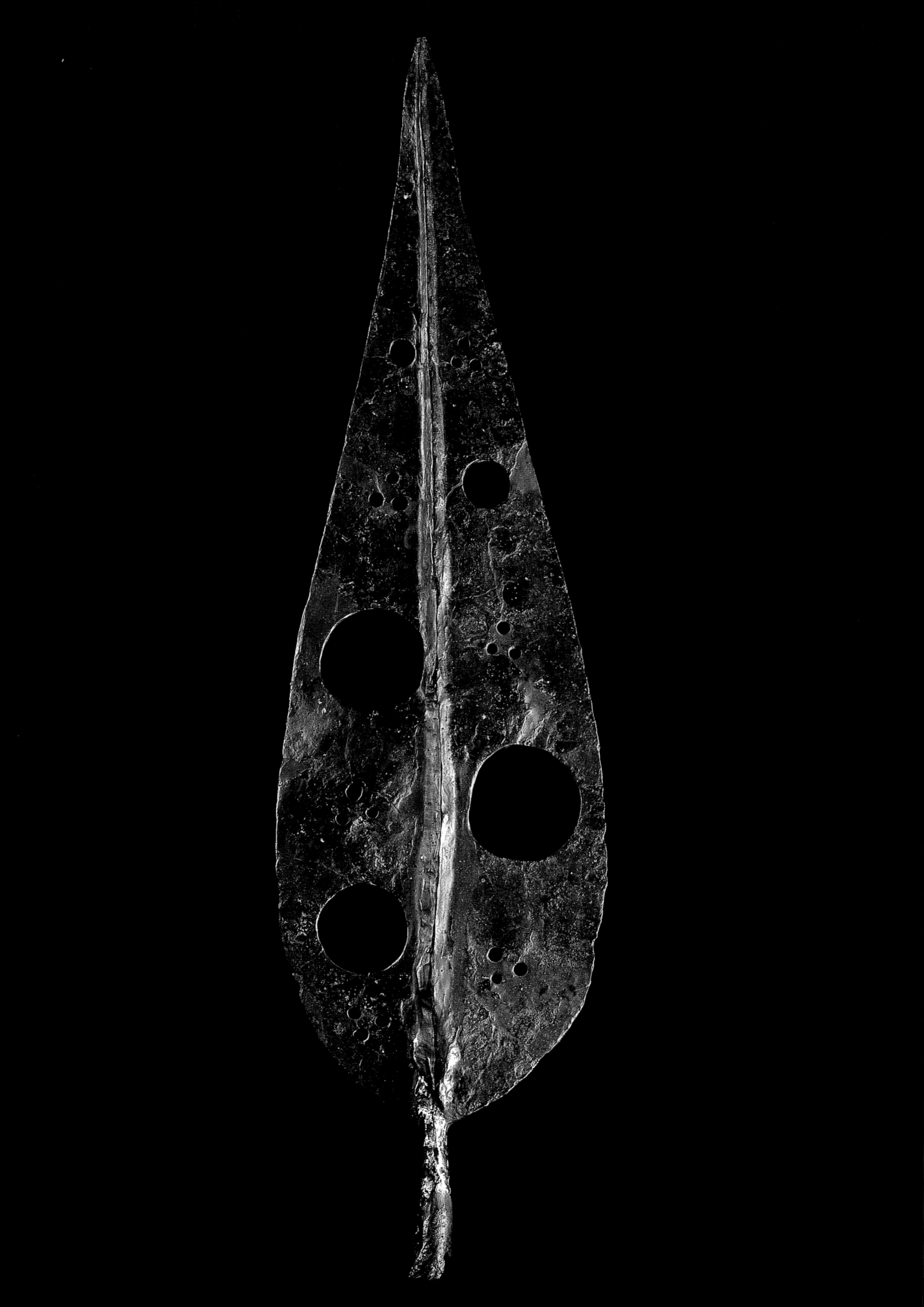

Left
Bronze cover-mount of a wooden flagon from Brno-Maloměřice (Moravia).
An unusual version of the paired serpentine monsters with griffons' heads: they are overlapping, the head of the second one appearing behind the only one visible at first sight; the curious crest is inspired by the Hellenistic image of the ketos *or sea-dragon. See p. 213.*
First half of the 3rd century BCE. Height: 90 mm.
Brno (Czech Republic), Moravské Muzeum.

Previous page
Detail of bronze armring from Troyes 'La Charme' (Aube), found in 1875 with a sword with a gold-inlaid anthropomorphic handle.
Here we see the theme of two heads joined at the crown.
3rd century BCE. Height of the detail: approx. 50 mm.
Troyes (Aube, France), Musée des Beaux-Arts et d'Archéologie.

Setting aside the exaggeration and the supernatural elements, the legend of CúChulainn undoubtedly provides a reasonably faithful picture of the life of a noble warrior in pre-Christian Ireland. First raised by his parents, the child would be sent to the royal court at the age of five. There he and other noble youths would learn various skills, including the use of wooden weapons, and would be trained through individual exercises and team sports, including the popular báine, which seems to have been an ancient version of hurley. He might also benefit from rudimentary literary instruction, but this was the special province of the druidic schools, where the country's intellectual elite was trained.

The future warriors were bound by the same rules as adults, and they established among themselves bonds of dependence. Thus, because he had neglected to ask for their protection, as a form of welcome CúChulainn was attacked by those who wanted to become his companions. Although he could easily overcome these assailants, the young hero had to submit; if he did not abide by this unwritten law, he would be refused entry into the group. Nevertheless, he immediately turned against the other youths and demanded that they put themselves under his protection. He thus became champion of the youth of Ulster, and later that of the whole kingdom. The decisive moment, when he took up arms, was exceptionally precocious in the case of CúChulainn, for he was only seven. This ceremony normally occurred at the end of the education with foster parents, when a youth was about seventeen. The young man then received his standard armoury, the *geissed*, which comprised a spear and shield. This could later be supplemented with javelins and a sword.

A warrior of rank used a chariot handled by a driver who cared for the vehicle and the horses but who did not take part in battle. The Irish term *eirr*, designating the hero, literally means 'man with a chariot'. There is evidence that this light two-wheeled vehicle, drawn by a pair of ponies coupled to a yoke, was used in European warfare as far back as the 2nd millennium BCE. However, Continental Celts seem to have adopted it only from the 5th century BCE onwards. Chariots found in the graves of local chiefs or petty kings from Champagne to south Bohemia were features of the development of La Tène culture. Their use in warfare was first documented in a passage about a chariot-charge by the army of the Italian Gauls at the Battle of Sentinum in 295 BCE. As has been mentioned, the chariot was abandoned in the following century, to be replaced by cavalry, but it remained in use rather longer in the British Isles, where it was used against both Caesar and, in the late 1st century CE, Agricola. Julius Caesar described the use of these chariots in battle in a way that corresponds remarkably with the Irish epics:

> Firstly, they drive about in all directions and throw their weapons and generally break the ranks of the enemy with the very dread of their horses and the noise of their wheels; and when they have worked themselves between the troops of horse, leap from their chariots and engage on foot. The charioteers in the meantime withdraw some little distance from the battle, and so place themselves with the chariots that, if their masters are overpowered by the number of the enemy, they may have a ready retreat to their own troops. Thus they display in battle the speed of horse, [together with] the firmness of infantry; and by daily practice and exercise attain such expertise that they are accustomed, even on a declining and steep place, to check their horses at full speed, and manage and turn them in an instant and run along the pole, and stand on the yoke, and thence betake themselves with the greatest celerity to their chariots again. (*Gallic Wars*, IV, 33)

Opposite
Bronze mounting (perhaps for a chariot or wooden bucket) from Stanwick (Yorkshire, UK).
A model of simplicity, this exemplary Celtic artwork creates the head of a horse from two leaves that simultaneously curve into large S's.
3rd–1st century BCE. Height: 109 mm. London, British Museum.

Opposite
Bronze facing of a ceremonial or votive shield, inlaid with red enamel, found in 1857 in the Thames at Battersea, London.
See pp. 128–129.
2nd century BCE. Height: 775 mm. London, British Museum.

The cost of keeping a chariot, horses and a permanent charioteer, as well as the demands of intensive training as described by Caesar, clearly indicate that this military elite was recruited from the ranks of the nobility, the only people with the necessary time and means. Their ideal peacetime occupation was not very different to that of the legendary King Conchobar, famed for his warrior qualities: 'As soon as he got up he began to put the affairs of the province in order. Then he divided his day into three parts. He began by watching the children of the nobility engage in feats of skill, he played, throwing bowls, then he played backgammon and chess [not the same game as the modern version; more like draughts]; he passed the third part in feasting and drinking until everyone was drowsy, when the musicians played them to sleep.'

Armed conflicts between different communities were numerous, and cattle rustling (or defensive measures against such pillage) must have been rife. The fundamental role that livestock played in the establishment of the social hierarchy, and the possibilities for advancement thanks to the bonds established made it highly desirable. The central episode of *Táin Bó Cúailnge* deals with the bloody battles that resulted from the theft of a magnificent brown bull coveted by Queen Medb (Shakespeare's Queen Mab), ruler of Connaught, who wishes to possess at any price an animal as fine as the white bull owned by her husband Ailill. What seems to have begun as a simple marital quarrel over personal prestige quickly degenerates into a widespread conflict between the kingdoms of Ulster and Connaught, where the most brilliant members of the warrior elite confront and kill one another.

This epic, distorted and exaggerated, seems to be an essentially mythological account of one of the many wars of ancient Ireland, but set within a specific historical and geographical framework. The role of CúChulainn, the tribal champion who must confront challenges in the name of his people and maintain constant watch over the frontiers of the territory, corresponds to an archaic concept of the hero. It is very different to that presented in the most recent Irish epic, called the 'Leinster cycle' after the south-eastern kingdom whose supremacy it exalts. This cycle became famous thanks to a pastiche published in 1760 by the Scottish poet James Macpherson, who attributed it to Ossian, supposedly a bard and warrior of the 3rd century BCE, a character inspired by Oisín, who appeared in earlier Irish texts.

The ideal warrior of the Leinster cycle is incarnated by the *Fianna*, young men of noble descent who dedicate their lives to hunting and the practice of arms, but who no longer form part of the traditional framework of the tribal community. Organized into a warrior confraternity led by Finn, father of Oisín, living on the margins of society, they traverse Ireland, acting as mercenaries for rulers. The *Fianna* respect a warrior code of honour similar to that of tribal champions such as CúChulainn, but, for them, war is an end in itself, a vocation that implies a definitive rupture of the bonds that unite the individual to a territory. Finn and his companions represent an idealized military class that values the power to break free from the constraints imposed by the tribal system of dependency. They are able to do this by exploiting their professional military competence at a time when many rulers need it most.

As with the Ulster cycle, the written version of this epic, with its geographical and historical framework, involved the transformation of an essentially mythological vernacular literature whose antiquity and origin remain obscure. But as the warrior function is dissociated from the tribal structure, it would seem to come from a society that has rejected those individuals who consider a military career to be the only one compatible with their status as noble freemen. This situation would probably have occurred later than the time of the Ulster cycle, but the two concepts could have co-existed. It is conceivable that rogue elements in the military elite (such as Finn) could have been marginalized in an attempt to provide a provisional solution to internal crises of the tribal system. This type of warrior ideology probably corresponds best to the professional status of soldiers observable among the Continental Celts of the 4th and 3rd centuries BCE, a period when military expeditions and mercenary employment offered many opportunities to those who sought riches and adventure.

Opposite

Detail of the openwork iron appliqué on a scabbard of the same metal, from grave No. 8 of the 'La Perrière' burial ground at Saint-Benoît-sur-Seine (Aube).

Two griffon-headed monsters are represented in reverse, the curved beak turned inwards, as on the Waldalgesheim handle (see p. 192).

First half of the 3rd century BCE. Length: 71 mm.

Troyes (Aube, France), Musée des Beaux-Arts et d'Archéologie.

Warriors and dragons

From the middle of the 5th century BCE, the motif of opposing pairs of highly stylized monsters, called 'dragon pairs' by archaeologists, began to appear at the top of sword scabbards. They are the monstrous guardians of the Celtic tree of life, the vegetal avatar of the solar god, dispenser of life, responsible for universal order, who also took the form of a horse, sometimes with a human head. The palmette, the symbolic representation of the tree, is sometimes shown between the monsters. This design was sometimes found decorating the scabbard plate; in the following century it became an emblem or protective sign that probably also signalled that the owner belonged to a supra-tribal organization of warriors, one of the brotherhoods that Polybius described as '*hetaireia*', similar to the *Fianna* in Irish legends. The term 'dragon pair' covers two distinct emblems: the dragon proper, with the body of a serpent; and another beast, generally with the head of griffin, the curved beak of a bird of prey and, sometimes, small pointed ears. This latter monster stands on hind legs – head turned backwards, body extended by a curved wing that meets the beak to form a ring. Sometimes the motif may have been transformed to the point of being difficult to identify, as, for instance, in the scabbard of Cernon-sur-Coole – where both monsters are represented, accompanied by a half-palmette and caught in a tangle of curves – and on some Danubian scabbards where the design is cryptically woven into a composition that, at first glance, seems purely abstract.

To date, more than 200 scabbards decorated in this way have been found throughout La Tène Europe, from Britain to the Carpathians and from north Bohemia to the valley of the Ebro, with concentrations in some regions where documentary and archaeological evidence confirm a Celtic military presence linked to mercenary service, expeditions or population migrations: northern Italy, the territories of the Danubian expansion, the Champagne region in the 3rd century BCE, the Rhône Valley and the site of Ensérune (also in France). The most recent examples decorated with this emblem come from the south-eastern periphery of the Celtic world and date from the beginning of the 2nd century BCE.

Decoration of an iron scabbard from Bölcske-Madocsahegy (Hungary).

Two allusive faces can be discerned: the larger one wears the double mistletoe-leaf headdress; the other is smaller and horned. Inverted, the scabbard shows an evocation of a face surrounded by the double-leaf, framed by a pair of griffon-headed monsters, beaks turned inwards. This is a good example of the supernatural representation typical of Celtic art at its height.

3rd century BCE. Length: 57 mm.

Budapest, Magyar Nemzéti Múzeum.

Left to right

Upper part of an iron scabbard from Casalecchio di Reno near Bologna (Italy).

The decoration is engraved (emblem of a pair of stylised griffons) and is created in relief with the aid of a mould (vegetal frieze).

4th century BCE.

Iron scabbard from incineration burial No. 6, Dobova (Slovenia).

3rd century BCE.

Iron scabbard from Magyarszerdahely (Hungary).

Second half of the 3rd century BCE.

Fragment of iron scabbard from Dvorovi kod Bijejline (Bosnia).

Emblem of a pair of serpentine monsters ('zoomorphic lyre').

First half of the 3rd century BCE.

Coral-inlaid iron scabbard, from inhumation grave No.163, Ensérune (Hérault, France).

First half of the 3rd century BCE.

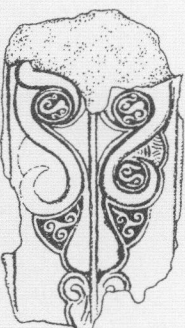
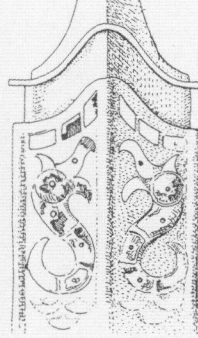

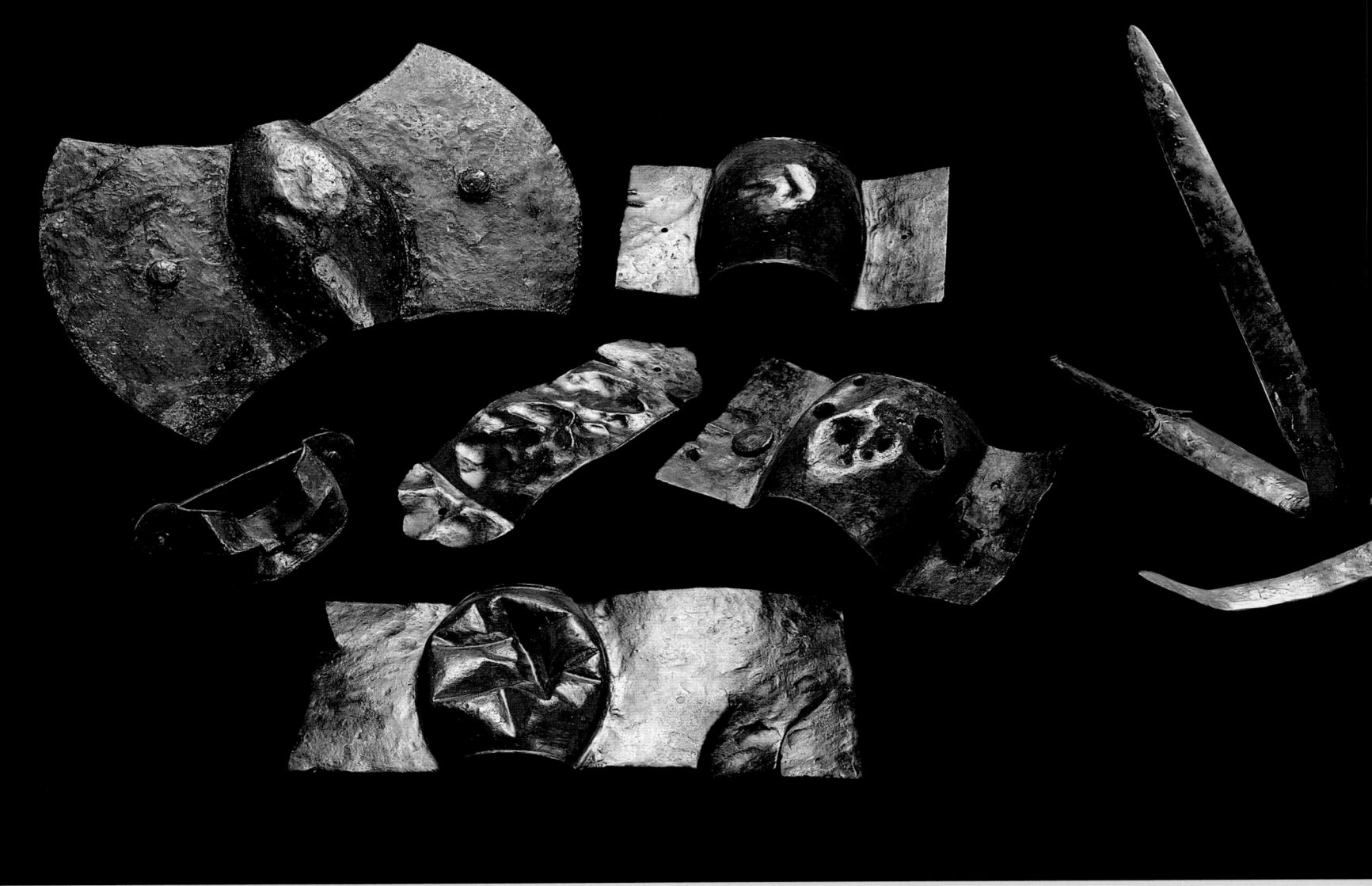

'Sacrificed' iron weapons, which were ritually deformed,
from the sanctuary at Gournay-sur-Aronde (Oise).
Left to right, shield bosses, swords, spearheads and tips.
3rd century BCE. Various scales. Compiègne (Oise, France), Musée Antoine-Vivenel.

Sacrificial arms and battle trophies

Excavations undertaken in northern France
at the end of the 20th century, especially in
Picardy, have drawn attention to particular
cult locations, directly connected with the
warrior ideology and unknown in other
parts of the Celtic world to date. These often
complex enclosures show traces of unusual
sacrificial practices and the display of
weapons and bodies.
At Gournay-sur-Aronde (Oise), weapons,
chiefly dating to 300–250 BCE, were first
displayed on an embankment, perhaps on

gruesome mannequins – which might have
been created from the bodies and bones of
enemies or sacrificed prisoners – then ritually
destroyed and thrown into a ditch, where
they accumulated. Skulls of cattle and
humans formed part of a kind of portico that
constituted the monumental entry to the
enclosure. Inside, facing the entry, was a
rectangular edifice under which was a ditch
containing the bones of cattle that had been
deposited whole and left to decompose on
the spot, probably after being sacrificed.

The ditch also yielded many bones of animals
that, unlike the sacrificed cattle, had been
cooked and eaten, seemingly during feasts
organized in the enclosure. This ditch also
contained several thousand La Tène weapons:
belt chains, tips and shafts of lances, metal
pieces from breastplates, swords and
scabbards (750 artefacts, of which a quarter
carry an identifying decoration).
A Ribemont-sur-Ancre (Somme), two distinct
enclosures seem to have separately received
and displayed the remains of more than a

hundred of the vanquished and around forty of the victors killed in the course of a great battle that probably took place nearby between 300 and 250 BCE. Complex rites of decapitation and dismemberment of the bodies and the weapons took place, transforming this trophy-memorial into a sanctuary. Julius Caesar eloquently described places of this kind: 'To him [a Celtic god associated by Caesar with the Roman Mars], when they have determined to engage in battle, they commonly vow those things which they shall take in war. When they have conquered, they sacrifice whatever captured animals may have survived the conflict, and collect the other things into one place. In many states you may see piles of these things heaped up in their consecrated spots; nor does it often happen that any one, disregarding the sanctity of the case, dares either to secrete in his house things captured, or take away those deposited; and the most severe punishment, with torture, has been established for such a deed' (*Gallic Wars*, VI, 17).

As has been discussed, the military expansion of the Celts that occurred at the beginning of the 3rd century BCE was driven by highly mobile groups operating outside the tribal system. The armed bands that reached the Balkans and eventually formed the Galatians in Asia Minor and the new tribes of the west were not dissimilar to the Irish Fianna. Initially comprising diverse elements, thanks to attracting new recruits from the regions they passed through as their expeditions proceeded, they ultimately formed new ethnic entities outside existing societies. When they finally settled, they based their communities on a model that was not centred on the tribe but on a confederation organized along military lines. The Galatian community, the *koinon Galatôn*, perfectly illustrates this model, which is probably the origin of the sudden emergence in different regions of Celtic Europe of new ethnic groups, such as the Belgae, the Volcae and others.

These military brotherhoods who travelled across Europe would have been inspired by a warrior ideal very close to that exemplified by the heroes of the Leinster cycle, but the tribal epic was nevertheless still appreciated. However, it became necessary to complete it with verses that reflected the shift in relations between certain warriors and society. Therefore, the epic of which the Leinster cycle is probably a distant echo might have been the literary equivalent of the development and remarkable expansion of plastic art at that time chiefly evident in the decoration of weapons.

The persistence of the ideal of a life dedicated to warfare, culminating in 'good death' in battle – one that led in the next world to membership of an elite of immortal heroes who feasted while recounting their glorious exploits – is well illustrated by an episode in the Battle of Telamon (225 BCE), which Polybius described, probably from an eyewitness account. At this battle the Gaulish coalition's army included 'naked warriors in front, all in the prime of life, and finely built men, and all in the leading companies richly adorned with gold torcs and armlets'. These were the Gaesatae – the Celtic name for mercenaries, according to Polybius – from the Alps and the Rhône Valley, who 'had discarded these garments owing to their proud confidence in themselves, and stood naked, with nothing but their arms, in front of the whole army'. The Greek historian explained the gesture by suggesting that 'some of the ground was overgrown with brambles which would catch in their clothes and impede the use of their weapons' (*Histories*, II, 28–9). This shows a complete lack of understanding of the motivation of these warrior aristocrats: they were indifferent to death and their heroic nakedness simply anticipated the eternal rank and glory they would earn by upholding to the end the principles that had guided them throughout life.

The aggression of these 3rd-century military groups led to many conflicts, particularly when they settled permanently in territories that might be coveted by other communities. Thus, the turbulent evolution of the tribes in north Gaul, the Belgae, who formerly comprised mobile armed bands, is reflected in that part of the Celtic world by monuments and sanctuaries where the weapons and spoils of the dead testify to the violence and frequency of battles up to 250 BCE.

The prestige of the Celtic heroic ideal was probably undimmed by the settlement of the armed groups that criss-crossed Europe in the 3rd century BCE in search of battles and adventure. Similarly, by establishing a warrior aristocracy, especially the cavalry, in the *oppida*, the old principles were maintained. And they would still be resonant many centuries later, among the knights of Arthur, son of the 'dragon chief' Uther Pendragon, the warrior king who waited on the isle of Avalon for the day when he could fight to liberate the oppressed Britons.

The Brno-Maloměřice flagon (Moravia).
See pp. 142 and 208–219.

*Left, detail of one of the openwork appliqués on the body.
Opposite, view of the upper part of the mount for the tubular spout.
The following pages show a detail of the main openwork mount on the body.*
First half of the 3rd century BCE. Brno (Czech Republic), Moravské Muzeum.

Images of the gods

The ancient Celts themselves, of course, never recorded details of their gods and their belief system. However, there are several secondary sources to which we can turn: classical writers discussed these topics, as did Irish and Gallic literature from the Middle Ages; and the ancient Celts' figurative works of art provide an invaluable first-hand testimony, albeit one that is open to widely different interpretations. Unfortunately, the religious images that we have almost certainly relate to only a fraction of the Celtic pantheon, probably the gods most venerated by the rich members of the social elite composed chiefly of the warrior aristocracy. Together with the rather esoteric character of Celtic art, this explains the preponderance and variety of the images of Gallo-Roman gods, compared with the much smaller number of themes identifiable in the previous epoch. From these sources we may form only a fragmentary and not entirely coherent picture of the ancient Celts' spiritual world. Indeed, it remains difficult to appreciate its evolution over time, as well as the impact of the beliefs of native peoples, generally of non-Indo-European descent, in the various regions where the Celts settled. Nevertheless, at least a sense of the antiquity and scope of Celtic religious practice may be gleaned.

Like the majority of the belief systems in antiquity, the Celtic religion was apparently flexible. It seems to have centred on several important, ancient gods, the protagonists in a mythological environment common to the various Celtic groups. This composite pantheon brought together a multitude of tribal gods, local pre-Celtic divinities and cults specific to certain social categories. The Irish mythological cycle demonstrates that the hierarchy of this divine world was thought to result from a series of fierce battles between successive generations of gods for dominion over the universe. This war began during the primordial chaos and led eventually to the establishment of an order maintained by the supremacy of the leading Celtic gods and the annihilation or submission of the others. The relationships of the divinities, based on an ordered hierarchy, were in part a model for those of humans. It was believed that the victory of one group of humans over another was due to the superior power of their gods, which implied a dependent relationship between the respective tutelary divinities. This, in turn, reflected the situation established on earth between the victor and the vanquished. Julius Caesar was the first to list the major Gaulish gods, and to define, clearly and succinctly, their functions. Unfortunately, he did not give their Gaulish names, but simply listed the Roman gods that, in his estimation, were their counterparts. In first place he cited Mercury, the most honoured: '[T]he inventor of all arts, they consider him the guide of their journeys and marches, and believe him to have great influence over the acquisition of gain and mercantile transactions' (*Gallic Wars*, VI, 17). In him we can recognize Lug, the great multi-functional and supreme sun god, whose name is found in several Celtic regions. He is Lugh ('the Shining One') of Irish mythology, the ruler of the Tuatha Dé Danann ('the People of the Goddess Dana'), the last generation of the gods. One of Lugh's epithets was 'Samíldánach' ('Many-Skilled'), and he was frequently called 'Long-Arm', which, together with his predilection for the javelin and the sling, confirms his solar nature. Like the bow and arrows of Apollo, the choice of these weapons symbolizes the ability of the sun's rays to strike from a distance. As a divine prototype of royal duty, Lugh lay with his mate Eithne, the land of Ireland, to engender the hero CúChulainn, whose earthly birth was accomplished by tricking Deichtire, the sister of King Conchobar.

Next, Caesar names Apollo, who 'averts diseases'; Mars, who 'presides over wars'; Jupiter, who 'possesses the sovereignty of the heavenly powers'; Minerva, who 'imparts the invention of manufactures'. The divinities cited by Caesar point to the expression of the three central functions of Indo-European theogony: sovereign and sacred (Jupiter), warrior (Mars) and productive (Apollo and Minerva). Mercury (Lug) effectively combines all three functions.

Opposite
The Brno-Maloměřice flagon (Moravia).
Side view of the mount for the tubular spout.
See pp. 208, 210–211 and below.
First half of the 3rd century BCE. Total height: 470 mm approx.
Brno (Czech Republic), Moravské Muzeum.

A masterpiece of Celtic art: the Brno-Maloměřice flagon

In 1941, remarkable bronze mountings that had originally been attached to an object made of organic materials (now decomposed) were discovered at Brno-Maloměřice in Moravia. They were excavated from a pit in a Celtic burial-ground dating from between 300 and 250 BCE. It was probably an incineration burial, and contained no other grave-goods. The 16 principal pieces in this group of artefacts (which also included 13 items in sheet bronze worked in repoussé and 38 small beaten-bronze nails) had been made by the lost wax method. Originally, the mountings were thought to be the metallic fittings of a wooden wine cask with a tubular spout, and they were unfortunately mounted for a time as ornaments on a wagon yoke. However, the latest reconstruction, the convincing result of sophisticated research, suggests a contemporary pottery shape that corresponds perfectly with the curvature of the chief pieces.

The moulded fittings display a remarkably high quality of workmanship, effortlessly fusing abstract symbols with human, animal and vegetal motifs. They undoubtedly represent a major triumph of Celtic art. All the principal themes of the Celtic repertoire are all included, skilfully integrated into compositions that the eye, blinded by the dynamic of the whole, cannot initially decipher. Thus, twin heads (also represented on another piece) decorate the base of the tubular spout. Near the base, a disturbing head with human and animal features bears a headdress of two long, striated S's that terminate, on the other side, in a trilobed palmette that forms the lower part of a upturned face. Its central part is hollow and the eyes are surmounted by a prominent horned forehead. These various natural elements appear or disappear, depending on the orientation of the object, how it is lit and the viewer's state of mind.

The second double head is more obvious. Soldered together at the neck and reversed like mirror-images, the two heads are framed in long leaves. One has lateral, horn-like protuberances; the other wears a palmette. The lid of the receptacle was surmounted with a curved piece representing a serpent-bodied monster, endowed with a decorated crest borrowed from the Hellenistic sea dragon (the *ketos*), the head of a griffin, a bird of prey's beak and the typical crests. The second of the two dragons who guard the tree of life, the companions of the god the Celts associated with mistletoe, is also represented. His body overlaps the first, his head is smaller, and his beak upturned, forming a protuberance behind the ring. One has to be looking for him in order to spot him. Different variants and assemblies of the dragon motif make up a net decorating the body of the vessel, a tangle of heads and bodies that is difficult for the eye to unscramble.

The final important figurative element is a human mask, whose oblique position in relation to a kind of four-pointed coiffure renders it particularly expressive. Compared to older Celtic flagons, the Brno-Maloměřice example is outstanding for its particular emphasis on themes cherished by the military elite of the period, notably the dragons that decorated their scabbards.

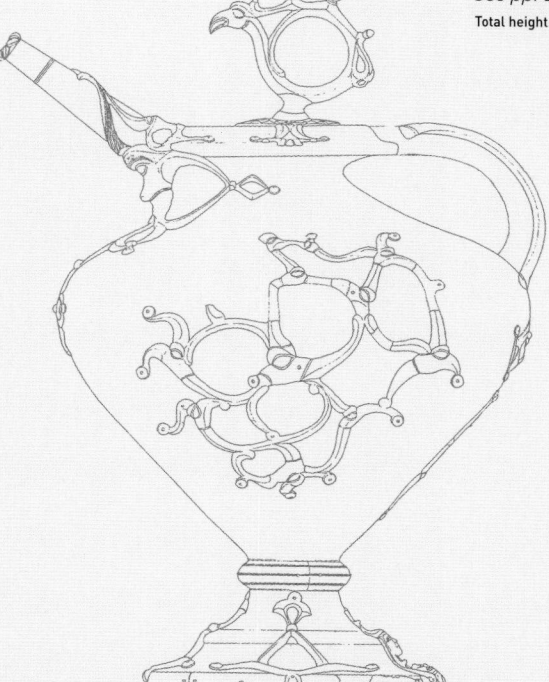

Diagrammatic reconstruction of the Brno-Maloměřice flagon (Moravia) with its bronze mounts.
The shape of the vase was deduced from the curves of the different pieces and in relation to the shapes of the most appropriate pottery vases of the first half of the 3rd century BCE. The exact position of the metal mounts is uncertain, except for those of the cover, the top of the handle and the base. See pp. 208–219.
Total height: approx. 470 mm.

The Brno-Maloměřice flagon (Moravia).

Left, detail of the ring with serpentine griffon-headed monsters that decorated the cover (see p.196).
Opposite, openwork mounting representing a double head.
Following pages, openwork mounting of the body (see p. 208).
First half of the 3rd century BCE. Brno (Czech Republic), Moravské Muzeum.

The second important classical text is a brief passage from the poet Lucan that cites the three great Gaulish gods to whom human sacrifice was offered: Taranis, Esus and Teutates. Taranis' name evokes thunder (*taran* in Gaulish), symbolized by the wheel, and he has been identified with Caesar's Jupiter. Esus means 'the Good God' and thus may be equated with the Dagda, an Irish god, second only to Lugh. (The Dagda sired the great goddess Brigit – almost certainly the equivalent of Caesar's Minerva – and he was one of the protagonists in the decisive mythical combat, the Second Battle of Mag Tured (Moytura). In this the Tuatha Dé Danann fought against the Fomori, a demonic, innumerable and monstrous group who claimed dominion over Ireland and tried to subjugate the successive legendary races that populated the country.) Teutates, meanwhile, has the same root as the Celtic word for tribe (*tuath* in Irish) and is associated with the Romans' Mars on several inscriptions. The Celtic god, therefore, led and protected the tribe in war. According to Caesar, it was to him that the Gauls consecrated the remains of vanquished enemies.

It will be noted that it is tricky to link Caesar's report with Lucan's, but it is even more difficult to assign precise functions to the Celtic divinities. These gods seem to have an aversion to being defined, and they systematically encroach on the attributes of Roman deities other than those that Caesar cited as their namesakes. Hence, linking Lug with Mercury is certainly justified because both dispense riches, are masters of all skills, and guide travellers, especially when they are journeying to the next world. However, Lug was also the *supreme* Celtic deity, while Mercury did not hold that exalted position in the Roman pantheon. In Gaul, Lug's festival, Lugnasad, when the council of the Gauls met at Lugdunum ('Lug's town'), was so important that it was later identified with that of the emperor Augustus. The association

of Lug with Mercury also diminishes his role as solar and warrior god. As Lug is equated *merely* with Mercury, some of the Celtic god's functions are assigned to Taranis (equated with Jupiter), while others are given to Belenus (equated with Apollo) and Teutates (equated with Mars). Teutates himself loses some of his warrior function to the goddess equated with Minerva, Brigit. None of this made much difference to the Gauls, however, who were used to venerating the great god Lug in multiple forms. Pre-Roman Celtic iconography reveals a systematic refusal to associate divinity with an explicit, fixed and unequivocal image. Nevertheless, Caesar and Lucan still offer some valuable insights.

Gods of light and shade

According to Caesar, 'All the Gauls assert that they are descended from the god Dis Pater [an underworld deity equated with Pluto, god of Hades] and say that this tradition has been handed down by the Druids' (*Gallic Wars*, VI, 18). We do not know the Gaulish name of this god, but his Irish equivalent is Donn ('the Dark One'), a god both fearsome and beneficent, isolated from the other divinities in the kingdom of the dead. He is the dark and subterranean mirror-image of Lug, lord of the daytime sky and of the earthly world. These complementary opposites fit remarkably well with the Celtic concept of universal order.

This pairing of sovereign gods probably explains the unusual coupling of two heads that is a recurrent theme in La Tène Celtic art. Such motifs are found on numerous brooches crafted in the 5th century BCE and on later artefacts. The heads are almost identical, as if to signify that the two gods are of equal importance and similar nature. However, one of them displays a distinctive element, often barely perceptible; it might be a vegetal (a palmette or a double mistletoe-leaf), or animal (ears or horns), or abstract symbol (the 'S' or the triskele).

Previous pages
The Brno-Maloměřice flagon (Moravia).
Detail of the principal openwork mounting of the body.
Views of the lower part of the spout mounting. A slight alteration to the angle of the object modifies the expression of the monstrous face, making it seem more human or animal. See p. 208.
First half of the 3rd century BCE. Brno (Czech Republic), Moravské Muzeum.

Left
**The Gundestrup cauldron
(Denmark).**
*Outer panel (g), a bust of a goddess
with small figures on her shoulders;
the one on the left struggles with a
lion. See p. 224.*
FIRST HALF OF THE 1st CENTURY BCE. Height: 200 mm.
Copenhagen, Nationalmuseet.

The elusive image of the gods

It is probably the luminous, Apollonian aspect of Lug that figures most frequently in Celtic art: the tree of life symbolized by the (generally trilobed) palmette, or the double mistletoe-leaf; his monstrous guardians, dragons or griffins; the horse; the bird of prey, generally a raven; the 'S' and the triskele. At first, these motifs are juxtaposed: for example, the statuette on the lid of the Reinheim (Saar) Flagon represents a horse with a human head wearing the double mistletoe-leaf, representing the three fundamental aspects of the divinity. This human-headed horse, a Celtic invention that owes nothing to the Greek centaur, later became one of the typical emblems on the reverse of coins minted in Armorica and Central Europe derived from the image of the *biga* on Macedonian staters. Celtic artists of the 4th century BCE created images in which the various aspects of the divinity became inseparable parts of an indefinable whole, at once anthropomorphic, vegetal, zoomorphic and symbolic. It was their way of expressing the gods' ability to adopt different forms in order to participate fully in the universal cycle.

The Greek historian Diodorus Siculus tells a story that illustrates the 3rd-century BCE Celtic attitude to their gods. He describes the astonishment of Brennos, leader of the Celtic armies that reached Delphi in 279 BCE, when he found himself in a temple in front of statues of gods represented in human form. It seemed to him laughable that the Greeks thought all-powerful gods could look like ordinary men and women; such a rendering could not adequately express the supernatural power that enabled them to adopt different forms. By contrast, the images of their gods left by Celtic artists of that age embrace that notion fully. When one glimpses the richness and the semantic subtlety of these original creations, it is easy to understand how the representation of a god as an ordinary human seemed to Brennos and his Celtic contemporaries to be an audacious and disrespectful act that revealed a profound ignorance of the complex nature and powerful forces that ruled the universe.

This singular concept of the image of the gods, so different to that of the Mediterranean world, reflects a system of coherent thought: the esoteric doctrine of the druids, the Celtic intellectual elite. According to Julius Caesar (see 'Gaulish society in the middle of the 1st century BCE, as described by Julius Caesar' in Part II, Chapter 3, above), part of this doctrine related to the principle of reincarnation, which Caesar thought led to the Celts' fearlessness in battle. Two slightly later texts supplement the information given by Caesar. According to the geographer Strabo, 'Not only the Druids but others as well say that men's souls, and also the universe, are indestructible, although both fire and water will at some time or other prevail over them' (*Geography*, IV, 4, 4). Pomponius Mela (1st century CE) wrote that a druidic doctrine 'is widespread among the people, the knowledge that souls are immortal and that the dead have another life, which renders them courageous in war. This is why they burn or inter with their dead all the necessities of life: formerly they left all settling of affairs and payment of debts to the other world. There were even those who threw themselves on the funeral pyre of their kin as if they were going to live with them' (*De chorographia*, III, 2, 18).

So classical writers had two views of what the Celts themselves believed: after death, either they went to another world separate from that of mortals, or their souls were reincarnated on earth. The first concept, which is very ancient, seems to have been general. The second may have been reserved to a small group of initiates, as is the case in comparable Greek doctrines such as the Orphic and Pythagoric teachings.

Preceding pages
Aber Valley Nature Reserve (Wales).
*Located in north Wales, facing the island of Anglesey 12 km
(7¹/₂ miles) east of Bangor, this National Nature Reserve preserves
a type of forestation probably similar to that of the Iron Age,
with a predominance of oak trees. Celtic artists' predilection for
contorted and equivocal images must surely have been fed by
the atmosphere of the temperate forest, where the vegetal
forms, changing with the light and the seasons, provided
inexhaustible stimuli for the imagination...*

The Gundestrup cauldron (Denmark).
*Above, inner panel (C) with, in the centre, the bust of a god with a wheel
(Taranis).*
*Below, inner panel (B) with, in the centre, the bust of a goddess, surrounded
by elephants and griffons.* See p. 224.

First half of the 1st century BCE. Height of each panel: 200 mm.

Copenhagen, Nationalmuseet.

The Gundestrup Cauldron: dumb images of a Celtic pantheon

In 1891 a group of narrative panels in silver (and other silver pieces) were discovered by chance in a bog in Gundestrup, south of Jutland (Denmark). They had originally formed the facing of a large, possibly wooden, basin (69 cm/27 in in diameter), and had been dismantled, then deposited, probably as a votive offering. Their original sequence is therefore unknown, and the present order of presentation is the result of guesswork.

The exterior of the basin seems to have been decorated with eight almost square panels (24.5 x 26 cm/9½ x 10¼ in), of which seven have been recovered; the missing panel may correspond with a fourth female deity. Shown in relief are four busts of male divinities (a, b, c, d), arms raised in a praying gesture; two of goddesses with arms crossed or laid on the breast (e, g); and one of a goddess on whose raised right hand a bird perches (f). Each is differentiated by headdress, beard, the shape of the torc (or its absence), as well as by secondary motifs featuring humans or animals, inferior divinities allied to the god or goddess, or allusions to a myth associated with him or her. Unlike the interior plaques, some backgrounds and details – hairstyles, beards, jewellery – have been enhanced by gilding.

Inside the basin, five large panels (40–43 x 20 cm/ 15¾–17 x 8 in) were arranged vertically around a circular base on which a bull is shown in high relief. The central theme of three of these panels is a divinity: a god with a wheel (C), generally identified as Taranis, who also features on the exterior (c); a goddess surrounded by elephants and griffins (B), also represented on an outer panel (g), this time with two probably male figures, one struggling with a wild beast; and a squatting god with antlers on his head (A), known in Gaul as Cernunnos ('the Horned One'), who holds a torc in his right hand and a ram-headed serpent in his left. Cernunnos is surrounded by animals (deer, boar, ibex, lions and even a large fish, or possibly a dolphin, ridden by a small figure).

Two other inner panels feature scenes. The first (D) shows three large bulls. In front of each is a figure pointing a sword at its throat. Three running animals (dogs or wolves, possibly) appear above and below the principal theme, generally thought to be a ritual killing. The second panel (E, p. 112) shows a sort of military parade: above, four riders follow the ram-headed serpent to the right; below, facing left, three men blowing carnyxes (Celtic war trumpets) are preceded by a man with a boar-crested helmet carrying his sword on his shoulder and six infantrymen with spears and long shields. In front of them, a giant man with carefully groomed, plaited hair holds an average-sized man upside-down over an object that may be a receptacle, a vat made of staves. A tree is laid horizontally between the two rows, its bare roots pointing towards the giant, above a dog standing on its hind-legs. This scene has been interpreted as a human sacrifice by drowning, and also as a representation of the passage to the other world, following immersion in the basin that procures immortality.

Three styles have been identified from the punch marks used in the ornamentation of the panels, probably meaning that three craftsmen were involved. This corresponds with stylistic analysis: one of the artists made four external plaques (c, d, e, g) and three internal ones (B, C, D); another created two exterior plaques (b, f) and two internal ones (A, E); the third executed the base with the bull. It has not been possible to attribute one external plaque (a).

The Gundestrup cauldron (Denmark).
Above, exterior panels representing male and female divinities
(from left to right: c, f, b, a, e, d).
Below, view of all the assembled panels of the Gundestrup cauldron; originally, they were
probably fixed on a wooden support. The order of the panels is speculative.

First half of the 1st century BCE. Height of each panel: 200 mm. Copenhagen, Nationalmuseet.

Opposite

The Gundestrup cauldron (Denmark).

Detail of the military parade panel (E).
*The oversized figure is clearly a god. Some interpret the scene as
a human sacrifice by drowning in a vat, others as the passage to
the other world through immersion in the water of immortality,
which gives the Sun the strength that enables him to renew
himself day after day.... See pp. 111–112.*

Above

The Gundestrup cauldron (Denmark).

*The central medaillon of the interior. The recumbent bull –
above which a small figure brandishes a sword, possibly
preparing to sacrifice it – has lost the formerly attached horns
that were possibly made of gold. On its forehead is a sort of
rosette, an obviously solar giratory motif.*

This work was created in the region known as 'Thraco-Getic', along the coastline of the Black Sea (present-day Bulgaria and Romania), but the images are clearly Celtic. It shows the typical hairstyles, the vegetal stylization of certain details (hair, beard), the usual animals, real or mythical, the carnyx, the characteristic equipment of infantrymen and cavalry, the prominence of the torc, and many other features. The similarity between the panel showing the military parade (E) and the only other narrative work of Celtic art that we have, the Hallstatt Scabbard (earlier by more than three centuries), should be noted. On the scabbard we also find a row of four riders, distinguished this time not by crests on their helmets but by their garments and the treatment of their horses; they are preceded by only three infantrymen. On the side panels of the scabbard are figures holding a wheel, which are reminiscent of the man to the right of Taranis on the inner panel of the Gundestrup Cauldron.

Even if the workmanship of the cauldron and certain details, such as the unusual presence of elephants, point towards an origin in south-western Celtic Europe, its place of manufacture will probably never be known for certain. It is generally thought to date from around 100 BCE, and may have been brought to Jutland, after long and adventurous wanderings, by the Cimbri, who originally hailed from that region. But this is merely a hypothesis: the cauldron might equally well be booty from the fall of the Celtic tribes of the Danube Valley after 50 BCE. However, it was certainly not designed for private use but for a ceremonial function in an important communal sanctuary. It seems likely that it was removed from such a place and from its sacred function during a fierce conflict.

While the cauldron undoubtedly illustrates the major divinities and the fundamental myths of the ancient Celtic religion, to date no convincing interpretation has been proposed to explain this belief system fully.

The Gundestrup cauldron (Denmark).
Inner panel (A) showing the god of the deer forests (Cernunnos), surrounded by animals.
First half of the 1st century BCE.
Height: 200 mm.
Copenhagen, Nationalmuseet.

Left
View of the nature reserve at Aber Valley (Wales).
A suggestive evocation of the forests known to the ancient Celts. See p. 220.

Not far away for ages past had stood
An old unviolated sacred wood,
Whose gloomy boughs, thick interwoven, made
A chill and cheerless everlasting shade [...]
Black springs with pitchy streams divide the ground,
And, bubbling, rumble with a sullen sound.
Old images of forms misshapen stand,
Rude and unknowing of the artist's hand

LUCAN, *Pharsalia*, III, 399-426.

The unexploited richness of monetary iconography

The richest and most varied iconography left by the ancient Celts is surely to be found on their coinage. There are thousands of images, and this somewhat daunting quantity explains their slight representation in the iconographic repertory of Celtic art. For many years the study of Celtic monetary images focused almost exclusively on their links with their Greek, Roman or other prototypes; little attention was paid to the deliberate modification of these models (something that can also be seen on other media, such as wine pitchers, and at other stages in the evolution of Celtic art). As has been mentioned earlier, it was assumed that the discrepancies between the 'originals' and the Celtic versions were due to the Celtic engravers' lack of skill, leading to simplifications and deformities, or to an innate predilection for abstraction, which had the same results.

The coins show that very different models were developed into comparable images. Thus, Celtic adaptations of the laureate head of Apollo originally on the obverse of a Macedonian stater were very similar to those found on an Etruscan-inspired flagon of the 5th century BCE. What is often incorrectly categorized as 'stylization' leads inevitably to comparable forms, to symbols that are omnipresent in Celtic art: the 'S', the foliate or mistletoe-leaf motif, the palmette and its Celtic version, the pelta. It is therefore a case of reconstituting natural forms, starting with the symbols used to represent anatomical details. The principle can be read on at least two levels: in overview and by studying the individual symbols that comprise the whole, each of which has one or several meanings. What may at first sight seem like a simplification of forms is in fact a means of enriching the content by offering the viewer the possibility of reaching multiple or equivocal interpretations.

Monetary images clearly belong to the iconographic repertory of Celtic art. Even a superficial examination shows that they present the characteristic themes seen on other objects: the god associated with the palmette and the mistletoe, the human-headed horse, the boar, the griffin, the bird of prey and many others. However, the monetary repertory is even richer than this. If it is systematically analysed, it could significantly widen our knowledge of the ancient Celts' spiritual world, because, like their other figurative works, Celtic coinage authentically reflects the beliefs that motivated these people.

Opposite
The sources of the Seine at Saint-Germain-Source-Seine (Côte-d'Or, France).
The ancient Gauls, who venerated this place, deposited numerous votive offerings here.

Epilogue

The Roman conquest of Gaul and the Danubian regions, the German and Dacian encroachments that precipitated the fall of the Celtic cities of Central Europe and the storming in 26–25 BCE of the last independent bastions on the Atlantic coast (Asturia and Cantabria), followed by the occupation of most of Britain, meant the beginning of the eradication of a visible Celtic presence in Europe. The new provinces they had populated, to the east and west of the Roman Empire, adopted the architecture and habits of the conquerors, which obscured the earlier foundations of their economies, the urban network and the territorial organization. This explains why 19th-century CE scholars could not grasp the importance of the Celtic legacy in the formation of these provinces.

However, the Roman conquest rarely led to a complete reversal of the previous situation. Even seemingly obvious Roman advances, such as the establishment of first-class transport networks that facilitated a remarkable growth in trade, were improvements rather than innovations. For instance, an efficient and well-equipped transport system had existed long before the Romans arrived: the bridges constructed between 300 and 250 BCE suggest that Celtic trade routes played host to heavy transcontinental traffic.

The Celtic heritage

The same goes for architecture: only large public buildings or those of wealthy private citizens – and the comforts associated with them, notably running water and under-floor heating – were Roman innovations. For the rest of the buildings, traditional construction techniques using wood and other perishable materials continued to be employed, with a skill that endured until the Middle Ages and beyond. Moreover, as with other woodworking crafts until the introduction of machines, tools remained the same as those invented by Celtic artisans well before the Roman conquest. The situation was no different for metalworking, especially utilizing iron, in which Celtic smiths' skill was unequalled.

In agriculture the principal innovation was the introduction of new breeds of domestic animal. The development of Mediterranean-type cultures was obviously restricted to certain zones, notably those adapted to viticulture, to which the troops' demand for wine and the flourishing market gave a spectacular boost. Crop-growing and animal husbandry remained the staples, especially the raising of cattle, sheep and pigs, stimulated by the development of a large market for wool and salted meat, two products for which the Celts were famous throughout the Roman Empire.

Although absorbed by the Roman administration, the well-established Celtic territorial organization did not change, except for the appearance of new cities, probably founded by former clients of powerful tribes whom the Romans encouraged to secede. The imprint of Rome was manifested above all in the elite class's adoption of the new lifestyle and culture: Celtic aristocrats sent their children to schools where they learned Greek and Latin, to enable them to find jobs in the administration and participate in political life. This led to the abandonment of traditional druidic education, followed by its inevitable decline. Gallo-Roman and Celto-Roman nobles immersed in Graeco-Roman culture abandoned their former beliefs to such an extent that only those elements embedded in popular folklore survived; and in the nobles' eyes these were peasant superstitions, devoid of interest. This is why, when the fathers of Christianity lifted their ban on a written record of druidic traditions, the scholars of the period no longer saw anything of interest to transmit to posterity.

Why was the Celtic world, formerly so powerful and so solidly anchored in its convictions, so rapidly obliterated? Part of the answer may be the very factor that allowed the Celts to travel and settle throughout Europe in the first place. They possessed a great capacity to adapt and to reach a modus vivendi with other races. This, coupled with the prestige their military strength had brought them, and buttressed by a warrior ideology, meant they were very efficient colonizers. Ever since their distant ancestors had begun their long march west, they had been able to insinuate themselves gradually; they acted like a kind of cement, ensuring a degree of ethnic, cultural and economic cohesion from Central to Atlantic Europe. Imposed by force of arms, the new Roman model totally overshadowed the prestige of this old one, which was isolated wherever Rome dominated.

Opposite
**Sunset on the coast of Finistère,
near the headland of Lostmarc'h.**
The fate the Celts most desired was to be admitted to the company of those who, having quitted this world, reached the Isles of the Blessed, the heavenly paradise from which sadness, illness and death were banished and where enchanted music accompanied the unending feast that reunited in peace and harmony the brave warriors and their beautiful companions, among trees laden with fragrant flowers and succulent fruits…

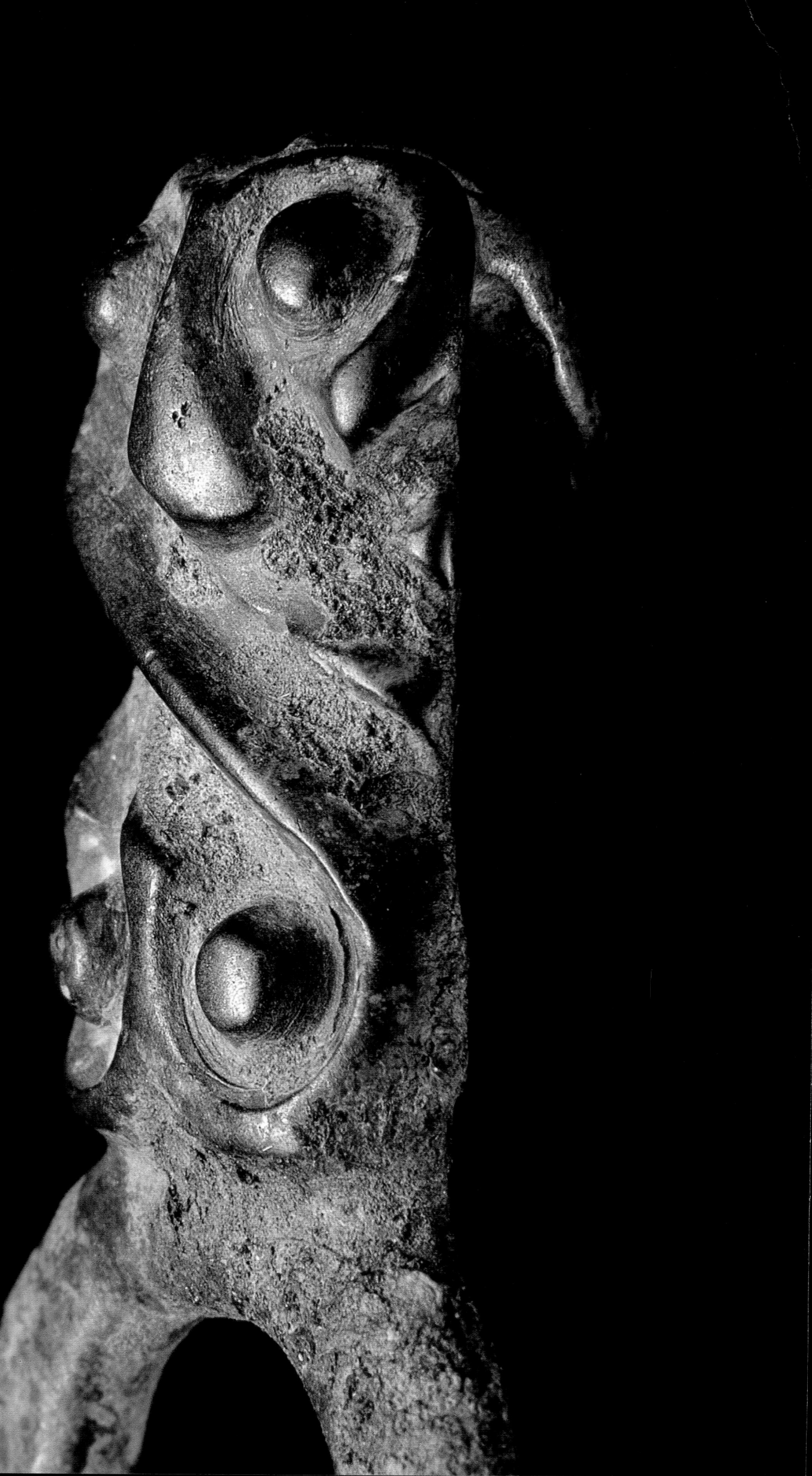

The Arthurian resurgence of the Celts

The decline and fall of the Roman Empire led to a return to traditional values and structures, as is indicated by the adoption of Gaulish names for Roman cities. Roman Lutetia took the name of the Parisii and became Paris; Durocortorum turned into Reims, after the Remi; Lemonum evolved into the city of the Pictones, Poitiers; many other modern towns followed suit.

In the British Isles, which had always remained partly independent and had not been so branded by their Roman conquest, a more spectacular renaissance took place. By combining the new Christian faith with elements of the old Celtic religion, medieval Europe was gifted a marvellous legacy. The heroic ideal that had led generations of Celts to achieve the fearless 'good death' was given a Christian sheen in the tales of King Arthur. This legendary king, his wizard Merlin and his knights embellished a millennium-old warrior tradition with the image of the sword Excalibur, which was decorated with dragons (just like the scabbards of the 3rd century BCE), and catered to a taste for supernatural wonders in the ethereal world of the enchanted forest, by turn hostile and benign, peopled with fleeting forms. The success of this fable was rapid and considerable. In the first decades of the twelfth century, Arthur and his companions, identified by inscriptions, featured as the chief subjects of the north portal of the cathedral of Modena in Italy; they were the only non-religious sculptures on the building. This is even more remarkable because they were carved some twenty years *before* the publication of Geoffrey of Monmouth's *Historia Regum Britanniae* (c. 1136–8), which, together with his *Vita Merlini*, contributed enormously to the popularization of the Arthurian legend in Europe, from Sicily to Scandinavia. Translated into many languages, these two works would later be highly adapted by French courtly writers of the Middle Ages, English playwrights, Richard Wagner for the opera stage and a host of modern film-makers.

Adopted by the Romantic movement in the nineteenth century, Celtic literature sparked renewed interest in the tribes who were simultaneously being unearthed by the new science of archaeology. Paradoxically, this research into ancient Europe tended to highlight the Celts' ability to adopt the Roman model while contrasting this 'progress' with their earlier 'primitive' state. Thus, pre-Roman Celtic art, the most authentic expression of their culture, was considered to be merely a clumsy adaptation of the art of classical antiquity, a 'barbarous' imitation of the only art form worthy of study.

However, with the evolution of modern art came a new awareness that Celtic art constituted one of the great creative movements of the past. These images, open to an almost infinite number of interpretations, stimulate a taste for the fantastic; they help to free the imagination from the constraints of definitive form. And they reveal that the spiritual heritage of the Celts, just as much as that of classical antiquity, constitutes a vital component of our European personality.

Opposite
Bronze belt-hook from Dormans (Marne).
The two alternating faces of the universal cycle: summer's burning heat and winter's damp cold, light and shade, life and death ...
Early 3rd century BCE. Height of the detail: approx. 25 mm.
Épernay (Marne, France), Musée Municipal d'Archéologie et du Vin de Champagne.

/chronology

the Celts		historical events

BCE

	the Celts		historical events
3rd millennium	Indo-European peoples, distant ancestors of the Celts, settle in Central and Western Europe.	**3rd millennium** [beginning of]	First fortified settlement on the site of Troy.
2nd millennium	Emergence of populations considered direct ancestors of the historic Celts.	**2800-2300**	Old Kingdom of Egypt (pyramids, hieroglyphic writing).
		1500-1100	Development and peak of Mycenaean civilization. Greek texts in Linear B script. Mycenaean voyages to the western Mediterranean.
		1400-1250	Apogee of Troy VI, model for the city in the *Iliad*.
		c. **1190-1180**	Fall of the Hittite Empire, Asia Minor.
800-750	Beginning of the Hallstatt period (first Iron Age).	**824-813**	Traditional date of the foundation of Carthage.
		754	Legendary foundation of Rome.
		c. **750**	Foundation of the Greek colony of Pithekussai at Ischia. Greeks start to colonize the western Mediterranean.
620-560	First Celtic-language inscriptions (Sesto Calende, Castelletto Ticino in Northern Italy).	**612**	Fall of Nineveh and the Assyrian Empire.
		c. **600**	Foundation of the Phoenician colony of Massalia (Marseille).
550-480	First writings on the Celts by Greek writers (Hecataeus, Herodotus).	**514**	Expedition of Darius I, High King of the Persians, into Europe. Establishment of a short-lived provincial government between the Danube and the straits.
		490	Athenians defeat the Persians at Marathon.
		480	Greeks defeat the Persians at Salamis and the Carthaginians at Himera (Sicily).
460-450	Beginning of the La Tène period (second Iron Age).		
400-390	Celtic tribes invade Northern Italy (Senones, Boii and others).		
387	Romans defeated at Allia, the sack of Rome.		
335	Alexander, at war with the Triballes, receives Celtic emissaries in the north-west of modern Bulgaria.	**336-323**	Reign of Alexander the Great.
298	Celts invade Thrace. Defeated at Haemus Mons (Stara Planina) by Cassander.		
295	Defeat of the Gauls of Italy and their allies at Sentium.		
283	Final defeat of the Italian Senones by the Romans.		
280	Celts invade Macedonia.		
279	Celtic expedition to Delphi.		
278	Galatians cross into Asia Minor.		
268	Romans subdue the colony of Ariminum (Rimini), starting point for the Roman conquest of Northern Europe.	**264-241**	First Punic War. Sicily becomes a Roman province.

the Celts

225	Roman defeat of the Gauls and Cisalpine Celts at Telamon.
218	Hannibal crosses southern Gaul and the Alps then enters Italy, where he is joined by local Celts.
191	Roman defeat and final surrender of the Northern Boii.
190-170	A network of *oppida* is built throughout Bohemia.
154	Revolt of the Lusitanians and Celtiberians against Rome. Roman expedition against the Salyes of Provence.
133	Siege and fall of Numantia.
124	Second Roman campaign against the Salyes. Creation of Provincia (Narbonensis).
121	Roman victory over the Arverni and Allobroges led by Bituitus.
c. 120	Probable start of the migration of the Cimbri and Teutones. Successful defence by the Central European Boii.
58-52	Gallic wars. Caesar's expedition into Britain.
42	Cisalpine Gaul is absorbed into Italy.
25	Galatia becomes a Roman province.
12	Pannonia occupied by Rome.

historical events

238	Carthaginians land at Cadiz; beginning of the conquest of the Iberian Peninsula.
218-201	Second Punic War. Rome occupies the Carthaginian territories in the Iberian Peninsula.
149-146	Third Punic War. Destruction of Carthage.
113-101	Cimbri and Teutones move between Norica, southern Gaul and north-western Italy.
44	Assassination of Julius Caesar.
31	Octavius defeats Antony and Cleopatra VII at Actium. Octavius becomes *Princeps Senatus* and takes the *cognomen* (surname) Augustus. Start of the Roman Empire.

CE

the Celts

43	Roman invasion of Britain under Claudius. Conquest of the southern half of the island.
61	Revolt of the Iceni and other British tribes against Rome, led by Queen Boudicca.
78-86	Agricola's campaigns in Britain.
407-411	Final departure of Roman troops from Britain.
432	Patrick is sent as bishop to Ireland.
c. 450	Eastern centre of Britain is occupied by Saxons. Insular Bretons emigrate to Armorica.
c. 539	Battle of Camlann, where Arthur is said to have been killed.

historical events

14-37	Reign of Tiberius, first successor of Augustus.
238	End of the reign of Alexander Severus. Start of the great barbarian invasions.
284-305	Reign of Diocletian. The Roman Empire is thereafter divided into the Empire of the East and of the West.
313	The Edict of Milan: Constantine grants Christians the same rights as pagans.
410	Capture of Rome by Alaric.
475	Odoacer captures Rome and deposes Romulus Augustulus, the last emperor.

/ index

A

Aar 25
Achichorius 76
Aedui 12, 15, 20, 106, 110, 180
Agris 72, 74
Ailill 199
Aix-en-Provence (*Aquae Sextiae*) 108
Alban Hills 67
Alesia 20
Allia 6, 60, 64, 236
Allobroges 82, 99, 237
Ambicatus 52
Amfreville 74, 162
Amiens 4, 102
Anas (Guadiana) 97
Ancona 62, 66, 75, 82, 84
Angles 129
Anglesey (Mona) 128
Ankara 32
Apennines 66, 105
Aquae Sextiae (Aix-en-Provence) 108
Aquilia 94
Arevacii 99
Arganthonios 35
Ariminum (Rimini) 94, 236
Arras 4, 91
Arthur 129, 130, 204, 210, 211, 235, 237
Arverni 99, 236
Asperg 4
Asterix 6, 16
Asturia 98, 232
Atrebates 4, 118, 128
Aulerci Eburovices 150
Aulnat 99
Aurillac 174
Autun 12, 102
Auvers-sur-Oise 67, 162
Avalon 204
Avaricum (Bourges) 115
Avebury 16
Avenches 100
Avila 93, 102, 240
Avon 128
Aylesford 124

B

Badbury Rings 130
Badonicus (Mons) 129
Basel 102
Basse-Yutz 70
Báta 154
Battersea 128, 199
Beine-Prunay 74
Belerion (Cape) 125
Belgae 86, 90, 118, 204
Belgrade 4, 88
Bellovesus 52
Belteine 23, 143
Bercy 88
Bergamo 102
Bergères-les-Vertus 50
Berne 4, 72, 102
Besançon 102
Bibracte 12, 20, 102, 106
Bituriges 52, 114
Black Sea 28, 229
Blasket (Islands) 204

Boii, 4, 15, 64, 66, 70, 75, 82, 85, 94, 100, 104, 105, 106, 108, 109, 115, 118, 186, 193, 236
Bolgios 76
Bologna (*Bononia*) 22, 94, 201
Borsch 62
Bosigran Castle 130
Boudicca 37, 128, 129, 172, 237
Bouqueval 88
Bourges (*Avaricum*) 102, 115
Boyne (*Buvinda*) 130
Bozouls 190
Bratislava 4, 102, 106, 109, 111, 186
Brennos 6, 15, 23, 64, 76, 78, 222
Bres 180
Brescia 102, 110, 145
Brigantes 128, 130, 172
Brigit 143, 216
Brno-Maloměřice 63, 142, 194, 208, 210, 212, 213, 215, 216
Broighter 124
Brythonic 16
Budapest 4, 64, 102, 106, 154, 193, 201
Burgundy 172
Buvinda (Boyne) 130

C

Cadiz 34, 94, 236
Caledonians 129
Camboglanna 130, 235
Camlann 130, 235, 237
Camulodunum (Colchester) 99, 126, 128
Cañete de los Torres 96
Canosa 75
Cantabria 98, 232
Cantium (Kent) 118
Caratacos 128
Carlingford 190
Carpathians 92, 115, 201
Cartimandua 36, 128, 172
Casalecchio 201
Cassivelaunos 20, 126
Castelletto Ticino 30, 236
Cathbad 190
Catuvellauni 126
Cenomani 30, 94
Cerethrios 76, 82
Cernunnos 224
Certosa (La) 52
České Lhotice 108
Cernon-sur-Coole 8, 161, 190, 200
Châteaumeillant 150
Chiusi (*Clusium*) 64
Chlum 40
Chouilly 51, 90, 134
Cimbri 100, 106, 108, 229
Civitalba 76, 82
Čížkovice 68
Clermont-Ferrand 99
Clonmacnois 121
Clusium (Chiusi) 64
Clyde 128
Colchester (*Camulodunum*) 97, 126, 128

Coligny 3, 136, 141
Como-Prestino 30, 31, 52, 102
Commios, king of the Atrebates 126
Condé-sur-Marne 72
Conflans 160, 161
Conn 179, 180
Connaught 199
Cooley 190
Coriosolites 100
Cornaux 25
Cornwall 14, 125, 130
Corseul 100
Cotini 115
Craggaunowen 152
Croatia 79
Crozon 133
Cruachan 23
CúChulainn 172, 190, 192, 193, 196, 199, 208
Cunobelin 99, 126, 128
Cymbeline 97, 126
Cynesians 28
Cynetes 28, 97

D

Dana 208
Deichtire 208
Ditzingen-Hirschlauden 26
Dobova 201
Donnersberg 102
Dormans 235
Dorset 119, 126
Douro 94, 99
Dover 118
Drava 79
Droužkovice 35
Dún Ailinne 133
Dun Aengus 118
Dundalk 190
Durocortorum (Reims) 209
Dürrnberg 32, 36, 62, 63, 155, 166, 168, 178, 180
Dvorovi 201

E

Ebro 83, 97, 201
Eigenbilzen 56, 57
Eithne 208
Elbe 26, 105
Emain Macha 23, 130, 133
Ensérune 85, 88, 201
Entremont 166
Epiais-Rhus 75
Eravisci 115
Erstfeld 46
Erkenbrechtsweiler 115
Escaut 125, 130
Essex 126
Este 58
Esus 217
Esztergom 193
Evreux 150
Excalibur (sword) 235

F

Fál 180
Fellbach-Schmiden 165
Fenouillet 79
Fère-Champenoise 91, 193
Filottrano 75

Fínegein's Night-Watch 179
Finistère 36, 58, 125, 133, 141, 149, 232
Finisterre (Cape) 28, 97
Finn 199
Finsterlohr 102
Firth of Forth 129
Fomori 217

G

Gaesatae 83, 91, 94, 99, 100, 204
Gajić 71
Gallipoli 118, 149
Geneva 4, 30, 102
Gibraltar 35, 125
Glauberg 60, 63, 166
Goidelic 16
Golasecca, 23, 29, 30, 31, 36, 37, 52, 66, 97
Gournay-sur-Aronde 202
Grampians (Mountains) 129
Guadiana (Anas) 96
Gundestrup 60, 94, 110, 111, 222, 224, 225, 226, 227, 229
Gussage All Saints 126

H

Haemus (Mount) 76, 236
Hallein 32, 62, 63, 155, 166, 168, 180
Hallstatt 20, 23, 60, 61, 111, 229
Hauviné 175
Helico 52, 75
Helveti 106
Heuneburg 28
Hirschlanden 166
Hlubyně 36
Hochdorf 36
Holzhausen 172
Hořovice 46
Hořovičky 37, 47
Hrazany 108
Huelgoat 58, 141
Huelva 35, 124
Hungary 154, 193, 201

I

Iberians 12, 97
Iceni 128, 172
Imbolc 143
Ingolstadt 102, 103
Insubres 31, 66, 83, 94, 186

J

Jogasses 51, 92, 136
Jura 25, 136
Jutland 108, 224

K

Kabaïon (cape) 125
Karaburma 88
Kélouer Plouhinec 36
Kermaria-en-Pont-l'Abbé 148, 149
Kleinaspergle 4, 63
Knock 121
Křivoklát 3, 204
Kšely 145
Kšice 43
Kyšice 54, 55

L
Lasgraïsses 78, 79, 158
Latovici 115
Léglise 58
Leinster 133, 199
Leinster cycle 199, 204
Lemonum (Poitiers) 235
Leonnarios 76, 82
Lepontines 30
Leval-Trahegnies 86
Libčice-Chýnov 51, 52, 54
Liguria 66, 70, 105
Linz 108
Lisbon 12
Lizard's Point 125
Loire 12, 106
Loiret 155
Loisy-sur-Marne 92
London 121, 130, 133, 199
Lostmarc'h 232
Lough Crew 23
Lug(h) 6, 143, 158, 208, 217, 222
Lugnasad 143, 180, 217
Lusatian (culture) 26
Lusitanians 99, 237
Lutarios 76, 82
Lutetia (Paris) 235
Lyon (*Lugdunum*) 141, 143

M
Macha 133, 193
Mag Tured 150, 158, 180, 217
Magdalenenberg 97
Maggiore (Lake) 30
Magyarszerdahely 201
Maiden Castle 121
Manapii 130
Manching 102, 103
Manerbio sul Mella 110, 145
Manětín-Hrádek 37, 39, 61
Marin-Épagnier 25
Marseille 31, 35, 124, 166, 236
Marson 86, 164
Marzabotto 3, 22
Medb (Mab) 199
Mediomatrices 186
Meilhan 150
Meillan 150
Menapii 130
Merlin 235
Merida 96
Meseta 94, 99
Mesnil-les-Hurlus 164
Métallifères (Monts) 35
Meuse 130
Mezek 91, 118
Milan 4, 32, 102, 150, 237
Minerva 217
Miolan 150
Molesme 158
Mona (Anglesey) 128
Montmeillan 150
Morava 82
Moscano di Fabriano 75
Mšecké Žehrovice 8, 94, 166
Münsingen 72

N
Nanterre 88
Naples 72

Narbonensis 108, 236
Navan Fort 130, 133
Nemi 67
Nerion (Cape) 28
Neuchâtel 20, 25
Neusiedl (Lake) 106
Neuvy-en-Sullias 155
Nevězice 99
Noreia 106, 108
Norfolk 128, 176
Noricum 104, 106, 110, 115, 237
Nová Huť 52, 55
Numantia 97, 99, 237

O
Odiel 124
Oestrymnides 124
Oisín 199
Oploty 66
Ordovices 128, 129
Orkneys 125
Osismes 58
Osismi 52, 125, 141
Ossian 199
Ostimioi 52, 125
Otava 158
Ouessant (*Ouximasa Uxisama*) 125

P
Panenský Týnec 156
Paris 4, 75, 88, 102
Parisi 91, 118, 121
Parisii 88, 91, 118, 185, 235
Pendragon (Uther) 204
Penmarch (Headland) 149
Pergamon 12
Pfalzfeld 166
Picardy 202
Picts 129
Pictones 4, 111, 235
Placentia (Plaisance) 94
Plaňany 145, 175
Plessis-Gassot 75, 88
Po 26, 31, 64, 94, 105
Podlešín 160
Pogny 121, 136, 150
Poitiers (*Lemonum*) 4, 102
Pont-ľAbbé 134
Port-à-Binson 6
Prague 4, 43, 102, 143, 146, 152
Přemýšlení 193
Prestino 30, 52
Přísnotice 154
Pyrenees 14, 83, 99, 125

R
Raz (Pointe du) 125
Reca 106
Regia 130
Reims (*Durocortorum*) 4, 51, 75, 102
Reinheim 63, 172, 182, 222
Remi 3, 4, 15, 51, 70, 75, 86, 235
Rhètes 32
Ribemont-sur-Ancre 202
Rimini (*Ariminum*) 94
Rise 126

Roanne 115
Roissy-en-France 88, 91
Roquepertuse 60, 166, 186
Rungis 88

S
Sado 35
St-Connan 158
Saintes 150
Saint-Benoît-sur-Seine 201
Saint-Gothard 64
Saint-Maur-des-Fossés 88
Saint-Vincent (Cape) 28, 97
Salamanca 102
Samain 23, 141, 143, 180
Samildánach 158, 208
Sancerre 106
Santonae 150
Sarre 63, 172, 222
Sava 82
Scordistae 82, 115
Scotland 128
Segovesus 52
Seine 230
Senones 15, 66, 67, 70, 75, 76, 85, 86, 91, 236
Senos (Shannon) 130
Sens 67
Sentinum 76, 118, 196, 234
Sequani 85
Sesto Calende 30, 236
Shannon (*Senos*) 130
Snettisham 176
Solway 129
Somme 203
Somme-Bionne 165
Staigue 126
Stanwick 196
Stara Planina 76, 236
Staré Hradisko 104 108, 110
Stonehenge 16, 17, 32, 34
Stradonice 3, 94, 98, 99, 100, 104, 105, 106, 108, 110, 115, 118, 150, 156, 163
Stuttgart 36

T
Tagus 35
Tara 23, 150, 158, 180, 182
Taranis 217, 223, 224, 229
Tartessians 124
Tartessos 35
Tasciovanus 126
Taurini 115
Tectosages 78, 79, 82, 83, 86
Telamon (Talamone), 58, 85, 204
Telce 163
Tène (La) 3, 20, 22, 25, 29, 26, 52, 58, 66, 121
Teutates 217
Teutons 106, 108, 237
Thames 99, 118, 121, 126, 128, 130, 199
Thielle 25
Thuizy 165
Thule (Iceland) 112
Tiber 64
Ticino 29, 30
Tigurni 108
Tincommios 126

Todi 30
Toulouse 78, 108
Touriñan (cape) 28
Tre'r Ceiri 16
Triballes 76, 236
Trinovantes 99, 126
Třísov 99
Troyes 196
Tuatha Dé Danann 118, 180, 208
Tübingen-Kilchberg 26
Turin 102
Turoe 149
Tyne 129

U
Uisnech 150
Ulaca 32
Ulster 133, 180, 190, 196, 199
Ulster (cycle) 199
Urnfield culture 26, 105

V
Váh 115
Vannes 4
Vascones 99
Veneti 182
Venutius 172
Vercellae 108
Vercingétorix 3, 6, 20
Verica 126
Verulamium (St Albans) 126, 129
Villards-d'Héria 136
Villeseneux 138, 139, 144, 172
Viriatos 99
Vix 37, 177
Vltava 43, 51, 99, 108, 158
Volcae 78, 79, 82, 83, 88, 99, 108, 204

W
Waldalgesheim 63, 66, 67, 168, 172, 182, 193, 201
Wandsworth 121
Westhall 133
Witham 118

Y
Yorkshire 91, 118, 121

Z
Závist 3, 4, 37, 43, 52, 67, 70, 102, 105, 108, 166
Želkovice 35, 39
Zennor 130

/ bibliography

select bibliography

Celtas y Vettones. Diputación provincial de Ávila, Ávila, 2001. An innovative synthesis of the Celtic presence in the Iberian Peninsula, published in conjunction with an exhibition.

The Celts, V. Kruta (Editor), O.H. Frey (Editor), B. Raferty (Editor), M. Szabo (Editor), Thames & Hudson, 1999.

The Celts (catalogue of the exhibition at Palazzo Grassi, Venice, 1991). Edited by Venceslas Kruta et al. Rizzoli, USA, 1999.

Classical texts

CAESAR, JULIUS, *Commentaries on the Gallic War*, tr. W. A. McDevitte and W. S. Bohn.

DIODORUS SICULUS, *Historical Library*, tr. C.H. Oldfather, 1933.

HERODOTUS, T*he Histories*, Penguin Classics, tr. Aubrey de Sélincourt

LUCAN, *Pharsalia* III.399, tr. Nicholas Rowe (1703-18).

PLINY THE ELDER, *Natural History*.

POLYBIUS, *Histories*.

STRABO, *Geography*, tr. Loeb, 1923.

TITUS LIVIUS, *The History of Rome*, tr. Rev. Canon Roberts. Everyman's Library; J. M. Dent & Sons, Ltd., London, 1905.

/ picture credits

Abbreviations / t : top ; m : middle ; b : bottom ; r : right ; l : left.

Dario Bertuzzi / pp. 2, 7, 9, 10, 23 b, 34, 35, 36 r, 37, 38, 39, 40, 41, 42, 44, 45, 48, 52, 53, 54, 55, 61, 68, 69, 72, 73, 92, 93, 95, 101, 105, 107, 108, 109, 111 b, 114, 115 l, 116, 134, 136, 137, 138, 139, 142, 143, 144, 145 t, 146, 147, 151, 153, 156, 157, 158 t, 160, 161, 162, 163, 172, 174, 175, 191, 193 l, 194, 195, 200, 205, 208 to 219, 234.

Erich Lessing/AKG Images / pp. 5, 12, 13, 18, 24, 26, 27, 28, 30, 33, 46, 47, 62, 64, 65, 66, 67 l, 70, 71, 76, 77, 82, 83, 86, 94, 96 t, 98, 100 t, 102, 104, 106, 110, 111 t, 112, 115, mb, 118, 120, 124, 125, 126 b, 128, 129, 130, 133, 145 b, 154, 155 r, 159, 164, 165, 166, 167, 168, 170, 173, 176, 177, 178, 179, 180, 181, 183, 184, 186, 187, 188, 190, 192, 193 r, 196, 197, 198, 204, 222 to 229, 231.

Werner Forman/AKG Images / pp. 16, 36 l, 59, 99, 100 b, 119, 121, 122, 126 t 127, 131, 132, 140, 148, 150, 152, 182, 206, 220, 230, 233.

Piero Baguzzi/AKG Paris / pp. 50, 51, 56, 58, 67 r, 74, 75, 87, 96 b, 115 r, 202, 203.

Archives CdA/Guillemot/AKG Images / p. 55 l.

AKG / pp. 15, 17, 20, 21, 23 t, 84, 115 mt.

Clichés V. K. / pp. 32, 103 bl, 149.

Archives V. K. / pp. 78, 79, 80, 158 b.

Römisch-Germanische Kommission, Ingolstadt / p. 103 t and br.

Carlos Valero, AFAN / pp. 88-91

Illustrations / p. 30-31: archives V. K.; p. 43: K. Motyková, P. Drda and A. Rybová in *Památky archeologické* 75, 1984; p. 60-61: K. Kromer, *Das Gräberfeld von Hallstatt*, Florence, 1959; p. 63: E. Penninger, *Der Dürrnberg bei Hallein* I, Munich, 1972; p. 75 : archives V. K.; p. 97: M. Almagro Gorbea and M. Torres Ortiz, *Las fíbulas de jinete y de caballito*, Saragosse, 1999, F. Romero Carnicero, *Las ceramicas policromas de Numancia*, Soria, 1976; p. 102: W. Krämer in Th. Müller and Weismüller, *Ingolstadt* I, 1974; p. 111: archives V. K.; p. 141: P.- M. Duval and G. Pinault, *RIG* III, Paris, 1986; p. 146: V. K.; p. 149: J. Waddell in *Studies on Early Ireland*, 1982 (Kermaria), M. Duignan in P.-M. Duval and C.F.C. Hawkes, *Celtic Art in Ancient Europe*, 1976 (Turoe); p. 160: V. K. (Casalecchio), M. Szabó and É. Petres, *Decorated Weapons of the La Tène Iron Age in the Carpathian Basin*, Budapest, 1992 (Bölcske, Dobova, Dvorovi, Magyarszerdahely), A. Rapin and M. Schwaller in *Revue archéologique de Narbonnaise* 20, 1987 (Ensérune); p. 219: M. Čižmář in *Pravěké dějiny* Moravy 1993.

/ acknowledgements

The author would like to warmly thank the sympathetic and efficient editorial team at Chêne with whom he had the pleasure of collaborating on this book, especially Colette Véron, Aurélie Dombes and François Chevret. Their considerable contribution was decisive. He also wishes to thank colleagues and friends who have facilitated successful new photography, particularly Mme Jana Čizmářová (Brno), M. Jean-Jacques Charpy (Épernay), M. Milan Lička (Prague) and M. Thierry Lejars, who kindly authorised the publication of photographs of the excavation he conducted at Roissy-en-France and of the remarkable objects discovered there.

Editorial director: **Colette Véron** /
Editorial assistant: **Aurélie Dombes** /
Artistic director: **Nancy Dorking** /
Graphic design: **François Supiot** /
Layout: **François Chevret** /
Page make-up: **Nicole Thiériot-Pichon** /
Photogravure: SELE OFFSET in Turin

© Éditions du Chêne-Hachette Livre, 2004.
Published in conjunction with Centre National du Livre
This edition published in 2004 by Hachette Illustrated UK, Octopus Publishing Group Ltd., 2–4 Heron Quays, London E14 4JP

English translation by JMS Books LLP (email: janem030@aol.co.uk)
Translation © Octopus Publishing Group Ltd.

A CIP catalogue for this book is available from the British Library

ISBN-13: 978-1-84430-098-3

ISBN-10: 1-84430-098-6

Printed by Toppan Printing Co., (HK) Ltd.